More Critical Acclaim for *When Rain Hurts*

A searingly candid chronicle of the heroic struggle of two adoptive parents to raise their multiply disabled son.... A useful, inspiring cautionary tale for prospective adoptive parents.
—*Kirkus Reviews*

Mary E. Greene shares her family's journey through the world of Fetal Alcohol Syndrome with a lucid candor free of self-pity (and a healthy wit). To anyone either struggling to make sense of the journey to adopt a child, or dealing with a skewed adoption system, Greene's book will offer both camaraderie and sustenance.
—**Edie Meidav**, author of *Lola, California*

What will a mother do for her child? If your name is Mary Greene, the answer is "everything possible." Greene's searing account of learning to parent her prenatal alcohol-exposed, bipolar, orphanage-veteran son is an unforgettable lesson in commitment, fortitude, and unconditional love. This riveting and candid story sheds a brutal light on the challenges faced by many post-institutionalized children and their families, and assures them, "You are not alone. There is hope."
—**Jessica O'Dwyer**, author of *Mamalita: An Adoption Memoir*

With vivid language and strong imagery, [Greene] describes the harsh deprivations characteristic of Russia's orphanages, the incompetence of its international adoption agency, and her frustrated need to be a mother.... [Readers] will find in Peter's story fertile suggestions for a public support system capable of addressing the complex problems of formerly institutionalized children.
—*Publishers Weekly*

D1082603

WHEN RAIN HURTS

An Adoptive Mother's Journey with Fetal Alcohol Syndrome

A Memoir

Mary Evelyn Greene

RED HEN PRESS | *Pasadena, CA*

Book layout and design by Aly Owen
Library of Congress Cataloging-in-Publication Data

Greene, Mary Evelyn, 1965–
  When rain hurts : an adoptive mother's journey with fetal alcohol syndrome / Mary Evelyn Greene.—First edition.
    pages cm
  Includes bibliographical references and index.
  ISBN 978-1-59709-262-3 (alk. paper)
  1. Children of prenatal alcohol abuse—Biography. 2. Adoptees—United States—Biography. 3. Adopted children—United States—Biography. 4. Fetal alcohol syndrome—Patients—Family relationships. 5. Orphans—Russia—Biography. I. Title.
  RJ520.P74G74 2013
  618.3'268610092—dc23
  [B]
                    2013003597

The Los Angeles County Arts Commission, the National Endowment for the Arts, the City of Pasadena Cultural Affairs Division, Sony Pictures Entertainment, the Los Angeles Department of Cultural Affairs, and the Dwight Stuart Youth Fund partially support Red Hen Press.

First Edition
Published by Red Hen Press
www.redhen.org

Acknowledgments

Many thanks to Dr. Ronald Federici, Dr. Jane Aronson, Dr. Glenn Castaneda, and Suzanne d'Aversa, for their continuing counsel, encouragement, and professional expertise. Many thanks also to the dedicated staff at Green Chimneys, my loyal and insightful blog readers, and of course, my husband and in-house editor, Patrick LoBrutto. My family and friends remain a continuous source of support and humor and I will always remain grateful for their presence in my life. I'm lucky to be part of such an amazing village.

FOREWORD
Joyce Sterkel, founder of the Ranch for Kids in Montana

WHEN RAIN HURTS is a rare and intimate look into the process of international adoption and the day-to-day struggles families face as they travel to adopt, bring their children home, and enter the world of endless rounds of consultations with professionals who claim to be able to help their struggling child. It is also a glimpse into the much underpublicized world of Fetal Alcohol Spectrum Disorders, a devastating but preventable birth defect that leaves caregivers isolated, overburdened, alone, and affected children forever destined to navigate hurdles in life that their brains simply cannot accommodate.

From the opening of the book and the details of the "paper chase" that the Greene-LoBrutto family endured in completing their international dossier for adoption, it became obvious that this family had done everything they could to prepare themselves for the adoption of a child from Russia. They read extensively, attended lectures, and sought the opinions of some of the leading physicians who were experts in the field of adoption medicine. Unfortunately these precautions weren't enough, and in the end they would not prepare them for the day-to-day struggles that families like theirs experience as they traverse the landscape of mental health and medical providers in search of solutions for the problems of their deeply troubled children.

Immediately I was struck by the accuracy of Mary's description of the family's journey to Russia and all they saw and experienced while there. Few people have been able to articulate this experience as honestly and poignantly as this mother has managed to do. I was transported to my own memories of travel and living in Russia, and the authenticity of this account, with its raw and graphic detail, was uncannily reminiscent of my own experiences and those of other families with whom I have worked.

Unless your life has intersected with that of a child who suffered early deprivation, loss, and prenatal exposure to alcohol, it's impossible to fully comprehend the daily struggles with which these families cope, often with little support or understanding from their extended families, friends, school personnel, or health care professionals. The cost of raising such a child can quickly outstrip many families' financial abilities as their insurance benefits, and bank accounts, quickly become depleted. The cost of psychotropic medications alone can exceed hundreds of dollars per month. The everyday stress can quickly overwhelm a family's emotional and physical capacities as parents such as the Greene-LoBruttos must be "on" 24/7. In addition, adequate respite care is frequently too expensive, or the caregivers are ill-trained to cope with these often explosive, unpredictable, and difficult children.

Prenatal exposure to alcohol can leave a child permanently impaired and needing care far beyond the traditional age of majority. More profoundly affected children, such as Mary's son, will require lifetime care and continuous adult supervision. Few parents are prepared for such a scenario. The toll on families is staggering. Divorce, behavioral difficulties with other children in the home, ostracism by their communities, schools, and even close family members further isolates these families and can lead to a breaking point where everything falls apart.

As readers delve into *When Rain Hurts*, they can imagine themselves in this situation. They ask, "Would our family be able to cope? Would we survive?" And they must consider the most pressing question of all: "Could we help our child to heal and learn to function within the greater realm of society?"

When parents adopt a child from difficult circumstances, they often believe that love heals, and indeed to a certain extent it does. But even the most loving parents cannot love away a child's genetic foundation, preverbal memories, or intrauterine exposure to alcohol. In the forefront of the adoption arena is a myriad of necessary programs that "educate" the parents regarding what they might expect when they adopt a child. It matters not if they involve group settings, individual readings, online courses, or support groups as long as they give the prospective adoptive parents a glimpse into the reality of raising a child who may have very specific foundational damage due to neglect, abandonment, lack of a primary caregiver, and/or prenatal exposure to alcohol or drugs. However, none of these avenues can provide the "walk in my shoes" opportunity that Mary's book so undeniably and eloquently offers.

When Rain Hurts is an incredibly accurate, honest portrayal of raising and coping with a son damaged by prenatal alcohol and institutional neglect. It is insightful, emotional, educational, and riveting in its details of the unfolding saga of parenting and loving a deeply wounded, neurologically compromised child. As the parent of three internationally adopted children and the former director of an adoption agency and current director of a therapeutic program for adopted children, I highly recommend that parents, professionals, and those seeking to adopt read this book and step into the intimate portrayal of the life of this one family whose struggles are so eloquently shared for the world to see and examine.

In addition, *When Rain Hurts* serves as a cautionary tale for women who drink alcohol while trying to conceive and at any stage during their pregnancies. Worldwide, there are more persons living with the damage caused by prenatal alcohol exposure than those who carry some form of autism diagnosis. Unfortunately, FASD has a judgmental aspect to it, and therefore this devastating disorder is largely swept under the rug and not openly discussed within communities, churches, and schools, or by medical service providers. This book clearly illustrates the need for change, both in terms of awareness of the risks associated with alcohol use during pregnancy and the resources and supports that must be made available to families struggling to raise these kids.

Unfortunately the Greene-LoBrutto family's struggles are far from over. Theirs is a lifelong journey, and only time will show how these children change and evolve within the life cycle and learn to cope with their disabilities. Having said this, it's clear this mother loves her child. Day in and day out she scales mountains to help him, using her professional expertise as a lawyer, researcher, writer, and teacher to advocate on his behalf and gain access to the services he desperately needs. What makes this book stand out among so many others is that Mary bravely shares her intimate fears, doubts, and low points without apology and without sugar-coating the reality of daily life with a post-institutionalized, alcohol-exposed child. She mourns the loss of the man her son was meant to be while remaining fully committed to helping him reach his potential. She gives voice to the thousands of warrior moms and dads silently struggling through challenge after challenge with grace, humor, and stubborn resolve. Thank you, Mary.

INTRODUCTION

MY FIRST BABIES were born under the spigot of my childhood home in St. Petersburg, Florida. Bored with actual dolls, I began filling up hot-dog-shaped balloons with the garden hose, transforming them into three-dimensional creatures in the quirky corners of my imagination. I'd draw faces on the multi-colored balloons with magic markers, strip my various dolls down to their white baked-on underpants, and liberate the dresses and bloomers for my water borne creations. Then I carefully placed them in extra long breadbaskets swiped from the kitchen cupboard, taking precautions with a dishtowel to protect their fragile latex skin. Snug in their baskets, I strolled my water babies around the backyard in a green wheelbarrow, singing lullabies and telling magical stories of my own devising. Sometimes Joy, my best friend then and now, would participate in the ritual. We'd pretend we were sisters and the water balloons were boisterous, rowdy cousins who required time-outs and occasional spankings.

Since my mother forbade me to bring them indoors, I'd carefully tuck them into their baskets, using dust rags for blankets, and lay them in the back of a garage shelf for the long, lonely night ahead. I loved my limbless babies and mourned each time one began to leak or, even worse, exploded into liquid oblivion. My obsession with mothering the water balloon babies began when I was in nursery school and ran its course by the time I entered first grade. I would wait thirty more years to experience again the loving, and at times harrowing, responsibility of motherhood.

I intend to skip everything that happened in my life between the water balloon babies and the decisions leading to Birobidzhan, Russia. Suffice it to say I met a man, fell in love, tried the traditional means of procreation along with cutting-edge medical ones, and finally set about creating our family through international adoption. Our odyssey has been at times ordinary and astonishing, evoking feelings of shining triumph that are sometimes dwarfed by moments of profound regret and sorrow. The vision of motherhood I developed as a young child and stubbornly clung to through my mid-thirties did little to prepare me for the challenge of loving and reaching a child whose brain was damaged by unspeakable hardship and poor prenatal judgment.

Red Hook, NY (Summer 2008)

Our son suffers from Fetal Alcohol Syndrome, the most severe condition along the continuum known as Fetal Alcohol Spectrum Disorders (FASDs).

Given the extent of his disabilities, it's clear his teenage birth mother drank throughout the entire pregnancy. Unfortunately, there's nothing unique about his circumstances. According to the Centers for Disease Control, there are more children and adults coping with the permanent effects of FASDs than there are individuals living with Autism Spectrum Disorders. In fact, the CDC acknowledges that the known incidence of FASD is grossly underestimated due to the stigma disclosure creates for birth mothers.

Unlike autism, FASDs are 100 percent preventable. A pregnant woman who does not ingest alcohol cannot give birth to a child with FASD. Despite knowing that nearly 60 percent of prenatally alcohol-exposed males will experience incarceration during their lifetimes, and just as many females will experience prostitution and unwanted pregnancy, many doctors remain uncomfortable asking their pregnant patients about alcohol use. In turn, many mothers live with the guilt and knowledge of knowing they harmed their children but are too scared and ashamed to look beyond denial and seek help. Prenatal alcohol exposure devastates both birth families and those formed by adoption. Crippled by poor memory and lack of impulse control, the vast majority of FAS children will never lead independent lives or even drive a car. Raising and loving an alcohol-exposed child is more exhausting than running a marathon, more expensive than sending triplets to the Ivy League, and more heartbreaking than all of Shakespeare's tragedies combined. It's a permanent, unforgiving disorder of thought, temperament, cognitive ability, health, and behavior.

Although ample literature regarding the effects and impacts of FASDs exists, none convey what it's like to parent these innocent, beautiful, yet profoundly damaged children. Orphanage life, along with the neglect, deprivation, and abuse that accompanies it, adds injury to an already inescapable insult. Children like our son can be ticking time bombs. But they're also resilient survivors who can learn to love and trust, to dream just like any other child, and who strive every day to live in a world that, for them, may lie beyond their reach.

Acknowledging the devastating truth of what it's like to live and love in the presence of this vicious brand of prenatal assault is the reason I wrote this book. Every day I work hard to transform myself into a mother who can successfully parent my son, a special needs child who was injured in the womb four years before we met. I can now say with confidence that this goal has been achieved, though constant vigilance will always be required to ensure its continuation. Today my son no longer actively resists the tug of intimate family life. Together, we have moved toward a more peaceful state of mind, one that accommodates his disabilities but is rich in love, secure in its foundation, and resplendent the way only hard-won endeavors can be. Looking for cues from my child, I do my best on any given day to meet his multiple and always changing needs, clinging all the while to the hope and growing certainty that there is a path that can lead us, hand in hand, toward an even richer, more balanced life. This is the story of my remarkable son, Peter, our search for a magical path, and my journey, forever in progress, toward forgiveness, acceptance, and peace.

For my children, Peter and Sophie.
To me, they are the finest people ever born.

❦

AUGUST 10, 2007. *We're eating at a diner this morning because a realtor has brought clients from Woodstock to look at our house and we can't be there. We've been told that buyers won't visualize a home as theirs if they see other people living in it. Sophie and Peter are coloring at the table as we wait for breakfast. The drawing of Sophie's big-headed person, with purple eyelashes and Tammy Faye Baker lipstick, brings crooked smiles to the row of construction workers sitting at the counter. Peter is drawing a racetrack and race cars. We know this because he tells us. What he's doing is running the crayon around and around the paper, as though the crayon itself is the race car. At six, he doesn't understand that a drawing is representational or that drawing is a form of communication. His thinking is too concrete to maneuver such concepts. He expects people to understand what he thinks and always seems surprised when they don't.*

Breakfast arrives and the children put the crayons away and pull their now-decorated placemats up for safekeeping before the waitress sets the plates down. Peter tells us that his pancakes taste like chicken. Pat and I trade furtive glances. Sophie's fork hangs in the air in a pregnant pause. Peter has sent the family a signal: from this moment forward, today will be a bad day. I struggle not to let this pronouncement color my mood, but the optimism for the day wanes all the same. I eat my meal even though I'm no longer hungry. We have long understood that Peter's demeanor at breakfast is a fail-safe barometer of temperament and ability for the day ahead. When he was younger he used to hum "da tee tee da da, da tee tee da da" to alert us that an inharmonious storm was gathering in his brain.

As predicted, breakfast was just the starting gate to a long day's endurance race. Today's personal low point is losing my temper at bath time. It's so hard to tell what Peter can't versus won't do, especially on tumultuous forecast days. Tonight, for instance, he's having trouble locating his hair for washing. We have been working on this skill for two years. No matter how I coach him, he can't do it. After I finally finish the job myself, visibly frustrated, he snickers. At times, Peter enjoys making Pat and me angry. Maybe it's merely a way for him to vent his own frustration, but the snickering is difficult to take all the same. The boy in the tub tonight can be hard to like and filled with disdain. Moments like this are tough for people outside the four corners of our family to understand. They are dark, lonely moments filled with doubt and self-condemnation. I'm so thankful Pat understands when I tell him what happened. He is my anchor at times like these, and our resolve to confront our obstacles together, with love forged from friendship and shared experience, is a precious lifeline, an immeasurable gift. I don't know what I'd do without his knowing touch and understanding eyes, the unassuming smile that gives me hope and consolation.

Chapter 1

The Philtrum

After Russia, I can't help but stare at philtrums. I think I'm doomed to obsess over this obscure but vital piece of human anatomy the rest of my life. I see beauty in philtrums, and on occasion I detect heartache. The philtrum is the vertical groove between the upper lip and nose. In the womb, a baby's normally growing brain differentiates into the left and right frontal lobes. Near the end of this process, if all goes according to plan, two folds of flesh grow around the skull and meet in the front of what becomes the baby's face. The philtrum is essentially a seam, the place where the halves of the face fuse. It's a mark of symmetry, a talisman of sorts. A well-formed philtrum is proof of our grand anatomical design and the centerpiece of a well-formed face. A poorly formed philtrum predicts abnormal brain development.

I have an ordinary, unexciting philtrum. My husband Pat's is a little nicer. Our daughter, Sophie, has a deep and luminous groove, beautiful and rich in its perfection. I smile with relief when I think of it. Peter, whom I've grown to love with a once inconceivable intensity, doesn't have one at all. He will always be the half boy underwater, swimming, always swimming toward something, not sure of where he's going because the weight of the water disorients him. His own air bubbles conspire to distort his vision and prickle his hyper-alert skin. Lost but plucky in the vast expanse of a backyard pool. He is not whole and never will be. The groove between his upper lip and nose is silky smooth.

Summer 2007

Well before science was able to explain the developmental significance of the philtrum, the ancients recognized its importance. The word *philtrum* comes from the Greek *philtron*, from *philein*, meaning "to love," "to kiss." According to the Jewish Talmud, God sends an angel to each womb and teaches the unborn baby all the wisdom of the world. Just before the baby is born, the angel touches it between the upper lip and the nose and all that has been taught is forgotten. Other folklores claim that the philtrum is the spot where the angel put his finger to "shush" the baby in the womb from talking about heaven, or from telling another secret. Still other stories say the philtrum is an indent left by the finger of God Himself.

I won't accept the cruelty of a god who would overlook my son, and so I have formed my own view. To me, the philtrum is a marker of hope. Not a guarantee of health or happiness or even normalcy, whatever that means, but a reason for optimism. Without a philtrum, there is no such thing as a healthy start. And a head start? That's out of the question.

I haven't always been consumed with talk of philtrums. The seed of my obsession sprouted in late winter 2004 and fully blossomed two years later. Before then, I can't honestly say I'd heard the term, and I was only vaguely aware of its presence on the human face—mine or anyone else's.

Sometime in the weeks before the tulips bloomed in Manhattan, and when we still lived in the city, Pat and I signed up for an information meeting being held by a local adoption agency, Happy Families, at a Jewish community center. We had long ago agreed we wanted to adopt a child, even if we successfully conceived, a possibility that was growing more remote with each passing month. And so our odyssey began that night, the first of many stumbles along the way toward adoptive parenting. The date on the advertisement was wrong, though we didn't know it at the time, and we were a little late. We slipped into the room and sat down at a long table with several other couples and a few singles. A woman with untamable gray hair, a compelling voice, and fiercely intelligent eyes was asking folks to say a little about themselves. Pat and I were nervous. We felt certain we had blundered our way into a Jewish studies seminar and our non-Jewish status was about to be found out. Worse still, maybe we had unwittingly joined a sex therapy group and were about to be asked to share intimate details about our marriage. We needed to leave, and quickly.

But the woman with the wild hair asked what we hoped to get out of the "class" just as we were making our escape. I blathered something incomprehensible about a Happy Families mix-up and scurried to the door like a panicked squirrel, Pat and satchel in tow. She laughed and asked us to stay. It turns out we had walked into an international pre-adoption parenting course being hosted by Kathy Brodsky and Dr. Jane Aronson on behalf of the Jewish Child Care Association of New York. Dr. Aronson, we soon discovered, is a world-renowned adoption pediatrician, top in her field and an adoptive mother herself. We learned so much that night we decided to sign up for the rest of the course. Of the thousands of adoption-related mistakes made by us, this was by far the most providential. We never did catch up with Happy Families.

In many ways, our entire story relates back to meeting Dr. Aronson that night. She is the person who explained the importance of the philtrum to me and everyone else in the room. I remember Pat and several other men nodding in agreement when she described it as the mustache area that men hate to shave. I looked around and realized, whether consciously or not, that every single person in attendance was locating and exploring his or her own ribbon of flesh between the upper lip and nose. I was doing it too. How odd we must have looked in the presence of each other, outlining the peaks and valley of our grooves with the pads of our fingers. I remember trying to catch a glimpse of Dr. Aronson's, as though the shape of her philtrum might reveal the mystery of the person inside.

As I learned about the philtrum, I struggled to process why this information, so seemingly obscure at the time, was so important for Pat and me to understand, and what it meant for our future child. After that night I knew I needed to make sure our own adopted children had one, that part was clear. Prospective children without philtrums are considered "high risk," an ambiguous term with clear implications, even to a novice like me. The risk of children born with missing or "indistinct" philtrums is greatest, we were told, in Eastern European countries. And why are philtrums so important? In the international adoption world, the presence or absence of them is a litmus test for four words I never before had heard, much less uttered: Fetal Alcohol Spectrum Disorder.

⟡

August 18, 2007. *Peter and I are going into the city today, just the two of us. We're taking the train into Manhattan and then spending the afternoon at the American Museum of Natural History. Afterward, we'll spend the night at a hotel. Pat and Sophie are headed to the Crayola Factory for an adventure of their own. Peter requested a trip alone with me a while back and I've been eager to oblige. I hear him wake early, but he doesn't come into our room, which I know from past experience means he took off his Pull-Up and peed on the bed. Sure enough, I smell urine as I turn the corner. What I don't anticipate is the blood. I find him shaking like a leaf, naked from the waist down, holding his soiled pajama bottoms and Pull-Up. Blood is smeared on his face and hands and all over his bed and walls. He has gouged his right nostril to make himself bleed, a shocking new trick he's been perfecting over the last several months. Did he do it because he purposely wet the bed and was nervous I'd cancel the trip? Or did he wet and gouge just so I would cancel the trip? As crazy as it sounds, maybe he is happy about the trip and this was his way of showing enthusiasm. Or more likely still, maybe the trip represents a chance for real intimacy, one on one, and this is more than his damaged soul can handle. One thing is certain, though: Peter is a skilled saboteur.*

I go about the business of cleaning up what looks like a crime scene and struggle not to look thrown. Our realtor is hosting an open house tomorrow while we're away and a generous amount of blood mingled with the smell of stale urine is bound to affect the ambiance. In a few weeks, Peter and Sophie will start school in Red Hook, across the river from where we now live. The 1733 Dutch Colonial stone house Pat and I fell in love with before the adoptions, the house we promised the kids was their "forever home," is now for sale. We're entering the last stages of building a new house, complete with geothermal heating and cooling. We want to plunge ahead with a clear carbon conscience. The decision to move, however, was driven not by ecological consideration but rather by Peter's educational and therapeutic needs. We fought his school last year to the point of emotional and financial folly; we should have taken our lawyer's advice and moved thousands of dollars earlier. There's always so much at stake, it seems, our children's welfare topping the list. Peter and I need this trip together, and we need it to go well. This is what I tell myself to stay calm. I leave the house ninety minutes later, yelling over my shoulder for Pat to make sure his cell phone is charged and turned on at all times. I kiss Sophie goodbye and wish I were taking her and leaving Peter with Pat. Maybe Peter knows this. Maybe it's the real reason he gouges his nose.

Chapter 2

What a Missing Philtrum Looks Like

Peter came to us in the form of three grainy digital photos e-mailed from our adoption agency, which in turn received them via e-mail from the orphanage in Russia. Seeing the initial photos of your future child is the adoptive mother's equivalent of looking at a sonogram for the first time. In those blurry images, with heart pumping faster than a pubescent salsa drummer, I saw an Olympic gymnast, a Nobel Prize-winning scientist, a poet laureate, or even the next Baryshnikov. Best of all, I saw my son.

Those were my giddy dreams, certainly. The kind of dreams that make your heart flutter with excitement and provide the adrenaline necessary to keep you painting the nursery (or in our case, bedroom) even though you're so tired your arms wobble like spaghetti noodles. My real dreams for Peter, however, were what nourished hope and provided the sustenance necessary to survive the adoption waiting game. I wanted him to be happy, healthy, secure in our family, and grounded and well-practiced in the values that would prepare him for adult responsibilities and a fulfilling life. He would be our Peter the Great, not because of his remarkable public accomplishments, but because he would overcome his difficult beginnings and grow up happy and well-adjusted, through the boundless—dare I say heroic—love, patience, and example provided by us, his parents.

When I look back at those photos, it's easy to remember why I first fell in love with the idea of Peter, and why I've worked so hard to fall and stay in love with the reality of him, our troubled little boy who came wrapped in a package so fuzzy and devoid of information that we were able, and eager, to see perfection. What was clear was that Pat and I thought the boy in those photos was one of the most beautiful children we'd ever seen. And in fact, he is an astonishingly handsome child, with twinkling eyes and an infectious, impish grin. He's blessed with big, almond-shaped, brown eyes and eyelashes long enough to harvest and sell in designer salons. At the time, I reveled in the perfect chubbiness of his cheeks, rosy and red the way nature intended. Peter smiled so happily in the pictures that I never gave the shape or quality of his philtrum (which his infectious smile camouflaged) much worry. His face didn't resemble any of the faces of the countless alcohol-affected children I had seen on websites or in books.

First referral photo, Birobidzhan, Russia (Summer 2004)

Although Peter would turn out to have certain classic features of Fetal Alcohol Syndrome, like an indistinct, flat philtrum and thin upper lip, he lacks the small eyes, funny ears, or dull expression that are equally as characteristic of the prototypical FAS face. At the time, I didn't realize there was little correlation between facial features and the severity of damage caused by prenatal alcohol consumption. Depending on what stage of pregnancy a birth mother ingests alcohol, her child may be severely impacted but show few if any dysmorphic features or growth deficiencies.

The most important thing I saw in Peter's face was a potential son for us and an older brother for our soon-to-be-adopted daughter, Sophie. I saw in Peter the little boy we would soon be cheering as he turned the corner on third base or kicked his first soccer goal. I saw a budding artist whose drawings would be proudly displayed throughout our home. And most of all, I saw in his beautiful face, which was framed in sparse, lusterless hair, a three-year-old child who needed and deserved to be showered with every ounce of maternal love I'd been accumulating for this long-awaited, precious moment.

So what does a child without a philtrum look like? He looks like Peter. A boy so seemingly divine he made my heart flutter and my imagination take flight. The story of our family necessarily includes an examination of the difficult reasons and way in which Peter eventually came to us. How on the heels of a truly remarkable failure of the international adoption system, and the profound grief and disappointment we endured because of it, Pat and I were given this moment of perfect possibility. Our journey toward parenthood, and Peter, was fraught with many twists and turns, highs and lows, and numerous surprises. In order to understand the final composition of our family, and the full circle of hope diminished, restored, and then redefined that Peter's adoption represents, I first need to tell the story of the series of babies that slipped through our hands and hearts before him. Especially Ben, who for Pat and me has become a sort of ghost child.

There's no doubt our experience with the baby we called Ben influenced our decision to adopt our son, as well as the eclectic range of emotions I harbored when we first met him. My journey with Peter will never be summed up in a Hallmark card; in fact, he and I have had very few greeting-card moments. I have scratched, snarled, and clawed my way toward loving my son, so our beautiful moments together feel nearly transcendent. Someday I may be able to receive a hug from Peter without remembering how far we've come, but for now I remember. For now, an easy, casual hug still feels like a remarkable achievement compared with the complex and immutable emotions Peter demonstrated in the orphanage and during our first eighteen months home. The child we were about to adopt ran to Pat and jumped in his arms, but he screamed with sickening alarm if I took even a single step toward him. He covered his ears and yelped angrily when I tried speaking, even in soft, hushed tones. I had no choice but to back away and watch like a polite outsider as he circled around my husband, movements stiff and robotic, rhythmically repeating his name as he marched to the inconsonant rhythm in his head.

I was worried when I first met Peter, certainly, but I didn't panic, not right away. He was interested in toys and Pat and he liked looking at the books we brought. After a few minutes, he worked up the nerve to come close enough to grab the keys and sunglasses that I dangled in front of him at arm's length. He was also beautiful, just as he was in the photos, though much smaller than we expected. As I watched from a safe distance, I tried to remember that this was scarier for him than it was for us. Who knows what the caregivers had told him, what he thought adoption meant, or, more to the point, where the dark corners of a deprived three-year-old's imagination can lead. He had been in the orphanage since he was five months old and had never left the premises, taken a ride in a car, been rocked to sleep, or even seen many strangers. Two adults oohing and aahing over him, speaking too loudly and in an incomprehensible tongue, naturally might overwhelm his fragile nervous system.

Peter surely didn't know what a mother was then, but he understood enough, or perhaps had endured enough, to know he didn't want another female caretaker. We were told at the orphanage that these children, especially the boys, are interested in strange men and disdainful and distrustful of unfamiliar women. I don't know whether this is because the women caregivers in their lives are unkind or act inappropriately or, more likely, whether the children simply don't get enough attention and nurturing and blame the gender with which they're most familiar. At the time, I was willing to chalk up Peter's obsessive interest in Pat and his active disinterest in me as common, even expected, orphanage behavior. It would be months and months before I realized my child's feelings toward women were complex enough to worry whether they may have had more sinister roots.

For more than two years, I would strive with varying levels of commitment and energy, and often without evidence of progress, to overcome the prejudice my son had against me, to teach him to relax in my arms, and to trust that a mother's touch is meant to soothe and not harm. The effort has been successful. Three years after his adoption, Peter is sitting cozily next to me on the couch, his arm hooked into mine. He's watching Winnie the Pooh as I write these very words. In the last year and a half, Peter and I have achieved intimate milestones I never dreamed possible based on our first hours, days, weeks, and years together. The two of us are living proof that love can blossom in the hostile, foreign terrain of a grossly undernourished, permanently damaged, and even genetically compromised brain. I've gone from being the person in the world my son most feared and distrusted to being the person he loves and needs above all else. I've fought hard for the privilege, but without hesitation I now can say that I am Peter's mother.

❧

SEPTEMBER 10, 2007. *I lay awake wondering how long we'll be able to keep Peter safely home with us. My thoughts race in the quiet hours before dawn, when worries and fears amplify beyond ordinary bounds. Our son lies and steals and sometimes destroys with an appetite that belies his tender age. The latest is that after ten days he finally confessed to throwing Sophie's prized birthday presents in the trash. I bought replacements to surprise her, but Peter wound up the more surprised. Looking like he'd seen a ghost, and making what lawyers call a statement against interest, he stared at the toys and shouted, "But they gone away in the garbage!" Sophie is too often the object of Peter's resentments, and though I'm glad he was caught in this particular deceit, I worry that nothing will change. He seems organically incapable of learning from his mistakes. I'm mindful of the time he hurled a fist-sized stone at close range, striking her on the temple with deliberate aim. He was restive and angry the remainder of that day, blaming Sophie, incredibly, for the injury he caused as he watched me ice the swelling knot on her head. He has a fantastical ability, when ensnared, to recast himself as the victim, the misunderstood innocent who should never bear blame. I'm tired of the lecturing, the picture drawing, the social stories, the role-playing, the disciplining, the resort to yelling, and the cycle that begins anew when none of those strategies work.*

To a large extent, Peter is right. He is a victim. How can he be held accountable if his brain won't allow him to learn from his mistakes? Who did this to him? Was his biological mother a teenage binge drinker or had she graduated to a more steady intoxication? What other wrongs has Peter suffered, wrongs so horrible that his psyche is imbedded, indelibly, with feelings of mistrust, contempt, and at times unchecked rage? Alcohol exposure alone can't account for all that's skewed inside his brain. My damaged child holds me hostage, just as Russia itself holds him in the iron-fisted, immutable bonds of alcohol damage and institutional neglect. Escape isn't possible. I belong to Peter and he to me. And so I continue to love him, knowing full well that love alone may not be enough. For my daughter's sake, I must remember that Peter acts on uncensored impulses, some of which are meant to harm. Lest I forget, Sophie gives me her unicorn to sleep with tonight, assuring me as we kiss sweet dreams that its magic horn will keep me safe.

CHAPTER 3

THE ADOPTION AGENCY

PAT AND I would be put through an iron triathlon of adoption-related obstacles before a strange marriage of fate and circumstance led us first to Sophie, then Peter. One of the first and most seminal decisions we made, the decision that put us on the eventual path toward our children, was picking an international adoption agency.

After months of interviewing, attending information meetings, reading every possible written word on the subject, and otherwise losing our minds over the decision, we chose to adopt through Adopt Through Us, which was located in south Florida but has since gone bankrupt. Before choosing our agency, however, we first had to decide what color, age, and sex we wanted our child or children to be, and then choose a country accordingly. Did we want to "pick" our own children in-country or did we want information referred to us ahead of time? Did we want to travel to the child's country or did we want the child escorted to us? Did we want an infant or would we consider a toddler or, better yet, an older child? The combinations seemed endless, like the logic questions I studied and answered twenty years ago to gain entrance to law school (if thirty-four people are seated at a round table, and blonde women cannot sit next to men under age thirty, and if tall men over age thirty cannot sit next to short men of any age unless they are also bald, then . . .).

Some decisions were easier to make, though difficult to admit. More than Pat, for instance, I wanted Caucasian children. I'm a little ashamed of this fact, but the truth is I wanted to be able to walk down the street without advertising that we are a family formed by adoption. I wanted a seamless blend, and on some level I suppose I resented the idea of having to wear our adopted status like a curious tattoo. I'm not sure why it mattered so much. I'm open with people and my children about the way in which our family was created, and I want Peter and Sophie to be proud of their Russian heritage. Although our adopted status has never been a secret, I suppose I liked the idea of letting it be one, of being able to blend into the anonymity of typicality in case the urge grabbed hold.

Also, I reasoned, we still had not surrendered the idea of having a biological child. Pat and I had tried for the usual amount of time with no success, but at thirty-eight, the occasional short-lived pregnancy allowed for lingering hope. And if we were successful at reproducing, I told myself I didn't want our adopted child to feel out of place because he or she "looked" different. This was ridiculous, of course; my desire to have kids of the same race was not rooted in some kind of misplaced altruism toward our future adopted children. Our new neighbors, who are Caucasian, have a biological son Peter's age and a younger daughter adopted from China. She is the most precious, happy, well-adjusted child I know. She is a half Irish Catholic, half Jewish, Chinese American. When her ethnicity and multicultural upbringing one day becomes a topic for self-exploration, I trust her parents will help guide her through it with grace and wisdom. No, I wanted white children for myself. I wanted to be able to raise the issue at a dinner party but not be badgered by questions at the mall. I wanted to be able to take my children to the zoo without having to bear that approving nod from strangers that says, "We know you have adopted those kids and we think it's wonderful!" I wanted to feel like a "real" mother and was scared beyond distraction that I'd feel instead like a fake. Crossing racial lines simply required more strength and character than I could muster.

Now I know how foolish I was, how much my own insecurities about what family means have caused so much of the heartache, exhaustion, and desperation that Pat and I experience on a daily basis. Peter and Sophie are Caucasians, true enough. We "pass" in the mall, at the zoo, and anywhere else. The world would never guess our children were adopted, and we—Peter and Sophie included—have control over when, how, and whether people should know. In fact, when Peter makes himself vomit in a restaurant or flails around the grocery store like a newly launched pinball, all eyes are on me, as if to implore, "You're his mother, make him stop." But I can't. It seems I naively have traded the appearance of normalcy for actual normalcy. Peter is permanently brain-damaged from the effects of prenatal alcohol exposure, his mind further compromised by neglect, abuse, and the stark rigors of Russian institutionalization. When he's like that, I can't make him stop. I'm not sure anyone can.

Natural History Museum, NYC (August 2007)

But I didn't know any of this at the time and felt only slight queasiness when I thought about the risks of adopting from Russia. We were taking all the right precautions and proceeding in an orderly, even lawyerly, fashion. We had a plan and felt empowered enough with knowledge gained from our adoptive parenting class to march ahead. The first items on our to-do list were to pick a country and then an agency. We had already decided on Caucasian children, or at least I had decided and Pat was too gentle and kind to make me examine my motives, and this decision left us few options at the time. We would either adopt from Russia or Kazakhstan. Kazakhstan was quickly eliminated, however, because all of the agencies we investigated sent parents overseas, blind, without information of any kind. When we asked why, we were told they believed that adopting parents should pick out a child themselves, as if somehow these flocks of bewildered, untrained people so desperate to parent will know when they walk into an orphanage halfway across the globe which orphan is meant to be theirs.

Pat is a fiction editor, a hopeless romantic and dreamer, and I'm a tree-hugging lawyer and teacher, champion of lost causes and stranded pond guppies. We both knew better than to put ourselves in that situation. I still can remember the faces of the puppies in the litter I turned down thirteen years ago in favor of the one I chose, a scrappy Jack Russell named Scout. I can still see the faces of all the children in the Russian orphanage we met during our trips, and if I close my eyes I can feel their hands reaching up my legs, soundlessly imploring to be whisked away. I would have taken them all had it been my decision to make. Pat too. At least we knew ourselves in that regard. Kazakhstan was out of the running.

We were going to Russia and decided that Adopt Through Us, doing business in my home state of Florida, would lead us there. They promised photographs, accurate medical records, videotapes, and clean, compassionate, well-staffed orphanages. They only dealt with the best, and their own staff had adopted children from the same orphanages from which we would be adopting. They knew and respected Jane Aronson, the adoption pediatrician we had met in the city whose expertise and insight had become important to us.

Like countless scores before us, we enlisted the aid of Dr. Aronson and arranged for her professional opinion to help inform our decision-making when the time arrived. She was a large part of our plan and, to me, a secret ace in the hole. She would help us keep a rational, steady course, and I was confident she had the chutzpah to shake me silly if I started acting like a crazed, child-deprived lunatic. It's not that I felt the lunacy brewing inside me so much as I had witnessed the effects firsthand and knew I could benefit from a strong inoculation. My year of fertility treatment, or, more accurately, my year of watching and listening to other women in the fertility clinic waiting room, taught me that otherwise sane people can be rendered senseless when confronted with the prospect of a childless life.

Dr. Aronson was our insurance policy against emotion, want, and biological need driving us toward foolhardy and tragic choices.

Once we had our country, our agency, and Dr. Aronson to guide us, all we had to do was comply with a daunting volume of procedural requirements and then wait for our referral, for the e-mail that would bring us a picture of the child that had been chosen for us, along with a brief medical summary. If the preliminary information looked good, then the agency would overnight the videotape and other records for a more intensive review. For a remarkably modest fee, Dr. Aronson would then intercede, reviewing medical records, photographs, and videos sent from the orphanage. If her e-mails to us are any indication, she does this work mostly in the middle of the night, in the few quiet hours, I gather, when her two young sons, partner, and busy medical practice stop vying for her attention.

Dr. Aronson assigns levels of developmental and health risk based on a number of considerations, such as available growth measurements, facial features, muscle tone, and review of medical records. She studies the child's videotape, searching for neurological signs and other clues in the two- to four-minute clips sent by the adoption agency that might indicate a problem. For instance, a baby's movements should be symmetrical, he should have a pincer with which to pick up Cheerios by ten months, and his fists should not be clenched beyond a certain age. She checks to see whether the child responds to his name, whether weight is borne evenly by the legs, and whether he appears to be nearing developmentally appropriate milestones. Like a prosecutor seeking truth from a hostile witness, she digs without apology for truths obscured by scant information and hidden behind the alluring façades of infants and toddlers in desperate need of rescue. She forces prospective parents to see the truth and counsels them when facts are murky and therefore potentially devastating. She is a fiercely devoted advocate for children, yet she knows and accepts that not every child can be saved and not all prospective parents are suited for all challenges.

With Dr. Aronson in our back pocket, we prepared to wait, smug with knowledge that we were in control of our adoption destiny. Pat is significantly older than I and was married once before, a father of two boys and a girl. Of the three children from that marriage, only his daughter Jennifer, now grown and married, survives. His two biological sons are dead. A car struck Joseph on his bicycle when he was twelve, and Vincent died from a hole in his heart before he learned to turn over. Pat was robbed of his right to see his sons grow up and I desperately wanted to give him one more chance. We requested a referral of a baby boy, the younger the better.

∾

SEPTEMBER 16, 2007. *Peter is so difficult on the way home from school Friday that I ask Sophie to go inside so he and I can have a private discussion, right there in the car, inside the garage. No distractions, no getting out of his car seat until he at least hears me out. Peter can't or won't answer "why" questions, so instead I offer several suggestions to open him up, hoping something finds purchase. When I finally ask whether he thinks I love Sophie more than him, the parroting stops and he answers clearly, "Yes." My heart sinks. We have covered this territory before, but Peter doesn't understand cause and effect. He doesn't understand his behavior affects how people treat and feel about him at any given point in time. For instance, he shouldn't expect to be showered with affection when he lies and steals and throws Sophie's presents in the garbage bin, but he does.*

    I try explaining again, a wrenchingly sad task because Peter doesn't accept or trust the permanence of love, but then I stop. What he does next takes my breath away. My emotionally blunted son, the boy who hurts himself and tells me I smell, crawls over the seat into my lap, takes a tissue, and gently dries my teary eyes. I suddenly ache with a pang of love for my son so big that it catches me off guard. I can't stop crying now, so he comforts me. "I know, Mom, I know," he says. "I'm sorry, Mommy." I tell Pat that night and cry again all over. But the same volatile, moody boy wakes us the next morning; the talk has had no effect, and my renewed hope wilts. The opportunity arises again later in the day, and the talk begins anew, as though Friday's discussion never occurred. This time Pat is with us. Twenty minutes later, we arrive at the same emotional, cathartic endpoint that we reached in the garage the day before. And again, Peter is wiping my eyes, gently following the path of my tears with his fingers. He's not faking or manufacturing a moment. It was as real to him last night as it was Friday after school, and so it is real for me too. I have no choice but to sway in time to Peter's rhythms, no matter how inconsonant.

This morning he runs into our room and tells me he loves me. The second talk, it seems, has taken hold. Sophie and Pat go downstairs to start breakfast, and we play a game where I hug all his parts. I hug his feet, and his knees, his thumbs, and even his hair, careful not to tickle or squeeze too hard. This moment feels so good, so natural. Peter feels it too. He smiles easily at me and my heart soars. A moment later I feel his body tense slightly, and he kicks me—not so hard that it hurts, but it's not friendly. He turns his face away and swings back, anger flashing, revealing, if only briefly, the aggression that lurks beneath the surface. He doesn't know why this happens. I ask and he says he doesn't know. He is sorry. I'm sure he is. He can't seem to hold a mood. He tries, but something dark inside grabs hold, snuffing his will away. The spell can be broken, though I'm not sure by him. Someone else has to intercede, and usually it's me. I've become chief guardian of Peter's happy moments and easy mood, all the while staying vigilant against the undulating lability of his mind. The boy I love traces my tears with his fingers while his own drip shamelessly down his face. That boy deserves protecting. That boy deserves to know, deep in his bones, that I love him with every fiber of my being; that my love, though imperfect, is complete. Whole and inalterable, just like my love for Sophie and Pat.

Chapter 4

The Referral

The first referral Adopt Through Us sent was for a ten-month-old boy whose name I no longer remember. The hoops people have to jump through just to be eligible to receive a referral are enough to overwhelm all but the most committed. Although we motored through the process with adrenaline-laced speed and an undeniable measure of excitement, precious months had passed and we were antsy. We happily had been fingerprinted, photographed, background checked, psychologically analyzed, medically probed, vaccinated against exotic disease, subjected to oversight in our home, and made to swear on the collective writings of humanity that we would be superlative parents. Even our cranky old dog had been scrutinized, and she failed to exhibit the good humor that we ascribed to ourselves during this time period. We were past ready when the e-mail with the baby's basic information and a one-page medical report finally came. The report said he was born five weeks premature but had made significant progress and was a "good boy," a nebulous phrase popular among Russian orphanages.

We had filled out countless forms, meant to provide the agency with a complete profile of our preferences, wishes, and fears, checking the box on one of them to indicate we only wanted referrals of full-term babies. But there he was, his picture brought to us in full color through the miracle of digital photography. Adopt Through Us undoubtedly understood the power of the picture, maybe even betting that our desperate desire to have a baby would overwhelm the more sensible side of us that had checked the "no premature babies" box. And if they were playing the odds, they gambled correctly. Lying on our bellies with the laptop on the bed, propped on elbows and ankles intertwined, we opened the attachment and held our breath. Like us, the baby was on his belly, smiling ruefully as he struggled against the weight of his head. He looked more like five months than ten. I remember he had straggly wisps of brown hair and a tiny hooked nose. Best of all, he had a philtrum. He wasn't cute by Gerber standards, but we were ready to fall in love.

We immediately forwarded the e-mail to Jane Aronson, with copies going to my brothers and sister. The youngest of five, I have always been close to my siblings. In the years following my parents' deaths, I found myself relying on them more and more, and I was anxious to share our long-awaited news. Pat, on the other hand, was more subdued. The concept of international adoption was foreign, even scary, to his Sicilian family. This genetically ingrained mistrust of the unfamiliar coupled with my husband's history with his own two boys rendered the LoBrutto clan lukewarm, at best, on the subject. In ways clever and common, and all ways in between, his mother, brother, and daughter made it clear they had no intention of championing the cause. Most of them would come around, especially Pat's mother, but not for a while.

The video arrived on our doorstep the following morning, overnight mail. Dr. Aronson would receive her duplicate copy a few hours later. We must have watched the videotape thirty-five times. The tiny person we saw in the photo came alive before us, head bobbing for the camera atop a wrinkly, chicken-thin neck. We watched as the Russian attendant undressed the baby, a strange but undoubtedly necessary part of the presentation. He was barrel-chested and skinny, not a single roll of baby fat to pinch. But we weren't concerned; a calorie-rich and balanced diet would produce a pinchable roll within a few months. We were transfixed.

The female attendant next propped him up to show that our future baby could sit, which in his case was more like a slump. Then she pulled him up on his legs and bounced him up and down so many times that the sight of his head jostling over and over left me wishing there were some sort of international child protective squad that could be summoned to his rescue. His legs buckled quickly under the G-force of the bounce, and finally he was allowed to sag back into an exhausted yet more sustainable position. And then it was over. Not a single sound was heard in the entire two-minute videotape. We stared at each other for a moment, both reaching to hit the rewind button at the same time. We watched, stared, talked, rewound the tape, and then watched again, with breaks here and there for meals and other distractions, until we received Dr. Aronson's e-mail at 2:30 in the morning.

The baby was a risk, she wrote. His measurements, if accurate, were encouraging, but there were other concerns. His fists were clenched and one of his legs buckled when he was pulled to a stand. Palms should be open at ten months and weight should be borne evenly by the legs. Also, the wobbly head was a problem, as was the lack of vocalizations. These and other signs indicated neurological compromise, a central nervous system out of sync, perhaps irreparably. Dr. Aronson concluded that the concerns noted upon review of the videotape suggested a moderate degree of risk.

The decision was in our hands. The next day we called Adopt Through Us and told Peggy, our caseworker, that we were turning the baby down due to Dr. Aronson's feedback. We reminded her that we had asked not to be considered for premature babies and to please keep this in mind next time. We hung up and then hurried to rid our home and hearts of the evidence. The e-mails were erased and the videotape was put in the trash bin. Relatives and close friends were called and asked to do the same.

We were disappointed and sad, but we also had resolve. We didn't cause the baby's problems and nothing in our karmas said we were required to fix them.

But that night I barely slept. The rational confidence I summoned during the day gave way to a night dominated by a restless insomniac's study in self-doubt and second-guessing. I had wakeful dreams about the clothes I would pick out for him, what the nursery would look like, and what color his hair would become once his health was restored. We had decided to name our baby Benjamin, a name we both liked and one that held special significance for me because it was the name of a favorite relative who died when I was in law school. I grieved that night over the realization that this child would not be our Ben. I lay awake, questioning the correctness, the prudence, and the coldness of our decision. Was I perfect at ten months? Was Pat? Would we have passed Dr. Aronson's scrutiny? Maybe the reason his hands were clenched was because his belly hurt that day and maybe all that brutish bouncing wore him out to the point that he needed to favor one leg. I lean to one side when I'm tired and I don't have any obvious neurological defect. Did I exhibit any of these signs as a baby? It's impossible to know since both my parents have died and can't be asked. Maybe, I told myself, we were wrong.

Daylight brought relief from this self-torture, and Pat and I thankfully managed to resume our normal lives for the intervening weeks before the next e-mail arrived. I had broken my ankle in several places while skiing a few months earlier. Although an impressive assortment of titanium hardware was needed to coax the pieces of bone into knitting, the coaxing worked. I had graduated by May to walking on a lunar-style boot without crutches, giving me hope that I would be mobile by the time we went to Russia. We knew that couples just like us, scattered mostly around the United States and Canada, were waiting for their first, second, or even third referral, and it was useful to keep this fact in mind. There is nothing unusual, in the unusual game of international adoption, about turning down referred children for any number of reasons. I knew our disappointment was not unique, but it did feel uncommon enough to allow the "why me?" mentality to permeate my thoughts. The fact that I was hobbling around on a bum leg didn't help.

But as usual, Pat stepped in, with his tenderhearted ability to intercede when he feels me slipping. Sometimes we talk about it, sometimes we don't. But always he jokes and cajoles and gently steers me toward a more hopeful vision. I remember him taking me on lots of car rides during the time my ankle was healing. Pat and I both love to survey the scenery in our beautiful Hudson Valley—the farms, the red barns, the rolling hills, the Catskills on the horizon, the occasional covered bridge. The noiseless beauty, the horses' manes ruffling with the breeze in the pastures, the copper tones of late afternoon: it's easy to get lost in the natural splendor and forget what, in the long run, are minor disappointments. Even with the kids, we still manage the occasional scenic drive, with Pat "getting lost" on purpose. They invariably fall asleep from sheer boredom, and for twenty minutes or so we glide around and about the endless country roads feeling snug and content, quiet and peaceful in splendid solidarity.

We didn't get the chance to put too many miles on the odometer in the days following that initial referral, however, because the second came close on the heels of the first. We were back on the road to parenthood. The boy was full-term and weighed nearly ten pounds at birth. He had an astonishingly healthy head circumference, enjoyed the height of a giant, and was eight months old. The photo showed he had a full head of dark hair, lush lips, and plump cheeks. His name was Igor. He stared back at us from the computer screen with intense, lively eyes. Igor was Gerber cute. Without hesitation, we called Adopt Through Us and asked Peggy to send the videotape to Dr. Aronson and us. She confessed she'd been so eager to rectify the last referral that she sent us Igor's medical report and photo before she had even received, or reviewed, the video. Copies would be sent, Peggy promised, as soon as the tape reached her office.

St. Pete Beach, FL (Fall 2005)

The news went over the wires of our family network with usual lightning speed. Jokes flew across computers about how Igor (our Ben) would tower over Pat and me by the time he was seven. We would need to buy an extra refrigerator to store his preschool snacks. Did we know a place where we could order custom-made baby clothes? Unlike the first baby, Igor looked so healthy and his measurements were so enormous that only the most pessimistic could find cause for worry.

But two days passed, then three, and still not a single word. By day four we were annoyed, though still too naive to be concerned. I called Adopt Through Us and was told Peggy would need to call us back. Several hours later she did, and the news was not good. The video arrived, but the agency would not be sending it. Half of Igor's face was frozen. Paralyzed. For medical reasons that have long escaped me, the defect wasn't noticeable in the photo. Peggy, of course, was sorry. So very sorry.

After a few moments of mumbled, stunned condolences, Pat and I took to our separate corners to cope. He disappeared into the consoling, silent world of his work. I watched as he plunked heavily down the stairs, head hanging in disbelief. I have always envied this ability of his, the ability to lose himself in books, to let the world drop away in favor of the stories he helps shape, the fictional lives and invented happenings of the written word.

What I needed was to slip into the tub and cry. More nights than not, I allow myself the indulgence of an evening bath. Most often I read while I soak, novels mostly, but some nights I close my eyes, dim the lights, and try to will my mind and body into letting go of tension and useless worry. Enveloped in my private sanctuary, I should have shed healing tears for the babies I saw in my dreams but would never hold, for the littlest hearts, including Igor's, that my love would never touch.

But I didn't take that bath. I was incapable of letting Igor and his ten pounds of hope slip from our fingers without a fight, so instead I spent an hour or two researching possible benign causes of facial paralysis. Eventually I landed on an appealing explanation. Delivery by forceps, I read, can temporarily damage facial nerves and cause reversible palsy. Eureka! I e-mailed Dr. Aronson immediately. I had barely heard the *swoosh* of the message being sent when her reply came back. Without being able to physically examine the baby, she explained, and without access to proper testing, there was no way to eliminate the more sinister (and likely) causes of the paralysis. Her message was sympathetic but firm: the facial palsy put him in the highest risk category. There was no need for her to see the video. Like the baby preceding him, this boy would not be our Ben.

The cold reality is that Igor probably will spend the rest of his childhood in an institution and, depending on intellectual functioning, perhaps his adulthood too. The Russian orphanage, our agency later explained, should never have referred him in the first place. His condition rendered him "unadoptable." The best thing to do, we were counseled, was to cast him from our minds and move forward. Good advice, but as I learned in law school, you can't unring a bell. Igor was in the world, there was no denying this fact. Pat told me recently that he rarely thinks about him; I wish the same were true for me. On occasion I still am struck by the unwelcome vision of his frozen face. In the nanosecond it takes for my brain to shake free of the offending, ghostly image, I wonder whether Igor's palsy has resolved itself. I wonder whether the orphanage has been able to provide his basic needs. But mostly I wonder whether he has anyone to love him, that beautiful baby boy who looked so perfect on picture day.

❧

SEPTEMBER 20, 2007. *Peter raided our bathroom in the middle of the night. Pat found loose pills and open bottles. Somehow he figured a way to bypass our safety precautions. In the past, his midnight adventures revolved around smearing the walls with lotion or shampoo and pouring Pat's aftershave down the drain. This morning he tearfully admits the mischief, which I take as a good sign because, like most kids his age, his strong inclination is to lie. He is still upset when I pick him up from school. His sister is also having a hard day, though I nearly miss learning why. Sophie wanted to share the adoption book we made last summer with her class but felt too shy when the time came. I try listening to her on the drive home but get distracted when Peter throws a soccer ball into the front seat. It grazes my head before bouncing to the floor.*

I pull over immediately to address the behavior and start to reprimand Sophie for interrupting. Then I realize what she's saying. She's trying to tell me she didn't show the book because she was afraid the other kids would tease her for being adopted. I'm so angry with Peter that I nearly miss the confused, timid tone in her voice. My daughter, who until now has soared through life with enviable confidence, is becoming aware of differences. We have always celebrated how our family was formed, but at five, Sophie for the first time is venturing beyond the protective confines of home, where other perspectives abound, and where differences aren't always celebrated. I spend so much time searching for a solution or even a temporary salve that might soothe Peter's tortured soul that I'm failing to focus sufficiently on my other child's entirely rational fears and needs. Sophie can be helped, really helped, and yet concern for Peter, a concern bordering at times on terror, preempts all else. This has to change.

Although it would be wrong to give up on Peter, the real crime would be surrendering Sophie's chance at emotional wellness in furtherance of his. As part of this family she'll always be more than just a bystander when it comes to Peter's troubles, but I have to minimize the collateral damage. I must learn to listen to Sophie even with soccer balls whirling overhead.

CHAPTER 5

BEN

WE FELT FULLY indoctrinated into the business of adoption by the time the third referral arrived. We had grown comfortable discussing peculiar Russian medical terms such as *perinatal encephalopathy, spastic tetraparesis, pyramidal insufficiency,* and *dyskenesia.* These and others are conditions, or more accurately, predictions, commonly noted on Russian orphanage medical reports that have no counterpart in Western medicine. Mostly they denote the poor circumstances of the birth mother, her lack of prenatal care, history of illness, or even the fact she gave birth at home. These labels are meant to signal the child was born from persons of unfortunate position; they are in many ways a judgment, a system of branding the unwanted.

Russian medicine enjoys a long history of assigning disease to otherwise healthy individuals. Combine this predilection with the vast number of children available for adoption and it's no wonder the official position of the Russian government, and the doctors it employs, is that these children are defective. To admit otherwise is to acknowledge a national crisis of family, opportunity, poverty, and hope. This is why Russian orphans by definition are presumed to have defects, and why the compulsion of orphanage doctors to find pathology where none exists seems itself so blatantly pathological.

As perplexing as it is infuriating, the Russian system of assigning dubious medical diagnoses to orphaned infants nonetheless fails to identify the numerous bona fide issues circling ominously overhead. These real issues, like habitual alcohol consumption during pregnancy, are overlooked and unacknowledged, yet they are the true harbingers that alter the destinies of these children. Already having made two informed but difficult choices rejecting orphaned babies in need, Pat and I understood these truths. We were seasoned veterans of the process, appropriately cynical and suspicious by the time the third e-mail arrived. We were no longer capable of being surprised or cajoled.

But there he was, Baby Number Three. Our hearts were tugged toward him the moment we opened the picture and saw his tiny, nearly translucent, ten-month-old face. He was our Ben. To this day, I can recall his delicate features as vividly as I'm able to remember the contours of my mother's hands, or the joy shining through my sister's exhausted, bloodshot eyes both times she gave birth. He had ruby red lips, cobalt blue eyes that did little to hide a certain vulnerable quality, and a musician's long, graceful fingers. Like a newly hatched chick, his head was covered with downy, yellow fuzz. His name was Aleksandr, a common name among Russian orphans, but he was known as "Sasha." The other bits of information, growth measurements and gestational length, were all promising. Other than the expected notation regarding perinatal encephalopathy, there were no red flags. The Russians were making sure we knew our Ben was born of suboptimal circumstances, but we already knew that. Not too many patrician children find their way into Russian institutions for orphans.

Peggy was called for the third time, and the video, which she assured had been carefully screened by her and others at Adopt Through Us, was sent via overnight delivery. The tape was beautiful to watch. He was a wonderful baby, tender and loving. He laughed and cooed and gently reached for his caregiver's fingers to grasp. His clothes were not taken off, which would have afforded Dr. Aronson an opportunity to examine his extremities, muscle tone, and nutritional status, but there were plenty of other encouraging signs. Pulled to a standing position by the caregiver, for instance, he was able to hold himself up using the crib rail for support. Not bad for a ten-month-old baby presumed to be neglected and nutritionally compromised. He also had wonderful eye contact and readily responded to his name being called.

We waited until we heard back from Dr. Aronson to let our families know, which was difficult because we felt so certain this child was Ben. I can't remember exactly what we did to fill the time, but I do remember how I felt. Edgy. Queasy. Helpless. Angry. I was becoming increasingly resentful of the fact that my destiny was tangled up with medical reports and video reviews and all the other clinical aspects of adoption, not to mention the intrusive, antiseptic year of fertility treatment that preceded it. We had already turned down two babies. The thought that a third child could follow suit and elude us was difficult to stomach. Though I wouldn't have admitted it, insisting instead to anyone who cared to listen that my life was rich and complete without children, my need to mother was as basic as my need to laugh or feel the warming sun on my face. Unwavering and elemental.

The business of acquiring children to love through adoption, however, was beginning to damage my soul in a way previously unconsidered. None of us are in control of our own destinies, not really. The trick is in maintaining the charade, but for me the illusion was starting to fray. I needed good news. I needed this baby to be ours.

My heart thumped wildly when word finally came, eyes scanning the few lines dashed out in Dr. Aronson's late night e-mail, lines that would change our lives forever. The baby was fine. All signs were positive, not a single finding worthy of concern. We didn't cry, maybe we were still too stunned, but we were overjoyed. Pat celebrated in his usual quiet way, the death of his sons having taught him long ago that good can turn bad all too quickly, the pictures in our bedroom reminding me daily of his solitary loss. First Vincent, whose infantile features blur over time with imperfect memory, and then Joey, the goofy, big-hearted prankster whose light shined so bright but much too briefly. It's a bitter lesson incapable of being unlearned.

I never had been directly touched, however, by such unspeakable tragedy, and so despite my respect for Pat's reticence, I felt like shouting our news from the highest rooftop. I was ready and eager to plunge headfirst into motherhood, completely confident in the adoption process that already had culled without mercy two helpless, deserving children. Though arduous, the process had worked. Ben was born! I wanted the world to know.

The first thing I did was stand in front of the television in our bedroom and record clips of the videotape with my digital camera, producing a fuzzy but animated vision of Ben that I e-mailed to my family and closest friends. Then I began my lists. What we would need to furnish the nursery, what

Ben would need in the way of clothes, shoes, blankets, toys, books, bottles, sippy cups, and diapers. He would also need a car seat, high chair, stroller, port-a-crib, and play gym. Then there was the list of what he didn't really need but I wanted him to have: University of Florida football outfits; Dr. Seuss plates and cups; personalized towels with embroidered dinosaurs; silly hats; stuffed dogs, horses, and monkeys; a puppy snuggle suit; Raffi CDs; organic baby food; and a genuine wooden toboggan.

Tweetsie Road, Blowing Rock, NC (July 2005)

These were the things that would mark him as mine, brand him as my own in a way that genetics, in this instance, could not. I'm certain Pat had his own list. Ben would first learn to love the things we loved, the favorites on our lists serving as loving placeholders until he was old enough to form his own desires.

An impressive pile of to-do lists began overtaking our rumpled bed when the phone started ringing. We took turns listening as the high-pitched squeals of congratulation poured in, one call following another for hours on end, our eyes finally wet with tears that no amount of dabbing could stop. Our child was real. He was in the world, in a city called Birobidzhan, a place in the far east of Russia that takes effort to locate on a map, waiting for a long ride home. With the click of a button, we could see his beautiful face and slender long limbs, hear his infectious laugh, and, best of all, dream of the day when the three of us would be together. As soon as the calls slowed, I abandoned my lists in favor of printing and framing his referral photos, carefully displaying them around the house so Pat and I could see our baby's face from any vantage. I fell asleep that night staring at his little face, feeling content and relaxed for the first time in months. I was becoming a mother. I could finally feel it. The most difficult part of the journey was over. All that was left was to bring him home.

❦

OCTOBER 2, 2007. *Dr. Federici, the neuropsychologist who evaluated and diagnosed Peter in May 2006, wants us to send our son to the Scar Residential Psychiatric Treatment Program in Jasper Mountain, Oregon. An enticing opening salvo on the Scar website states "Achieving Success with Impossible Children." One fact-finding phone call and I'm convinced the people at Scar have seen children like Peter before. In fact, there are so many "Peters" in the United States, children adopted mostly from Eastern European countries who are "scarred" beyond the realm of what even extraordinary rehabilitative efforts can address, that an entire (and expensive) medical, psychosocial, and educational system has evolved to support them.*

Until recently, Pat and I never had considered the possible need for residential treatment, but the idea has crept into our consciousness like a slow but steady cancer. Peter at some point may well require residential treatment, and if so, then it becomes a question of when, how, and whether we'll be able to afford it. The thought of existing, indefinitely, on a roller coaster ride would fill any normal person with dread. But imagine the roller coaster was designed and operated by a person with frontal lobe damage, a person who can't remember the peril he put his passengers in yesterday so is destined to repeat the same misstep today that he'll in turn repeat tomorrow. This is life with Peter. I can cry and hug and hold and reassure until I'm more tired and drained than I ever imagined possible, and little changes. I still believe Peter is reachable in those moments, but I've come to realize, and grudgingly accept, that sustained emotional growth must be measured in minuscule increments. His brain lacks storage capacity for the kind of complex, emotional learning that even newborn babies are equipped to internalize. The old behaviors return the next day, or the next hour, not because Peter is defiant or merely shedding crocodile tears, but because the moment is gone. Vanished. His mind is more permeable than Swiss cheese but much less malleable, at least when it comes to shaping healthy concepts of love, family, and respect.

Sometimes I worry that we've missed our opportunity, if there ever was one, to leave our imprint inside the echoing, dark caverns that form the mystery of Peter's brain. I'm not sure how residential treatment would alleviate this problem. I imagine, rather shamefully, that the mollifying aspect of a place like Scar accrues not so much to the children themselves but rather to the benefit of parents, like us, who have reached the zenith of their capacities. At some point, if ever we need to set this course in motion, we'll have to acknowledge a painful paradigm shift: the welfare of Pat, Sophie, and me may become inconsistent with and need to take precedence over the welfare of our son. Our beautiful but damaged son. The very thought of sending Peter away is anathema, and yet sometimes I feel myself yielding, all the same, to the slow caress of temptation.

CHAPTER 6

OH YEAH (THE DOMESTIC DEBACLE)

IN THE MIDST of our frenetic effort to complete the additional requirements necessary to receive our travel date, the sacred day on the calendar when we would fly to Russia and hold Ben for the first time, we received a phone call that stopped us dead in our tracks. I had been so consumed with the new round of paperwork that I had forgotten about the little seed we'd planted a few months earlier. I didn't even recognize the name of the caller when I answered the phone.

Around the same time we signed up for the international adoption meeting in Manhattan, we spread the odds of winning the adoption game by also getting ourselves on a domestic list. We put together an adoption package complete with photos, personal histories, and a dear birth mother letter. We filled out numerous questionnaires in which we indicated our desire to adopt a Caucasian baby through closed adoption. The birth mother needed to be free of alcohol, tobacco, and drugs from conception through delivery. Because most birth mothers who contemplate adoption prefer an open arrangement, which allows some contact and periodic updates, we knew our chances of being picked were slim. The fact that we also would accept nothing less than a substance-free pregnancy closed the door even further. Be prepared, we were told, to wait two to three years, possibly much longer.

That was fine with us. We were planning to adopt from Russia. We'd be ready if and when a domestic opportunity arose to help complete our family. If not, then Pat and I would either be content with our one child or we would return to Russia to adopt a second baby. Our plan read so logically on paper. But then the phone rang. A birth mother had picked us. She was due in three weeks and preferred a closed (meaning no future contact) adoption. The baby, a boy, was already over six pounds and due July 4th. She requested that we be with her in Tampa, Florida, for the delivery.

In the few beats it took before my brain aligned with this unexpected news, the qualifiers began popping from the phone like backyard fireworks. The birth mother had grappled with substance abuse in the past—cocaine, marijuana, and alcohol—but swears she's been clean for nearly a year. She is thirty-eight years old and on her fifth pregnancy. Yes, all her other babies were given up for adoption. The agency placed them all and each continues to thrive. The birth mother knows who the father is but won't say. The agency is in the process of investigating this issue so they can obtain the necessary paternal releases. Not to worry, these things have a way of working themselves out. To sweeten the pot, the woman on the phone whispers conspiratorially that the birth mother is beautiful and so are the four other children. And best of all: even though we were in the midst of planning our first trip to Birobidzhan to meet Ben, a trip that Adopt Through Us was predicting would take place in mid- to late July, and no matter that there were hundreds of unanswered questions regarding this birth mother, we needed to make a decision within twenty-four hours.

My poor husband nearly collapsed when I told him. I really had wanted to experience mothering a newborn, a wish he didn't passionately share but was willing to support and respect. He had already parented three newborn babies, after all, and I loved him for the selflessness of wanting me to have this opportunity even though he must have dreaded the sleepless drudgery it entailed. For a man in his mid-fifties, the prospect of going to Russia for Ben was daunting enough. But we both wanted our new son to have a sibling. For me, there was never any doubt, but Pat did not feel similarly until a New York City cab ride with his mother helped reorient his thinking. During a drowsy late-night talk, he shared with me how he had been listening to her melancholy reminiscences about growing up as an only child and realized he didn't want this for his son. And as it turned out, a sibling for Ben was landing in our lap, scheduled to drop in on the world, and possibly our lives, in a few short weeks. Never mind that I was still in a walking cast and facing another surgery in late summer to remove an assortment of hardware in my lower leg from the ski accident three months earlier. We would find a way.

Fall 2006

The news had an intoxicating effect, despite the poor timing and my hobbled condition. Pat walked around with his eyes bulging in disbelief, and I found myself giggling like a schoolgirl. However, we knew this was no time to behave like love-crazed teenagers or, better yet, a couple of geriatrics who had just won the lottery and decided to buy a hacienda in Costa Rica, sight unseen. To slow ourselves down and force a more rational consideration of the risks (such as history of drug use) and impossible logistics of the situation, we hastily scribbled a list of questions and criteria that we then ranked in order of priority. Making sure we did nothing to jeopardize the timely adoption of Ben was at the top of our list. In our hearts and minds and in every cell of our bodies, he was already our son. The thought of Ben wasting away in some Dickensian institution a minute more than necessary was simply unacceptable. Obtaining empirical proof that the birth mother wasn't using drugs or drinking was next. Finding the father was third.

Figuring out how we could fly to Tampa for the birth, accept temporary custody during the mandatory waiting period under Florida law (knowing this time period would likely overlap with our expected Russian travel date), leave the baby in the care of one of my siblings (probably my sister, Patty, who would have to come to Tampa from Atlanta and stay there with the baby in the home of one of my brothers, both of whom live in the area, as the baby would not be allowed to leave the state of Florida), fly to Russia, meet and confirm that we wanted to adopt Ben, fly back from Russia and return to Tampa, appear in Florida court to finalize the domestic adoption, fly back to New York with the baby, and then, six weeks later, travel back to Russia to bring Ben home? Well, that was number four. Obviously we chose not to prioritize in order of complexity.

As it turned out, number four on our list was solvable, especially when we pushed back and persuaded the agency that twenty-four hours was an unreasonable amount of time to determine whether this could work. We talked to adoption lawyers about temporary custody, the transfer of temporary custody to my sister, getting leave from the court to travel from Tampa to Russia, and a host of other legal gyrations that would be required to accomplish this feat. My sister, Patty, would have to take time from her law practice and make arrangements for the care of her own two children (her husband constantly travels), but she would find a way to make this work. My brother Mark and his wife, Paula, would set up a temporary nursery in their home in Tampa. Unfortunately, more than a year earlier, they had scheduled a two-week trip with their kids to the Grand Canyon that could not be canceled or rescheduled. This meant my sister would be on her own with the baby in my brother's house once we left for Russia to meet Ben.

The more difficult part was related to the issues the domestic agency assured us would work themselves out. The birth mother had not come to the agency until very late in her pregnancy, so the quality of her prenatal care, as well as confirmation of her drug and alcohol status, could not be determined. Despite this, the agency continued to assure us that the birth mother was cooperative and willing to undergo any and all drug and alcohol screens. An emergency appointment for her to see the agency's obstetrician had been made. But that appointment was missed, and so was the next one. We were told she had a fear of taking public transportation, which is why she didn't make the first appointment. The next time, the agency sent a taxi-cab, but the driver left after fifteen minutes when she failed to come out of the apartment the agency had placed her in and for which we were expected to pay. A few days passed. Someone from the adoption agency went over to the apartment, and after explaining to the woman that she would not enjoy any of the expected fees or paid expenses if she failed to cooperate with the medical protocol, she agreed to be escorted to the doctor.

My brother Mark is the kind of loud, lumbering guy who in his frater-nity days used to get thrown out of football games for drunk and disorderly conduct but who has always had one of the biggest and best hearts on the planet. He's an attorney now who represents product manufacturers against claims for liability. A seasoned litigator with an innate talent for identify-ing fraud, he was becoming more and more suspicious of the birth mother's behavior and growing list of ill-disguised excuses. While the agency was do-ing its best to corral a difficult client, Mark hatched a more practical, if not extreme, plan. He offered to send out his private investigator to find out who the birth mother was, the extent of her past (and present) drug use, the name and background of the father, and anything else we wanted to know. "Don't worry," he said. "I promise you, my guy can find out *anything*." Although I didn't have much experience with this side of Mark, and was a little alarmed to learn he knew how to gather information in this fashion, I was deeply touched by the offer.

In the meantime, the agency wasn't making much progress with the birth mother. She went to the doctor but refused to submit to a drug screen. The obstetrician did perform a sonogram, however, and was able to con-firm the baby was male and probably not due until early August. Anyone but the most desperate to believe in the fiction of this situation would understand what was happening. This woman was on drugs, and probably drinking and smoking as well. She was a professional birth mother who used the nine months of housing, groceries, medical care, and cash—all part of the private adoption package—to clean up, rest, and finance the times between pregnancies.

Unlike the wrenching emotions we felt when we turned down the two Russian babies before Ben, Pat and I knew in a matter of days that this was a con and we were the intended victims. I remember the relief I felt on the morning Pat and I decided over coffee and bagels that neither of us wanted to pursue this "opportunity" a minute longer. The initial excitement had passed and we had finally sobered up. That's not to say, however, that I didn't feel any regret or disappointment. I knew there would be no other chance to cradle a newborn, an infant that would be mine to hold and keep from the moment of birth. But thoughts of Ben, the baby in Birobidzhan we had claimed by name and in our hearts only weeks before, softened this blow and helped obscure thoughts of this latest bungled experience. He was all we really needed.

The phone rang before we ever had a chance to announce the decision to walk away. I listened to the adoption agency woman explain that the birth mother had gone into labor overnight. As she spoke, I watched a woodpecker accost the wooden swing that hangs under the large oak in our front yard. The baby had been born five hours later, and about five weeks premature, with cocaine and marijuana in his bloodstream. Consistent with Florida law, the state assumed custody and was taking mandated steps against the mother. Seconds after I hung up the phone, the woodpecker flew away, frustrated with the effort of pecking at an uncooperative swaying object. I looked over at Pat, who was smiling wryly. He knew what I knew. Topping off our mugs with hot coffee, we went about our business of planning for the day ahead. A day that was warm, sunny, and waiting to be absorbed. The domestic debacle was over.

&

OCTOBER 10, 2007. *I spend endless hours on the phone trying to wade through the gooey mess of countless mental health and social services departments, a task as impossible as swimming upstream in a river of Jell-O. Finding a human who can give me useful information, all the while decoding subtle clues offered or withheld, is a Herculean undertaking. I resent my descent into this world, the intrusion into our personal lives it represents, and, most of all, the reality that it's a system with which I know I'll become intimately familiar, whether next month, next year, or in the coming decade. Peter will need these supports, he'll need these people, and I have no choice but to learn the system and connect with those who are in a position to help. Right now I have the time to be overwhelmed by Peter and his daily challenges. Perhaps that's part of the problem. In the coming weeks I'll start practicing again part time with a small environmental law firm. Despite how busy I am with trying to manage the children's needs and all that is required to finish our new house and move from our still-unsold existing home, I need to get back to work. I need my mind to be flexed, several hours a day, by challenges that leave no room for brooding over my enigmatic son.*

In the doctor's office today for his well-checkup, Peter grabbed two hypodermic needles while the nurse turned her back. He pushed the plungers and sprayed the contents of the vaccinations around the room. I was talking to the doctor and did not have my eyes on him, a fact he undoubtedly registered in the split second before making his move. Afterward, in a flustered state, Peter's pediatrician wrote on his school health form that he was mentally retarded. Surely he must have seemed so in the moment, but he isn't. I had to go back and have her change the form. I was angry, of course, but later I asked myself, what should she have written instead? That he is impulsive, without judgment, lacks self-control, doesn't appreciate danger, can't access his intelligence, and is destined to repeat the same mistakes over and over? Today I leave a half dozen messages for various social workers, mental health professionals, and school officials, and while I wait to hear back, I become distressed by the thought that in some ways Peter's deficits are more substantial (and dangerous) than mental retardation. I often get lost in these emotionally risky cogitations without the antidote of work to coax my mind toward other thoughts. Work problems, no matter how complex, are eminently more solvable than those facing our family. The sooner I return, the better.

CHAPTER 7

SOPHIE

LIFE HAS AN odd way of instructing sometimes, and the takeaway lesson from the failed domestic adoption was unexpected and, as it turns out, a blessing in disguise. I was talking to my girlfriend Suzanne in Atlanta one afternoon, catching her up on the status of our still-unscheduled Russian trip and the surreal experience with the Tampa baby. She and I worked together as enforcement attorneys at the Environmental Protection Agency's regional office in Atlanta for eight years before I moved to Manhattan and married Pat. I smile fondly whenever I think of Suzanne's sassy voice and those impossibly tight curls that assume the same position no matter how her haircuts change. She is one of those wonderful New Yorkers living happily in the Deep South with the same brilliant pizzazz and gumption I once saw her display as she wrangled to snag the last pair of size 7 boots at a Macy's shoe sale. She has an uncanny ability to make lemonade out of lemons, and I rely on her greatly, despite geographical distance, when I need a lift.

On this particular day, and in typical Suzanne style, she let me ramble just long enough to feel better and then posed a question. Now that we had accepted the idea of adopting two children at once, and even figured out a way logistically to manage the insanity of the Tampa circumstances, why not ask Adopt Through Us whether we could bring another baby home with Ben?

A puckish question, to be sure, and one that made me smile. Uncharacteristically, I kept this idea to myself for a number of days. I tend to share almost all my thoughts and ideas with Pat, in stream-of-consciousness style, because he's usually a sympathetic but logical sounding board. But I was having a hard time gauging the possible range of his response, and he does have his limits. Take animals, for instance. Had there been no one to stop me, I might have acquired many more than we currently own over the last several years. Our very old house sat on eight acres and was plenty large enough for the furry friends of my dreams. But Pat unequivocally has drawn the line at two dogs, two cats, one gerbil, and a small school of fish. (Sophie caught most of the aquatic members of the family.) I can't much blame him. He's the one who lets the dog out in the middle of the night, disposes of the dead creatures the cats catch, and rescues the occasional minnow found flopping on the floor.

Adopting another child isn't the same as acquiring a zoo, but for Pat, the time, patience, and commitment required were essentially the same. The past year of our life together, on the best of days, conjured up images of riotous chimps and squawking birds, causing Pat to duck for cover at nearly every turn. Between fertility treatments, the ski accident, the decision to adopt, the rejected Russian referrals, and the Tampa fiasco, we both felt like we'd been plopped, unceremoniously, into a pressure cooker and left to boil. Just when we thought the worst was behind us, Pat's eighty-year-old mother fell and broke her shoulder while visiting from Florida. Scared and hurt, there was no way she could fly home and fend for herself. Although I was still in the walking boot, weeks away from being able to drive again, I found myself conscripted into caring 24/7 for my mother-in-law, a woman I barely knew at the time. She has since moved to New York to live near us and has become truly one of the great blessings in my life. I miss my own mother with waves of intensity impossible to bear at times, and yet this spunky little Sicilian woman, unexpectedly, has become mother, friend, and confidante. I value her opinion and insight, admire her sage sense of humor, and love her deeply. She has indeed become a mother to me, in the best possible sense of the word. But at the time, in all honesty, the situation overwhelmed me.

Night after night, when Pat and I lay in bed, we didn't know whether to laugh or cry. Thankfully, most often, we laugh when given the option, dissecting the absurdities of the day with what I've come to believe is restorative deprecation. We've made an art of poking fun at ourselves, often and without mercy. But still, there was a lot on our plates, and I didn't know whether in good conscience I should raise the issue of adopting another child just then. We were dodging catastrophes right and left, and, no matter how comic the events of our lives might play out on the big screen, I knew better than to assume that Pat's highly evolved sense of humor and gentle disposition were limitless.

So, before I made any decisions that would involve Pat, I called Peggy at Adopt Through Us to see whether a second child was even possible. The short answer was "Yes, of course!" The less clear, sticky part had to do with fees and expenses and whether a second referral would substantially postpone or even jeopardize our trip to meet Ben. Peggy promised to call back as soon as she had more information. Before we hung up, she asked whether we preferred a girl or boy. "A girl," I blurted. As long as gender selection was an accepted (and expected) part of the Russian adoption equation, there was no doubt in my mind. I wanted a snuggle bunny with whom to cuddle and play dolls with on rainy Saturday mornings, a daughter with whom I could one day share the secrets of my water balloon babies.

I remember distinctly the moment when the subject could no longer be forestalled. Peggy had called back with the answers to all my questions and asked in return that we make a decision by the next day. Only that morning, according to Peggy, the agency had received a referral of a two-year-old girl living in the same orphanage as Ben. The referral was ours to take, but we needed to move quickly. Other prospective parents were waiting in the wings. The message was clear: talk to Pat.

I found him in the kitchen making lunch out of hot sauce, goat cheese, and Italian bread. With the help of Vicodin, his mother was sleeping fitfully in the nearby sunroom, propped up with a dozen pillows so she could watch the swarm of ladybugs that had been crawling up and down the windows for days. Busying myself with emptying the dishwasher, I quietly explained Suzanne's idea, my phone calls to Adopt Through Us, and the news of the referral waiting to be delivered to our doorstep.

Pat didn't say a word, though he continued to shake neon-green hot sauce out of the narrow bottle with more energy than the task required. Although he didn't look angry, he wasn't exactly combing the drawers for celebratory cigars. Instead, he walked out of the room, still wordless, went into the bathroom and came back. "I'll think about it," he said. I didn't have the gumption to tell him he'd have to think quickly. My decision had already been made, as the thudding in my heart confirmed. This mattered, more than I realized, and the clock was ticking. The possibility of completing our family in one fell swoop very much appealed to me.

It seemed as if the possibility of a second referral quelled the nagging ache that surfaced whenever I thought about whether, realistically, we would find the time, energy, and money to go back to Russia to adopt another child. Hard as it was for me to accept some days, Pat was in his fifties and I was nearing forty. (In my heart of hearts I'm only twenty-five and Pat is twenty-eight.) Without the driving, raw desire to have a child propelling us through the adoption process, I wasn't sure we'd be able to rekindle the desire, and energy, to do it again. We naturally would become contented with Ben, overjoyed and satiated by his presence in our lives. I knew it would be all too easy to convince ourselves that he was enough, that he didn't need a sibling with which to share his childhood or lean on in the years of life that would stretch beyond our own.

The storm that had been threatening all day finally unleashed and jolted us both from our pensive revelries. A bolt of lightning stirred Pat's mother, and I heard her moan weakly from the other room, though she didn't awaken fully. I imagined the ladybugs losing their grips on the window screens as staccato sheets of rain hit the house, one slanted burst after another. Pat put his sandwich down and looked at me.

"You really want this, don't you?" he asked. His eyes were soft but full of worry.

"I don't want Ben to be alone."

"A girl?" He knew the answer but wanted to hear it anyway.

I nodded.

"A girl would be nice."

The conversation ended without another word, and life resumed its hectic pace. The storm woke Pat's mother for good, and she needed help changing positions. Pat may have needed the sizzling comfort of hot sauce to become sufficiently steeled for the conversation, but in the end he never even flinched. I would have been happy to adopt two boys when the chance arose, and I managed to walk stoically away when that chance blew up in our faces. Pat understood, more than anyone, the extent of my efforts to achieve motherhood and build a family. He also knew the Tampa debacle had been my one and only opportunity to experience a baby from birth. To this day, I'm not sure whether he wanted to adopt a second child at the same time as Ben or whether his goal was simply to make me happy.

Every day Pat gives me the extraordinary gift of knowing I'm completely loved. He nourishes my soul in a way that's more valuable and enduring than any possible combination of possessions. I'm very lucky in this regard, and I know it. That day he chose to illustrate this poignant fact by agreeing to adopt a second child. The reason I don't brood over whether Pat's decision was coerced is because it turned out to be the best decision we ever made, a wondrous gift to us both. Sophie makes us laugh on days when only tears come naturally and reminds us why we began this journey in the first place. She is perfect in a delightfully imperfect way and has brought immeasurable joy to our lives. She doesn't, though, go in much for dolls. On rainy days we snuggle and play, but we're more likely to play a zany version of zoo with her mounds of stuffed animals dressed in the clothes she stripped from her flung-aside dolls.

The correctness of our decision, however, was not so apparent at first. In fact, when Adopt Through Us sent Sophie's picture and medical report, we were a little taken aback. She looked more like a ten-month-old baby than an almost two-year-old child, and she was wedged into the bed of a large toy truck, making the poor baby look like a Thanksgiving bird. She was not pretty in the classical sense, and she looked bloated and distressed. These are not kind thoughts to have about an orphaned child in need of a family, but they were our initial impressions. Luckily, Pat and I are not such horrible people that we ever allowed a child's physical appearance to impact any of our adoption decisions. If she was healthy, we wanted her.

But there were aspects of the photograph that contradicted the medical report. For instance, despite her robust appearance in the photo, the report stated her birth weight was low and her current weight barely reached the third percentile. Later we found out that the orphanage made a practice of extreme layering, meaning she wore panties, an undershirt, a pair of long underwear followed by wool tights, thick socks over the tights, and then a pair of long pants, a long-sleeved shirt, and a wool sweater. Knowing this explained her balloon-like appearance and the distressed expression on her face, but we weren't aware of this practice at the time.

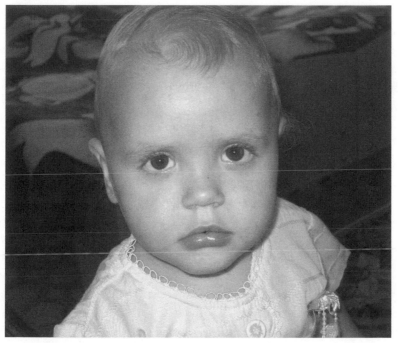

Meeting Sophie, Baby Home, Birobidzhan, Russia (August 2004)

Instead, we just thought she had a very large, puffy head. Though we joked about it, we never gave it serious consideration. My older sister and brothers still claim I was born with a rectangular-shaped head, and they gleefully produce photos to substantiate these ugly, mirthful allegations. They do this to tease me, of course, but what if they were right and I had been orphaned and put up for adoption in Russia? Would I have been rejected by middle-class Americans because of the shoebox shape of my head? Maybe these imaginary parents would have thought I had *perinatal enceph-alopathy* or some other alarming medical condition. As long as Dr. Aronson gave her a positive review, we would say yes. She would be beautiful in our eyes, if not to the world at large, and that was enough.

The video arrived a day or two later. Her physical appearance had changed in the intervening months. The film was recorded in summer and she had been liberated from the suffocating layers of clothes. Also her hair had lightened from dark brown to golden blond and her face looked slimmer and much livelier. The video showed her tottering around the edge of a play hut, holding onto the rim for support. Her eyes were closed the entire time, about three and a half minutes. We could hear a caregiver in the background urging her to do something, presumably open her eyes, and we held our breath as we watched our future daughter pause to consider the request. Then she smiled slightly, chortled quietly, and continued with her business, eyes closed.

We shared this video, as we had all the others, with friends and family. While waiting to hear back from Dr. Aronson, we were anxious to know what people thought of her unusual behavior. Most scratched their heads and offered various theories regarding why a toddler in a Russian orphanage might act this way. Some were simply stumped and offered no opinion at all. But one person whom I won't name suggested that Sophie had certain brain damage, and another chimed in that we would be making the biggest mistake of our lives if we persisted on this course.

One of the problems with planning a family through adoption is that it transforms what should be a closed-door experience between two loving people into business conducted in a public forum, complete with fans and hecklers. But in this instance, the anger and resentment I felt toward the naysayers in the stands was of my own making. We had asked for these opinions, and I unfairly had expected those within our inner circle to have the good graces to keep their mouths shut in the absence of having something instructive to say.

Luckily, Dr. Aronson was not worried, and we were overjoyed with the news when her e-mail finally arrived, as usual, in the middle of the night. She was amused by Sophie's decision to navigate the taping session blind. What Dr. Aronson saw in her behavior were streaks of independence, a sense of humor, a keen (and brain-preserving) ability to make her static environment interesting, and an overarching stubborn disregard for authority. In short, Sophie intrigued her. "This one is smart," she wrote. "She's very determined."

As usual, Dr. Aronson was right. Now that we know Sophie, there is no doubt she was controlling the situation, striving to unnerve her caregivers and make her dull world more interesting. Strangers routinely stop us on the street, in restaurants, and at playgrounds, mesmerized that someone so young has such presence, acumen, confidence, and beauty. Yes, the homely orphan in the referral photo turned out to be a breathtaking beauty. Icing on an already prize-winning cake. Despite having walked out of the same violent storm that pelted our son's brain with horrifying debris and relentless purpose, Sophie emerged from the Baby Home in Birobidzhan with abrasions but hopefully no deep, untreatable gashes. This is the real miracle imbedded in our daughter's remarkable, palpable spirit.

In the end, the decision to adopt Sophie has too many layers of significance, even salvation, to express adequately in words. If Pat and I ache over the enormity of Peter's problems, if we stare at the ceiling at night because the responsibility of caring for a child like Peter robs us of sleep, then Sophie often is our sweet elixir. When younger, she liked to say, "Mommy, I love you so much my heart grows big." I feel the same way. She is joy and cause for celebration, her rascally face a constant reminder that there is good in the world and room for applause in my heart.

At the time, we thought Sophie would make the perfect companion for Ben, who was thirteen months her junior. Little did we know how our ordinary dreams were about to spiral exponentially beyond our imaginings.

◌﹏

OCTOBER 28, 2007. *Jack Dann is visiting from Australia. He and Pat have been best friends, writer and editor, since their early twenties, though we've not seen him since the adoptions. The children were giddy waiting for his arrival, as though they could feel Jack's enormous energy pulsating toward them. Yesterday was humid and rainy, an uncanny fall day, with layers of leaves plastered against sopping wet lawns. Jack intuits instantly that we're not the same people he hugged and kissed goodbye four years earlier. And so the story unfolds across the vista of his visit, and Jack listens. Really listens. He doesn't try to downplay our fears or say everything will work out. He knows it won't. The devastation he sees in our faces is all the confirmation he needs. But he does talk about scripts, and stories. He is a writer, after all. He says people carry different scripts throughout their lives and they choose the version of themselves they wish to portray on any given day, much the way people choose shoes to match an outfit. He challenges us to recast ourselves so that he can see his old friends in a more peaceful, less turbulent script. We don't have to like the situation with Peter, or look for beauty or strength in our son's misfortune, but we can choose the script that gives us permission to still find joy in life and in each other.*

Thank God Jack is back. I need to hear this and so does Pat. Though we may have accepted our fate with Peter intellectually, we've yet to internalize this knowledge emotionally. We desperately need to, however. Jack sees to the core of this with his loving, keen, troubleshooting skills. This morning Peter graced us with some predictable, nerve-wracking tricks. But Jack is here and so it's okay. The front that brought the rain yesterday has given way to dropping temperatures and blustery air. The leaves, now dry, swirl drunkenly in the wind, and Jack has us poised for frolic. I prepare a full Thanksgiving dinner for our friend because he's an American living in Australia and misses the holiday. While the turkey is cooking, we take a ride up the street to a nearby farm stand. There is a pressurized pumpkin launcher that sends gourds flying incredible distances at astonishing speeds. Cars line the road for a half mile on either side, hoping to catch the "ba-boom" of home-grown, country fun. The contraption looks like something developed by army intelligence, and when activated, it bellows with such magnitude that the uninformed might worry that a new world war was suddenly underway. We watch for a while and eat roasted corn, and then we load the kids and ourselves onto a haunted hayride. Jack, Pat, and I are behaving like schoolchildren without proper chaperones. It feels good. Really good. If we can do this while Jack's here, we can do this when he's not. Jack brought a script for us to work from, but he's leaving tomorrow. It's time to write a new one of our own.

CHAPTER 8

RUSSIA, PART I (WHERE'S BEN?)

ON AUGUST 8, 2004, Pat and I stepped off the ten-hour Delta flight from New York to Moscow, hand in hand, and walked into the airport. The day we would meet our children was thirty-six hours away, and my knees wobbled in anticipation. Ben and Sophie. Although Peter wasn't then part of our adoption story, all paths were leading inexorably toward him, like snowmelt trickling through the forest to a mountain lake below, waiting quietly for the rebirth of spring. Peter would be reborn to us soon, but not yet. First we would meet his adopted sister and Ben, the boy whose cruel misfortune would become Peter's salvation. Russian roulette, orphanage-style.

The airport in Moscow makes JFK look like an exemplary model of civil planning. We began realizing this as soon as we tried passing through the double doors of the gate. Most double doors in large public places are designed to promote orderly egress and ingress. This is not the case in Russia. One of two doors is locked at all times, forcing stony-faced people to ram their way through the narrow single opening, Saran-wrapped luggage in tow, while others are doing the same from the opposite direction. Though Russians are a very warm and genuine people in the intimacy and comfort of their homes, their public demeanor is the reverse. This gruff predisposition coupled with the constant frustration of having to navigate buildings, roads, airports, sidewalks, and hospitals in a constant state of disrepair lends an angry pulse to the communal rhythm of the masses.

Pat and I struggled to elbow and shove our way through what resembled a glass-walled cattle chute, furtively searching the crowd for our Russian guide as we followed the herd into baggage claim. We found him before too long, thanks to the handwritten cardboard sign that read LIBUTTI and the I LOVE USA baseball cap perched atop his balding head. The spelling of Pat's last name, LoBrutto, wasn't that close a match, but it was encouraging enough to make us lunge toward him with relief, grinning like the dumb, bewildered Americans we were. His name was Sergei and he was one of the true jewels of our trips. Three years later, we're still in e-mail contact.

Our overnight stay at the Renaissance Moscow was brief but memorable. Shortly after we checked into our room we met two other couples traveling from Florida, also Adopt Through Us clients. Both had completed the first required trip, which Pat and I were just beginning. The purpose of this trip is to meet the child, spend time together, and officially decide whether the adoption should be finalized. Many people scoff at this requirement, asserting that the Russians are capitalizing on the adoption trade, eagerly collecting the additional fees, charges, gifts, and donations that two separate trips can provide. The fact that American adoption agencies counsel their clients to bring duffle bags stuffed with "gifts"—perfumes, handkerchiefs, wallets, small electronics, and "clean" cash (meaning no marks, tears, or folds on the bills)—heightens this suspicion of impropriety.

So many aspects of this journey bothered or at times even offended me, but not these particular requirements. Adopting a child is very serious business, and prospective parents should be made to jump through as many hoops and over as many hurdles as necessary to demonstrate sufficiently their stamina and commitment. Though tempting, it's a mistake to attribute the incredibly complex set of social and economic factors that lead to abject neglect and deprivation, such as that seen in Russian orphanages, to mere apathy and greed. Americans and Canadians and the occasional Europeans are taking away Russia's unwanted children by the planefuls. People like Pat and I have been invited to help relieve this national burden, one child at a time, because Russia can't care for its own. Not an easy thing to admit for a former superpower and not an easy obligation to assume for people with ordinary means, talents, and coping skills, pursuing the very ordinary and natural dream of becoming parents. Because of what happened with Ben, our agency struck a deal with the local Russian government to allow us to adopt Peter on our second trip within twenty-four hours of meeting him. There was no time allotted so that the idea of Peter could blend with the reality of the boy we met, to reconcile the twinkle-eyed smile in the pictures with the stiff, robotic child we found ourselves facing in the orphanage. Two trips are good.

As for the gifts, the idea didn't bother me so much after meeting the recipients, mostly kind, weary people who lacked the money to buy vegetables or even replace a pair of socks. The abject poverty was humbling to experience. But that night in Moscow, the gifts, the multiple trips, and a myriad of other complaints were hashed and rehashed over a four-hour dinner with the two couples we'd just met. The six of us sat around a table eating gristly cheeseburgers and drinking beer and soda. Pat and I were thrilled to find ourselves in the company of other American adoption couples. Listening eagerly as they shared stories of their first trips to Tumen, an oil-rich region that is prosperous compared to Birobidzhan, we later peppered them with questions about what we could expect. One couple, Jackie and Sam O'Riley, have become lasting, long-distance friends. They have a knack for injecting levity into situations where most would resort to tears or violence, and, luckily for us, the O'Rileys were with us on our return flight to New York, along with their newly adopted daughter, Natalie. Their humor and unabashed joy for their five-month-old baby brought welcomed reprieve from our worries on more than one occasion.

The other couple we met that night was as memorable as Jackie and Sam, but for vastly different reasons. Epitomizing all that is out of proportion with American society, they talked about buying babies, showing cash, making the deal, and "getting a kid." They expressed anger over the fact they were adopting a boy even though they had requested a girl. The baby, as it turns out, had been quiet and withdrawn during their first trip. "He was floppy," the woman said, shrugging her salon-tanned shoulders. "Like a rag doll," the husband added. "The kid wouldn't do anything." They admitted without apology that they had consulted no one regarding the child's medical records, photographs, or video and rolled their eyes when Jackie meekly asked whether they were concerned. Had Jackie and Sam's impressions been different, or had the photograph of that baby's hollow eyes not been stamped into my memory, I might have thought I dreamed them up. They were that crass, that naive, and that cartoonish. Unfortunately for the child, they were also very real.

The other interesting aspect of our one-night stay in Moscow had to do with Pat's tooth crown, which came apart in multiple hunks during dinner with the beauty and the beast couples. Pat has an early history of poor attention to dental health and is paying the price now, in locations grand and modest, across the globe. Sergei was scheduled to pick us up at 11:30 the next morning for our eight-hour flight to Khabarovsk, the nearest airport to Birobidzhan. Pat would have precious little time to find a dentist in Moscow who could repair his broken crown. Exhausted and suffering a toothache that was only partially quelled by a handful of Motrin and two bottles of Chinese beer, he tossed and turned throughout the night, grumbling in his sleep about the injustice of dental problems with the verve of a television evangelist. The next morning the concierge, in halting English, gave him directions to the American Clinic. I kissed Pat gingerly on his swollen cheek and wished him well as I watched him trudge toward the inner belly of the city.

Having nothing else to do, I waited in the lobby for Sergei. The couples from the night before had already checked out, and I was too nervous and exhausted to read or make meaningful use of the time. But I did have the energy to people watch, which was both fascinating and stimulating. The hotel catered to an odd mix of business people, tourists, and families in various stages of adoption, and none of these factions seemed comfortable with the presence of the other. The crisp click-click of high heels and pointy men's dress shoes were juxtaposed against the nervous, squeaky shuffle of the sneaker-clad adoption couples. The imposing, austere countenance of the predominantly Russian staff sharply contrasted with the soft humming drawl and comfortable clothes of a group of elderly tourists from South Carolina. I found the whole scene a wonderful study in juxtaposition.

I became so engrossed in my observations that Sergei had to come and tap me on the shoulder. He whisked us in a panic to the American Clinic as soon as he heard his latest charge had ventured out on his own. At the time, he didn't appreciate Pat's confidence in this foreign city or know that he had grown up on the tough streets of Brooklyn and spent the majority of his youth happily combing every odd corner of New York City. Except for the excruciating pain part, my husband was thrilled to be given two hours alone to explore Moscow.

While we waited for Pat to emerge, well past the 11:30 scheduled departure time for the airport, Sergei and I became acquainted. He asked what we did for a living and literally jumped off his chair when he learned Pat was a fiction editor. It was a remarkably demonstrative move for a Russian out in public. But Sergei, as it turns out, is a voracious reader of American fiction, particularly science fiction and thrillers, two of Pat's main genres. I also learned this unassuming, soft-spoken man who drives adoption couples around Moscow, orchestrating the endless appointments and appearances required to complete the process, held a Ph.D. in cryogenic engineering. But working as an engineer, Sergei couldn't afford internet access or pay for his nine-year-old son to attend a week-long science camp. As an adoption co-ordinator paid with American dollars, he lives a respectable middle-class life in Moscow. He has a flat in one of the newer high-rises and is proud the building has two working elevators.

When I asked why he doesn't work as an engineer, Sergei paused to consider how to explain the former Soviet Union's philosophy regarding the education of its citizens. He told me that the Russian government, for instance, chose him and 30,000 other youngsters to enter university to study cryogenic engineering at no expense. His "selection" derived from his secondary school grades and achievement scores. Once his and the others' education was complete, the government chose the five or six most accomplished among them for state-sponsored projects. The rest of the newly minted cryogenic engineers were left to fend for themselves, feverishly competing for the handful of remaining jobs in an incredibly specialized field. Sergei, though not one of the wunderkind, was lucky and talented enough to land one of those coveted remaining positions. But his salary was so low he couldn't afford to stay in his occupation and give his son the better life he envisioned for him.

We would encounter this phenomenon of overeducation throughout both trips. Nearly every Russian we met as part of the adoption process was a doctor, lawyer, accountant, or engineer, but few were working in the field in which he or she had been educated. In this respect, Sergei and those like him aren't much different from the hordes of discarded children warehoused across the landscape in decaying orphanages. Their hopes, talents, and potential contributions have been pulverized and forgotten under the impossible weight of a crumbling, dysfunctional system that notoriously assigned little value to the dignity and worth of individuals.

Pat and I were confronted with the harsh reality of this lesson when we arrived in Birobidzhan the next day, exhausted, excited, and with his temporary crown intact. An indifferent, gum-chewing young woman and her driver met us at the airport in Khabarovsk and loaded our luggage into a clunky ZiL automobile. I was desperate to go to the bathroom, but the facilities in the airport consisted of a series of holes in the ground with foot imprints on either side to guide your stance. I couldn't figure out how to manage the situation and was terrified I would slip and slide into layers of filth impossible to describe. So I decided to wait. As it turns out, I would wait, with legs tightly crossed, for over half a day. There are no rest stops on the poorly maintained road from Khabarovsk to Birobidzhan.

The young woman and driver ignored us completely for the next three hours, talking loudly to themselves in Russian, pausing only to put their seatbelts on at police checkpoints and then unbuckling them as soon as we pulled away. I don't recall either of them saying more than a handful of words to us the entire time. Pat and I whispered conspiratorially to each other at first, trying not to laugh at the absurdity of our situation, but then we fell quiet, letting our eyes and thoughts roam. The landscape was desolate and overgrown, and the road was littered with potholes and debris. Old women and young Asian men walked along vast stretches of road where there was no place to turn off for miles on end. There were groups of scruffy men sitting atop forty-year-old trucks filled with watermelons, offering toothless grins as we passed. I also caught my first glimpse of the *dachas*, the little wood huts passed from generation to generation that Russian city dwellers escape to in summer. Despite cheery curtains and a few ragged pots of flowers, for the most part these were grim, one-room structures without running water or electricity. There were few signs of life as we passed. I saw only one woman pumping water into a bucket by hand and another smoothing the hair sticking out of her kerchief as she emerged from what must have been an outhouse.

Although to an outside eye the *dachas* look like shanties slated for demolition, these rural huts are coveted. People in Russia, especially in the larger towns and cities, live where they are told. Only recently has the concept of property ownership come into existence, and for most, it's a dream far beyond their reach. But the *dachas* belong to them by birthright and can't be taken away. So with dedicated attention they continue to patch the leaky roofs and tack sheets of metal or plastic tarps over rotting exterior walls, keeping the elements and rodents at bay. Sergei told me that he went to the *dacha* belonging to his wife's family on the weekends, about an hour's drive outside Moscow. He hated going there—he found it depressing and claustrophobic—but I had the strong impression that his was a minority view. The air is free from industrial fumes, and the land, a swatch of dirt no bigger than the average American driveway, belongs to the Russian family and not the government. For that alone, I can appreciate their value.

After hours of monotonous, bumpy driving, we knew we had arrived in the birthplace of our children when we passed its only noteworthy landmark, a behemoth sign in rusting Yiddish letters. Birobidzhan is also known as the Jewish Autonomous Region, created by Stalin mainly to resettle Jews from the Crimea, Belarus, and the Ukraine in the early 1930s. Five thousand miles from Moscow and approximately twice the size of New Jersey, it was envisioned as a Zionistic alternative to Palestine. Like so many things Russian, the experiment failed miserably.

A few minutes past the sign we pulled into a housing complex, and the aloof young woman turned around and announced our arrival at the apartment where we'd be staying. She pointed to the fourth floor of one of the buildings, handed us a key, and said someone would take us to the orphanage the next day. Pat and I had been extremely patient during this leg of our unsociable journey, but we balked at this news. Our agency unequivocally told us that we would meet the children that afternoon. We only had three and a half days in Birobidzhan and refused to surrender a single precious hour of time reserved for meeting and bonding with Ben and Sophie.

The woman seemed surprised that we weren't willing to accept this news and said she'd come inside the apartment with us to make a phone call. She had someplace else to be, she explained, impatiently twirling the frosted blond tips of her dark hair, and she wasn't the person who was supposed to be dealing with us anyway. The actual guide and interpreter was sick. After much back and forth, the woman said she would drop us off at the orphanage and the driver would pick us up an hour and a half later. Hands on hips like the petulant adolescent she was, she said this was the best she could offer.

Baby Home, Birobidzhan, Russia (October 2004)

Galina, the woman whose apartment we were staying in, was at work and there was no one else we could consult. We had rented an international cell phone that was guaranteed to work in Birobidzhan, so we dug through our luggage, pulled out the leather case with the phone and instructions, and tried calling Adopt Through Us. Although we'd later be able to make a few calls, the reception was hit or miss. At the moment, there was no connection.

As promised, they dropped us off at the door of the orphanage, which was about a mile down the road from the apartment, and drove away. Pat and I stared nervously at the structure before us and paused to consider our next move. Like every other building in Birobidzhan, the orphanage was a four- or five-story complex, built during the Soviet era in the late 1940s or early '50s. When people ask him to describe the condition and architecture of the buildings, Pat has devised a standard response. "Imagine this," he says. "They were built in a month without plans or inspections, then abandoned for ten years, at which point terrorists came and bombed them; they were then abandoned for another ten years, at which point the Russian government, without repair or upgrade, brought in the people to work and live."

The complex was surrounded by overgrown vegetation, and the "playground" consisted of truck tires cemented into the ground and the rusting metal frame of what had been a swing set. The grass was thigh-high and the weeds grew unchecked, choking out the few neglected ornamental bushes that some hopeful person planted years earlier. There was no sign on the building or other indication of the entrance, so Pat and I approached what we thought was the main door and walked inside. A light-haired man about my age approached us and politely asked in halting English whether he could help. We told him we were there to meet our children, and we gave him Ben and Sophie's Russian birth names. He was confused and didn't understand why our translator wasn't with us, and all we could do was shrug and agree that the situation was not what we had expected.

The next thing he said sent my heart racing and the contents of my undigested airplane lunch gurgling toward my throat. "The girl is here," he said. "But it's nap time. You'll have to come back later. We don't wake the children up." And then, without a pause, the bombshell dropped. "Also, there is no boy here by that name."

Pat and I stared at each other, dumbfounded and incapable of response. *Where was Ben?*

❧

JANUARY 29, 2008. *Through mutual Bard College friends, we finally found native Russian speakers to translate Peter's adoption videotape, which was recorded when he was two years, nine months old. Three years ago, our adoption agency failed to have the tape translated. Nor did they try to find Russian speakers to watch it with them, though they enthusiastically assured us that Peter's vocalizations were age appropriate, which, we were told, was very good news. I resist the urge to weep as I speak with this kind stranger on the phone about his and his wife's impressions. He is reticent and choosy about the words he uses. He doesn't want to hurt or cause strain. I tell him that we're aware that Peter has developmental delays and that he won't hurt our feelings. He sighs and starts in.*

"First," he says, "the woman in the periphery of the video is heavily prompting him. She is very skilled at making him seem verbal." There is apology in his voice. "And the tape seems heavily edited." Then he pauses before continuing, "The truth is, he's not saying many words at all. What words he says are prompted. You can hear the woman directing him to repeat what she is saying." He gives me some examples. "Da, da, da, da," he says. Yes, yes, yes, yes. "The same simple words, he repeats them over and over." Three years later, Peter still repeats himself and parrots what he hears. The term for this is echolalia. Our Good Samaritan finally talks about the well-known children's poem Peter tries to recite in the tape. "Peter intones the words," he says, "but he's not actually speaking. He has the rhythm of the poem, but he's not speaking the words. He's only making sounds. Mostly this is what he does on the tape. He makes sounds. Not words." Sprinkled throughout our conversation are reminders to me that he's not a psychologist or trained in "these matters." I think I understand why he needs to make

sure I know this, and I feel a modicum of regret for pulling such obviously kind people, unwittingly, into our troubled lives. My instinct is confirmed when he tells me, "My wife, well, she thought his movements were odd. Not quite right. He was afraid of a ball. Why would a child his age be afraid of a ball?" He's uncomfortable expressing these observations, and I try to reassure him that I've taken no offense. We say goodbye with a promise on my part to e-mail photos of Sophie and Peter so they can see how well our children are doing. I check e-mail before bed and see his message in reply. He thanks me for the photos and ends by saying that he and his wife have the strange feeling they've known us for some time. The message haunts my dreams.

    Peter has profound effects on some people, and clearly they must have felt the gravity of our situation. For Peter, of course, as well as our family, but also perhaps for Russia itself. Peter is quintessentially Russian in every way. Magnificent, beautiful, and undeniably damaged. It's also our last night in the old house. The children are asleep and our dog, Scout, is pacing nervously amid the boxes and rolled-up rugs. I lay awake, too excited about our move to sleep. I try willing this man's thoughts aside in exchange for the knowledge that we're holding our own. My son needs me and I need him. He has taught me humility and patience, and in turn, I have given him my imperfect yet dogged love. No matter what choices Peter makes in his life, no matter how circumstances affect him or what opportunities arise or forestall, I know he'll carry my love and devotion inside his heart. He has put me through the ringer, certainly, and in turn, I have asked more of my son than he ever was emotionally and cognitively equipped to provide. In order to mother Peter, I have had to become a better person, more patient, more forgiving, less judgmental, and entirely more flexible. In order to be our son, Peter has had to abandon, one by one, every maladaptive survival mechanism accumulated from living three years in a Russian orphanage. Peter and I are ready for this new transition, our family's new beginning. I know we are. In fact, the four of us will walk into this new house, poised to fulfill a new set of dreams tailor-made to fit the diverse potentials of our family, hand in hand and with common purpose.

Careful not to wake him, I reach for Pat's hand, a hand I carry always in my heart, and count my blessings. I have everything I need: a beautiful man to love and hold and two children whom I love, boundlessly, in different ways and for different reasons. Love has blossomed and endured even in the sometimes untamable terrain of our family. Love is everything. And with love, tomorrow we start anew.

CHAPTER 9

RUSSIA, PART I (MEETING SOPHIE)

ONCE I RECOVERED my voice, the questions, along with a few colorful insults, flew toward the man at the orphanage like poisoned arrows from my mouth. I was done with pleasantries. *What do you mean he's not here? Where is he? We came from New York, damnit. New York. Did you know that? It's halfway around the world. Can I show you a map? Find our child. Find him now!*

The casual arrogance in the man's voice, which I first mistook for politeness, infuriated me. I became increasingly hysterical and wild-eyed, the words spilling from my mouth coming from someone I barely recognized. Pat knew I was dangerously close to blowing my lid, so he put his hand on my shoulder to signal that he would take over the questioning. When he did, his voice came from the bottom of his register, like distant rolling thunder.

Whatever Pat said had some effect, because we hastily were ushered into the man's office, where we learned his title was head doctor. We would meet other orphanage doctors throughout our trips, but we never spoke to this man after that first fateful day. Pat and I sat down in his computer-less office, both of us riffling through stacks of papers in a desperate search for Ben's paperwork. A woman came in and wordlessly offered me bottled water and Kleenex, though I wasn't crying. I was too incensed and terrified for tears.

We had traveled halfway across the world and without hint of apology were being told that a mistake had been made. I was coming unglued.

"You should call your agency about the boy," the doctor said, skimming our documents. "There is nothing I can do. Come back at 3:30 when the children wake. You can meet the girl then."

After that, he made a brief phone call, barking orders of some kind or another in Russian, then stood up and escorted us outside. Pat and I scanned our grim surroundings and wondered whether we were expected to walk back to the apartment. All the buildings looked the same. Without signage or even slight differences in architecture, there was no way to distinguish the indistinguishable shades of decay. I wasn't at all sure we could find the apartment.

Thankfully, the surly teenager and driver pulled into the circular driveway within a few minutes of our expulsion. The head doctor must have called them. They drove us back to the apartment, where we found a small crowd of women standing just inside the door. Heated discussion stopped as soon as we stepped inside. After introductions and repeated apologies for both the mix-up and the frigid treatment by the girl with bi-colored hair, a woman named Tamara explained the genesis of the confusion. Tamara, who would be our translator for the rest of our time in Russia, told us she had located the baby and would take us to him after we met Sophie. She discreetly chose not to reference the screaming match that took place earlier at the orphanage and that had culminated in threats against the entire Russian state. The orphanage didn't know who Ben was, she explained, because he lived at the hospital, which was in a separate section of town and not part of the orphanage system. The head doctor must have read this on Ben's paperwork but obviously decided to let someone else break the news. Tamara couldn't tell us why or what was wrong with the baby, but she did know he had been hospitalized since birth.

None of this, of course, had ever been mentioned to us. Ben's medical report did in fact state that he resided in the Baby Hospital, but when I asked what that meant, Peggy at Adopt Through Us assured me that it was the name they used for the infant ward at the orphanage, end of story. Even Dr. Aronson accepted this explanation. But Peggy was wrong. I tried contacting Adopt Through Us using the rented cell phone, as there were a number of urgent questions Pat and I needed to ask. This time I managed to get through, but no one other than the receptionist was in the office. After listening to my distressed voice and frantic plea for help, the woman assured me that someone would call back soon, either on the cell phone or Galina's direct line. Those were the first and last words we heard from Adopt Through Us until we were back in the States, ten days later.

We left with Tamara, saying goodbye to the other two women who were "coordinators" of the process in Birobidzhan. Because Tamara was allowed to navigate the orphanage unescorted, she marched us straight into a large hall with brightly colored murals and sunlit floor-to-ceiling windows. I recognized the room immediately from the referral photographs. Birobidzhan can sizzle in the summer, and I knew those windows would act like a heat lamp on blistering hot days. In terms of weather, at least, we were lucky the entire trip. The temperature never rose above the low 80s and the nights stayed comfortably cool.

Sophie walked in right after we did, shoulders back and leaning forward, eyes locked onto ours. One of her caregivers followed and, after saying hello, took a seat next to Tamara. Although this was a once-in-a-lifetime moment for us, albeit with a strange Russian twist, for Tamara and the caregiver the scene was simply part of their daily routine. A chance to sit down, catch up, or maybe gossip.

Pat and I smiled at Sophie and began saying ridiculous things like "What a pretty girl you are" or "Come show me your dress" in over-enthusiastic English, which we knew she couldn't understand. She wrinkled her nose and narrowed her eyes, confirming that we really were making fools of ourselves. She looked like a baby much younger than two except for her eyes and facial expressions, which were those of a much older soul. The keen intelligence so evident in her face made Sophie stand out from the rest of the orphanage children as much as a freckled redhead must surely stand out in the middle of a bustling Beijing market. Whenever the opportunity presented itself, the other children predictably ran up to us, wrapping their skinny, mosquito-bitten arms around our legs as they plaintively called to us, "Mama, Papa." There is nothing more heart-wrenching than being the object of an orphan's unattainable desire, and Pat and I choked back tears nearly every time one of their little bodies clamored to grab hold. Sophie, however, was not of that ilk. She was a cool cat who kept a watchful distance. By the end of our trip she would claim us with possessive entitlement, but not just then. We had yet to earn the honor.

Spring 2005

Instead, she studied us with the intensity of a scientist puzzling over a newly discovered organism, careful not to express any opinion until all the facts were gathered and analyzed. She had gumption galore. We made a game of scrutinizing her with the same curious vigor with which she approached us. I pored over every aspect of her, instantly memorizing the hue of her skin, the shape of her ears, the deep, perfect groove of her philtrum, even the clumsy, comical way she teetered around the room. But in truth, this was no game. Despite the plaguing worry over Ben, the moment was pure bliss and has become indelibly stamped into my memory. For the first time, I was meeting our daughter. I felt the way a new mother must feel in the moments after birth, when she first lays eyes on the miracle that is her child.

Unlike newborns, however, Sophie appeared in a pale pink cotton dress, tight enough across the chest to make the seams stretch, and a worn pair of boy's sandals. Her full face and fiery eyes belied the fact that she was significantly underweight. The little bit of hair she had was light golden blond, with a swirling cowlick prominent at the center above her brow. Her thin, mottled skin further was speckled with angry bruises and countless weeping mosquito bites.

She was also beautiful. The way she circled around us, studying Pat and me as though we were laboratory animals, inching slightly closer with every lap, enthralled us beyond expectation. Though hopelessly hooked, we weren't sure how to approach her. What do you say to a two-year-old child you've just met and who's never heard the English language? Our initial attempts failed miserably. As though reading our minds, Tamara broke off her conversation with the caregiver, took Sophie by the hand and explained that we were her new Mama and Papa. The talk did not have the intended eureka effect. So in desperation I pulled a Fisher-Price cell phone out of my bag, hoping it would entice her toward us. The flashing buttons and shiny colors did the trick. She darted over, grabbed the phone, and retreated hastily to a safer distance. We watched and smiled broadly as she pushed the buttons. Then she began to "ooh" and "aah," her eyes softening from frank mistrust to unabashed joy. The phone would become a prized possession.

My digital camera was another source of fascination. She examined the lens with an analytical expression befitting a physicist. When the flash went off, she blinked with surprise, lost her balance, and plunked heavily onto her bottom. This made her laugh lustily. I smiled at Pat, confirming what he already knew. The chinks in Sophie's armor were already showing, her guard was slipping away.

The next thing she did was truly amazing. Grabbing the camera, she turned it over and stared at her image. "Katya," she said, matter-of-factly. Her Russian name was Ekaterina Shumilova. At barely two, and despite having spent the majority of her life in an institution, she recognized herself on the LCD monitor and implicitly understood the concept of photography. We would give her a new name, Sophia Katherine, but it wasn't until the next trip that we started the transition, calling her Katya-Sophie at first, then Sophie-Katya, and finally just Sophie. Our precious Sophie.

We would have more time with her in the two days that followed, time to take walks and play and get a more complete sense of her mischievous personality, but we didn't stay long that first day. We were promised an opportunity to see Ben in the hospital, and we didn't want to be late. Kissing Sophie goodbye, to the extent she would permit, we left her with a small Winnie the Pooh photo album that showed pictures of Pat and me, our house, her room, and our cranky dog, Scout. We promised, with the help of Tamara's translation, to return the next morning. We also gave her a little pink gingham pillow with a photo of us I had slipped into the sewn-on plastic sleeve. Three years later, she is still sleeping with it.

❧

MAY 11, 2008. *While I spend Mother's Day with my children and husband, relishing their homemade cards and the flowers they picked out one by one with Daddy's diligent help, I can't avoid thinking of my own mother. The other day, I screamed at Sophie so loudly, and for so long, I nearly scared myself. She kept pushing my buttons, and then pushed them again, until I reached the very edge of my patience. Talking under her breath, saying, "Oh come on," or my favorite, "What the . . . ," every time I asked her to do something, arguing about every little word I uttered, and outright refusing to listen and take direction. Despite knowing she copes with significant anxiety, it's still hard for me to understand the anger and attitude that leads an almost six-year-old to respond this way without interruption for weeks on end. I know I tend to be generous with my personal history, especially in terms of the relationship with my parents and siblings while growing up, but I honestly can't think of a single instance that I spoke to either of my parents the way Sophie speaks to us on a daily basis. And my lack of smart-mouthed remarks and eye rolling was not because they instilled the fear of death in me or because I was timid and afraid of my own shadow. Quite the contrary, I was plenty talkative and full of mischief. But I was also respectful, and probably more aware of others' feelings than most kids my age.*

So today, on Mother's Day, I wish my own mother were here so that I could talk to her about these problems. I also wish the depth and solidness of the relationship with my children might one day be as strong as the one I shared with my mother. I can't help but reminisce about that time not so very long ago when the roles were reversed, when I was the young child revering my mother. The cat-eye glasses, the way I used to twirl her charm bracelet during church, how I never understood why my mom wouldn't get her hair wet in the ocean, the way she shyly covered her mouth when she was embarrassed, but mostly how I knew in my heart that she understood and loved me more than anyone in the world. If I had a bad day at school, my mother would know the instant I set foot in the door, no matter how hard I tried to hide it. She knew me better than I knew myself, and there was tremendous security in that truth.

As Mother's Day comes to a close, I wonder whether Sophie will long for me when my life is through the way I yearn for my mother, dead nine years now, every single day. I don't mean to sound morose; I'm talking about love, respect, connection, acceptance, comfort, and beautiful family bonds. I didn't give birth to Sophie, though I wish I had, and I sometimes fear that my lack of maternal authenticity could create the smallest crack in our bond that might one day lead to a gaping, painful wound. After all, Sophie has already lost her birth mother, as has Peter, a fact neither of them has connected yet, at least not consciously, to this annual day of honor. I want Sophie and Peter both to feel as loved and cherished as I felt by my mother, an imperfect woman just like me. But because my mother's love and commitment to us was entirely unassailable, she was everything to me, therefore she was perfect, and still is. I want to be that kind of mother to my children, and especially for my daughter, who I have so much to teach and from whom I have so much to learn. But maybe the loss she's already suffered, a loss I didn't endure until I was grown, is too much to set aside. Until we adopted, I had little experience with anger and primal wounds, scars that run so deep they travel the speeding course of the very blood that fuels our children's hearts and souls. I hope I'm the one whose unfailing love can show Sophie that there is a happier, freer, more content way to live. For Peter, I hope he knows each day that he's loved, that he's accepted for who he is, and that his "real" mother, me, will fight entire armies to guard against harm to his beautiful but damaged heart.

No one ever told me how difficult being a mother would be, and I guess I'm glad. Maybe Mother's Day is really a day of reconciliation. Maybe that's what honor means, because all of us, from time to time, deserve a little forgiveness in favor of the good, the triumphs, the happy moments we string together to form for our children a ribbon of silky, lovely, flowing memory.

Chapter 10

Russia, Part I (Something's Wrong)

The hospital where Ben was kept looked like all the other buildings in Birobidzhan, except it was more dilapidated. We walked up two flights of steep stairs, careful to avoid the crumbling holes and badly splintered handrail, and came upon a very old woman sitting in a chair. Her job was to block the door to the pediatric and obstetrics ward. Still in a walking boot and badly swollen from traveling, my ankle screamed displeasure with every step. We had been in Russia for four days and had failed to encounter a single elevator.

Tamara caught her breath at the top of the stairs and said something to the seated woman that made her scowl. She scowled even more as she stood arthritically and dragged her chair aside. We passed through double doors, one of which was locked, and nearly ran into a teenage girl holding her rounded belly with pained concentration. Eyes bulging and bent at the waist, she was definitely in labor. We would see her leave two hours later, hair mussed and wearing the same clothes, now bloodied. There was no baby in her arms, and I watched hypnotized as she gingerly lowered her exhausted body down the stairs. She was the first but would not be the only person we saw covered in blood or dirty bandages during our three horrifying days with Ben.

Tamara took us to a waiting room so filthy I was afraid to breathe. A broken couch that smelled like mold and was littered with round, suspicious stains sat against a windowless wall. The rug next to it was threadbare, its last strands of fringe knotted with hairballs and globs of matted dust. There was a sink in another corner with rusted fixtures and green baked-on guck covering the drain and metal pedestal. Splatters of dried blood were evident everywhere. Looking toward Pat, I reached for the security of the hand sanitizer inside my purse as I waited for someone to bring us Ben.

When I saw him, my heart ached. He was dressed in one of the many pairs of footy pajamas we had brought with us from home. Someone must have sent them over in an effort to ameliorate the bungled events earlier in the day. Even though they were size six to nine months, and Ben was twelve months old, the pajamas hung loosely off his skeletal frame, like a windsock waiting for a breeze. Gaunt and nearly translucent, his delicate blue veins wound visibly beneath the surface of his skin. If not for his eyes, which glistened with the same gentle kindness that stole our hearts in the video, I wouldn't have recognized him. The nurse brought the baby to Pat, carefully setting him in his arms, and smiled kindly at the two of us. Then she handed me a diaper, said something to Tamara, and walked away.

He was so fragile we found ourselves whispering in his presence. Except for the eyes, this was not the cuddly baby we had come to know and love in our dreams, the Ben in the referral photos generously displayed throughout our home. Something clearly had gone awry in the months since the referral. One of the first things I noticed was the way his hands shook when he tried to lift his wobbly arms. Unlike Sophie, he was hungry for touch and showed no hint of distrust. When it was my turn to hold him, he weakly but without hesitation reached for my face, outlining my nose, eyes, and lips with long, slender fingers. Despite his physical condition, he was tender, gentle, and peaceful, just as we remembered him. He was also seriously ill.

When I look back at this moment, I can't help but compare Ben with Peter. Ben's issues were substantial, as we were about to learn, and we would be subsequently advised not to take them on. But two months after Ben, the same set of experts told us Peter was in relatively good shape, so I forced myself to resist and ignore powerful instincts telling me otherwise. Ben is destined to have unfortunate, unfair, and enduring problems, just like Peter. Of this there is no doubt. But strong intuition tells me that he's free of the psychic wounds that ravage Peter's soul and mind, the demons that without apology try their best to scratch and gnaw at the very fabric of our family.

After giving us ten minutes to just quietly hold and look at Ben, Tamara dangled the diaper in the air and asked whether one of us wanted to change him. I laid a receiving blanket I had brought in my bag to cover the filthy floor, and Pat put the baby gently on his back. We pulled off his pajama bottoms and were surprised to find he wore nothing else except a diaper. The hospital must not have embraced the orphanage's practice of multilayer dressing. His knees were so knobby and his legs so thin they looked like Tinkertoy sticks attached at the middle with mini tennis balls. In fact, the sight of his legs alarmed us so much we asked whether we could remove his top and look over the rest of his body.

I don't know whether the hospital would have allowed this—the nurses and doctors wouldn't even let us see where he slept—but Tamara is a truly kind soul who wants the best for both child and prospective family. "Just do it," she said. "But quickly." And so we did. We found that he had an equally thin torso and a significantly sunken chest. As my mind began to scan the dozens of articles I'd nearly memorized about international adoption medicine, my sense of worry escalated. A "concave" chest is a prominent feature of Fetal Alcohol Syndrome. At that point I had no choice but to assume a more investigative role, so with apology in my heart I pored over his downy body, inch by careful inch, for worrisome signs, taking photos to send Dr. Aronson. I noticed features of his face that weren't obvious from the video or referral photo and noted them in a little notebook. His chin, for instance, looked underdeveloped, at least to my untrained eye, but he did have a philtrum.

Dr. Aronson sent a sheet of square stickers with instructions to place them in the center of Sophie's and Ben's foreheads and then take photos from the front and side, with face and lips relaxed (not smiling). She would use these photos in conjunction with a computer program that evaluates facial features against norms for purposes of FAS identification. The sticker on the forehead provides a scale from which to calibrate the measurements. The program allows the physician to more objectively evaluate the philtrum, the upper lip, the length of the eye openings, the position of the ears on the head, the shape of the ear folds, and a few other anatomical anomalies suggestive of alcohol exposure.

After spending half an hour with Ben, I knew we needed to get the photos to Dr. Aronson immediately. Tamara had already told us the post office in Biro had fee-based public Internet access. I would spend much of the evening downloading the pictures and composing an e-mail to Dr. Aronson that could be sent from the post office in the morning. Although Pat was concerned too, his alarm bells weren't sounding as loudly as mine, and, for his sake, I struggled to keep my anxiety in check. I wanted Ben as much as Pat, but I was terrified of his physical condition. He was sick, certainly, and we needed information on his medical condition, but there were other worrisome signs unrelated to illness. I took the pictures as Pat tried to distract him so that we could capture the baby's face and profile at the appropriate angles. Although we would later take the sticker pictures of Sophie, neither one of us felt the need to put her through the strange ritual that first day. With proper food, medical care, and love, we felt she would be just fine. More than fine, in fact.

Despite having been introduced to her only hours earlier, I could appreciate that Sophie's mind was her most exquisite, intriguing feature. I also was comforted to know, as I had learned in our adoption class, that the kind of cerebral prowess with which our daughter is possessed is incompatible with FASDs. Unfortunately, Ben was a different matter.

I finished my unmotherly probe as quickly as possible, and then Pat and I fumbled to change and dress him. We played for a few minutes more, all the while trying to assess where he was in terms of developmental milestones. At twelve months Ben could stand and take a few shaky steps holding onto our fingers or the edge of the tattered couch. We took this as a good sign. But when we pulled out a new toy from my bag, a hard plastic figure that came apart in three places, he made no move to pick it up. When we held it to his face, he would look at it, and when we put it in his hand, he would hold it, but he wouldn't pick it up or manipulate the toy in any way. I knew this wasn't good. But then he also was intently interested in Pat and me. He made eye contact, he smiled, he explored our faces and outlined the curve of our fingers, and he reached out to us an hour later when the nurse took him away. This part seemed wonderful, so wonderful, in fact, that the entire episode left us weepy, happy, scared, and hopelessly confused.

That night, I wept quietly while Pat slept. We played Crazy Eights and Spades for an hour, watched an episode of *The Family Guy* on our laptop, split an Ambien tablet, and finally turned out the lights. My racing thoughts, however, were no match for the mild sleep aid our doctor encouraged us to bring on the trip. Although I had written the e-mail to Dr. Aronson and attached the photos, I was frustrated that I had to wait until morning to send it. I might have been less troubled that night had we been able to talk to the doctor before we left the hospital, but a cursory search by Ben's nurse failed to locate her. We had endured a ten-hour flight and then a three-hour drive on a partially paved road, had been dumped on the steps of the Baby Home by a disgruntled teenager, had been told there was no baby at the orphanage fitting Ben's description, had screamed and panicked until he was located, had been driven back to the orphanage to meet Sophie, had been taken to a nightmarish hospital to find Ben, and had been confronted with a baby who had deteriorated significantly since May and who I now realized was afflicted with FAS. In short, it had been a very difficult stretch of days.

The rest of our time in Biro was spent getting to know Sophie and trying to unravel the mysterious circumstances of Ben's health, including why his present condition contradicted *all* the information in the medical report Adopt Through Us had sent us. Later the second day, Dr. Aronson e-mailed back and said it was imperative that we measure his head circumference and get a current, accurate weight. She didn't want to say too much more until she had these additional facts before her.

The doctor at the hospital was neither kind nor helpful. She told us Ben had a digestive problem that prevented him from eating and that we should take him to a specialist in the States when we got back. She explained that he had to drink formula in very small quantities several times a day because he couldn't hold down much at one time. I later asked to feed him and was brought a bottle with an ounce or two of watered-down formula and a nipple with a hole so large I could have popped a blueberry through it. He didn't want the bottle when I offered it to him, but later, when he finally took a few choking slurps, the contents rocketed back up.

After that, Pat and I asked to see his medical records, but the doctor refused. We measured his head circumference ourselves and wrote down the results for a later e-mail to Dr. Aronson. Current weight was given in kilograms, and when I pulled a conversion sheet from my bag, I was devastated to realize that Ben weighed slightly less than twelve pounds at twelve months of age.

Having an emotionally charged argument is especially interesting when the parties arguing need a translator to convey what they're screaming about. The doctor refused to show us the medical records, Adopt Through Us was incommunicado, and no one else could tell us what was wrong with Ben. I was near the end of my rope, but having to pause every few words so that Tamara could translate made it difficult to sustain my target level of outrage. When I threatened to find the mayor of the town and told the doctor she was breaking all kinds of international laws by withholding adoption information, she finally yielded. I'm not aware of any actual laws that were broken, but I was improvising and on a roll. Pat later told people that he was thinking of finding a priest to perform an exorcism. I was mad, really mad.

After conveying my thoughts, concerns, threats, and intentions in very clear and specific terms, the doctor said the records did exist but were archived and would take some time to locate. Pat and I said we could wait. This infuriated her even more. Eventually she left and came back twenty minutes later with a fat file that she handed us, knowing full well we didn't speak Russian. When we asked Tamara to translate the reports, the doctor stopped her, saying she had no right to review the records because she wasn't a prospective parent. At that point Pat lost it. He turned red as his facial muscles tensed and his hands opened and closed reflexively in preparation for a possible rumble.

We eventually won this inane fight, and Tamara read us the records while I jotted down notes. The medical report forwarded to us from Adopt Through Us, it seemed, belonged to a baby other than Ben. I had the report with me, and none of the measurements or birth information matched his real records and the disparities were not in Ben's favor. The real medical records showed that his weight and head circumference measurements had been dismally (and consistently) deficient since birth and that he'd been given a very low Apgar score. There were also copious notes about his inability to feed and tendency to vomit.

When confronted with the evidence, the doctor refused to offer any explanation or assume any responsibility for the hospital having sent the wrong baby's records. Perhaps she knew all along and this was a common scam to lure people into traveling, figuring once they were in Russia and spent time holding a baby, they would come back for the second trip and finalize the adoption no matter what the child's condition. Maybe she was doing it *for* the baby. I like to think it's possible, however improbable. One aspect of this part of our journey, however, will forever leave me scratching my head. How was sweet, gentle Ben able to appear so lively in the referral video, given the compromised state of his health? Maybe the nurses tucked a few extra layers of clothes under his outer layers to make him look more robust. Unlike the women in the other videos, the woman with Ben did not undress him but rather spent a lot of time tickling him, which in hindsight may have been a deliberate move to disguise troubling signs. Whatever the case, the reality is that the video even fooled Dr. Aronson, which I imagine is a very difficult thing to do.

The other reality is that Pat and I were alone in Birobidzhan, thrilled with Sophie but heartsick over Ben. There was a horrible decision looming over our heads, and we spent our last two nights in Biro taking walks and talking late into the night in the quiet of our hostess Galina's bedroom. We had e-mailed Dr. Aronson the measurements and other information and had no choice but to wait and keep calm until she replied. There was nothing else to do, as Birobidzhan had no real restaurants or other venues to distract us.

Galina proved a lovely hostess, and though she spoke little English, she knew something was terribly wrong. She did her best to ease our strain, cooking three meals a day and washing and ironing our clothes. She even ironed and starched Pat's boxer shorts, something he never hopes to experience again. She had a lovely seven-year-old grandson, Bogdan, living with her on a fold-up cot in the corner of a room.

We knew in advance of our trip that our hostess had a child, so we brought a Spider-Man Lego set for him. I enjoyed watching Bogdan play with the Legos before dinner and marveled at the extent of his appreciation and enjoyment of such a modest gift. A couple of nights, Pat and I even watched Russian soap operas with Galina after dinner.

Then it was time to leave, and leaving proved difficult. The day before, a little boy came up to me while I was playing with Sophie and held out a picture of a man and woman. Tamara said he wanted me to know that he was being adopted and that the people adopting him were also adopting his infant brother. He kept asking Tamara to make sure I knew his brother was going with him. He also said he was Sophie's best friend, that he loved her, and that she was his "sister." I was so struck by this precocious child's ability to understand the concept of family, and his ability to bond with Sophie despite the stark environs of the orphanage, that I asked Tamara whether she knew how to get in touch with his new parents. I had taken some pictures of the boy holding the photo of the couple, and I wanted to e-mail them.

My mother and I, Linville Falls, NC (Summer 1967)

Pat and I have since become friendly with this couple and their two boys, and even though they live in Colorado, we manage to see them on occasion. But that day, the encounter with Sophie's best orphanage friend had a profoundly unsettling effect on me. We were about to say goodbye to Ben, and I knew intrinsically that we wouldn't be seeing him again. I was hoping for a miracle, of course, but my instincts told me that Dr. Aronson's report, which we were still awaiting, would be grim. We had left for Russia with Ben's nursery completely finished and waiting for him. We had lived for months as though he was already part of our family. With naive hope and optimism, friends and family had given us baby gifts, some even mono-grammed with the initials BGL, for Benjamin Greene LoBrutto. But there I was, resigned to walk away forever. I knew I was about to trim the corners of what family meant to me in a way Sophie's little friend in the Baby Home steadfastly refused to do.

Saying goodbye to Sophie, knowing we were leaving her in that desolate place for an indefinite period of time, was incredibly difficult. Casting Ben from the place he held in my heart left me feeling even emptier than I felt on the days, seven years apart, that my mother and father died. The fact that Pat hadn't yet allowed himself to confront this reality made grappling with my feelings even more difficult, and precarious. He still was consumed with worry over what we would need to do to make Ben well, what specialists we would need to consult, and whether we could get him help in Russia dur-ing the month or two before we came back. We were scheduled to spend a few days in St. Petersburg as a side trip on our way back to the U.S., and Pat wanted to get on the phone and track down medical help as soon as we ar-rived. As tempting as it was to cancel this leg of our journey, St. Petersburg offered modern conveniences, like e-mail and Internet, and kept us in Russia longer in the event in-country steps needed to be arranged.

I kissed Ben goodbye and choked back the tears. If I didn't stay strong I would crumble, maybe even disintegrate right there on the filthy floor of the hospital's pediatric and obstetrics ward. I needed to focus on Sophie and my husband. Pat's state of mind worried me terribly because he was still cling-ing to the idea of impossible hope, even redemption, when it came to Ben. I knew he was going to crash, that the facts would soon prevail over wishful desire, but I didn't know when. All I could hope was that I'd be there to catch him when he fell.

&

SEPTEMBER 7, 2008. *Saturday we went to Mudge Pond, one of our favorite watering holes, to fish, picnic, swim, and enjoy the day. Autumn arrives early in this part of the country, often in spits and spurts, and so even though the temperature was in the 90s most of last week, yesterday the high struggled to reach 70. Considerable wind and low clouds rolling across the horizon further conspired to strip us of one of our official last days of summer, but we didn't mind. With fresh prosciutto and rolls packed for picnicking, and the kids busy with catching minnows and frogs, we had the park mostly to ourselves, relishing the brief snatches of sunshine as they appeared. Two parallel floating docks jut into the lake and form the sides of the designated swimming area. For a while, I teetered on one of them, intent on catching a fish for the kids, despite not knowing what I was doing and feeling like the wind was about to launch me into the choppy water. At one point, a youngish man in khakis and a blue shirt walked out on the dock directly across from me and made a call from his cell phone. I didn't think much of it, but as we packed up to leave, Pat's mother pointed to a pile of clothes on a bench. Earlier, she had watched the man in khakis strip to his bathing suit and dive into the lake. Apparently, he hadn't come back, and by then we were the only people foolhardy enough not to be driven away by the worsening weather. As we looked at his clothes neatly draped across the bench, we puzzled over what to do, searching the expanse of empty lake for signs of human activity.*

Pat tromped to the parking lot and reported that one other car besides ours was still there, with a rear-facing car seat in the back. I checked the clothes at one point for a wallet, I'm not sure why, but there was nothing but a few dollars and his cell phone, which we dared not use. Eventually, a woman in Levi's appeared next to me as I continued to scan the lake and companionably asked whether there were many swimmers today. "Not many," I replied. "But there's still one out there." After we told her what we knew, she explained that she often swam across the lake and back, and that it could take half an hour in good weather and considerably longer under rough conditions. "I wouldn't chance it today, though," she added, concern rising in her voice. "I'm going to run home and get my kayak and look for him. Give me fifteen minutes." Her presence and knowledge both relieved and worried us. It was possible our mystery man could still be exercising, but here was an experienced lake swimmer telling us she wouldn't risk it in that kind of weather. Was he merely taking a foolish chance or had he drowned? We didn't know. With Grandma wrapped in a few beach towels for warmth, we huddled near the picnic tables waiting for the woman with the kayak to return. She was gone longer than fifteen minutes, which turned out to be a blessing. "I see him!" Pat shouted excitedly. "He's coming in." And sure enough, he was. I could just make out his bobbing form a hundred yards or so from the shoreline.

I'm not sure why, but I met him on the dock with his towel like a scolding mother and told him in a cheerful voice that he had given the LoBrutto family and another woman in Levi's a real scare! Luckily, he was a jovial guy, and we all had a good laugh about the experience, though the woman with the kayak was not pleased when she eventually returned. "I guess I shouldn't have done that," he said, an impish smile crossing his face as he toweled off in the quickly chilling air. "Well, at least it'll make a funny story to tell your wife," I offered. "I, uhm, think maybe I better keep this one to myself," he replied. "She might not think it's so funny!" We all said our goodbyes, and he volunteered that he would never again take off alone across a lake in bad weather. It was an afternoon destined to become part of our family's lore, especially because there was such a benign resolution. Driving home that evening, my thoughts, as usual, drifted back toward Peter. Our mysteriously missing swimmer, a young father with a cell phone and a few dollars in his pockets, did something a little foolish and caused a few well-meaning strangers, us, a bit of anxiety in the process. My bet is that he, whom Pat and I have dubbed "the almost dead guy," won't do it again. He's learned from the experience and will adjust his future decision-making accordingly. What grips me with sudden, unyielding anxiety, whether in bed, driving the car, or working in the garden, is the realization that the wiring in our brains that allows us to make such adjustments, to learn from our mistakes, is either missing or irreparably damaged in Peter. Our son's brain lacks the protective checks and balances so necessary for survival. He's destined to live, thanks to his birth mother, in a permanent state of intoxication. If compelled to do so, by desire, impulse or stubborn drive, he would swim across that lake and back, no matter what the danger, again and again, until one day he finally vanished, for good.

CHAPTER 11

GOODBYE, BEN

PAT AND I flew back to Moscow on Domodedovo Airlines and then flew to St. Petersburg the next day. My seat on the flight to Moscow was a middle seat next to a very old, round woman with long gray hair who wore at least three layers of clothing, despite the summer weather, and carried a cane. Gauging from the smell, none of her garments had been washed for at least a year. Because the cozy proximity was making me queasy (I was a mere day away from exhibiting unfortunate symptoms of giardia), I got up to use the restroom and get some air while the plane was still boarding. As soon as I walked down the aisle, Pat switched seats with me and refused to move when I came back. I had no choice but to climb over both of them to the window seat as I gratefully chided his stubbornness. Once I was settled, the old woman draped her coat across Pat's lap, spread her hips well into his seat, dropped her cane between his legs, and then promptly closed her eyes. Pat looked at me, we tried not to laugh, and then he removed the cane, using only his thumb and middle finger as he leaned it gingerly against her. After that, he shook and slid the coat off his lap and scooted it toward her with his foot. Ever ready with hand sanitizer, I discreetly slipped the small bottle into Pat's palm and kissed his newly disinfected hand as he passed it back. The exchange caused the woman to stir and say something incomprehensible in Pat's direction. When he didn't answer, she hoisted up her skirts, shoving them expertly between sturdy legs covered in saggy knee-high stockings, and scowled like a bulldog. She must have been senile or drunk because she kept speaking to Pat in Russian throughout the long, uncomfortable flight, becoming increasingly agitated when he wouldn't answer.

After this treacherous trip, during which the rest of the passengers drank and smoked while Pat endured the demented babushka, we spent a sleepless night in Moscow. Despite our shell shock, we were happily relieved when, after a short, uneventful flight, we arrived at our hotel in St. Petersburg, which was on a picturesque little canal. After resting a while in a fabulously large bed, we felt semi-human again. We were able to get online in Moscow before leaving and had scheduled a phone call with Dr. Aronson. I don't recall whether we had to stay up late or awake early to make the call the next day, and it hardly matters. Pat and I slept very little during this entire leg of our trip. Crossing multiple time zones on an almost daily basis was nothing compared with the anxiety we felt for the baby and what Dr. Aronson would say. I had e-mailed her the pictures of Ben a few days earlier, and despite the resignation I'd felt in Birobidzhan, I irrationally interpreted the fact that she wanted to discuss her impressions on the phone, rather than by e-mail, as a hopeful sign.

The travel agency we used to book our trip to Birobidzhan arranged for a driver and interpreter for us in St. Petersburg. Unlike Sergei in Moscow, this man was petulant, disdainful of Americans, and utterly bored with our presence. But he did take us to the sights, which provided some much-needed distraction, including the fantastic State Hermitage Museum, where we easily could have spent the entire next three days, despite the coat incidents haunting me.

I carried with me a short, olive-green trench coat, and it seemed that wherever I went, starting with the Hermitage, a security guard would pull me out of the entrance line. I use the term "line" loosely as what really happens at Russian venues is that people elbow and push their way toward an entrance or ticket gate, tossing the young, infirm, and elderly aside to gain a better position with the affable casualness of Roman gladiators. Once I was pulled out of the line, the coat enforcer, whether an old lady in a chair or a young man with a crisp security uniform, invariably would order me to remove my unassuming frock and either carry or check it. The fact that four people next to me wore coats or baggy pants with scads of pockets that easily could have concealed any number of contraband items was of no matter. It was either something about me or something particular about my raincoat.

Whatever the reason, Pat and I would have several other opportunities to test our hypothesis regarding the visceral disdain my olive-green trench coat evoked among Russian venue attendants: at the tourist-trap ballet (the dancers were so old, they stood and explained what they would be doing had they the energy to actually dance); at Peterhof, the summer palace and gardens of Peter the Great; and at the Alexander Nevsky Monastery, where many famous Russian musicians are buried, including Tchaikovsky, Rimsky-Korsakov, and Glinka. I continued wearing my coat, not out of sheer stubbornness but rather because the wind, as early as mid-August, was impatiently blowing autumn our way. And for this, I was stopped at every turn.

After our day at the Hermitage, Pat and I roamed the streets of St. Petersburg looking for a restaurant. The city is beautiful, and very European compared with other parts of Russia, but peeling paint is everywhere, alongside cracked sidewalks and crumbling brick façades. Our interpreter confirmed what we already knew: that St. Petersburg has suffered in the years following the collapse of the Soviet Union. Whether it was due to the coat, or perhaps just the fact that we were Americans, the establishments we tried, one after the other, told us they were out of everything on the menu except caviar and vodka. Pat could have survived on this fare, but, since I don't like either, we continued looking until we came upon a Pizza Hut, where we ordered a large pepperoni pizza. Although my New York husband normally abhors national chain pizza, and despite the fact that the Russian Pizza Hut is a very poor relative of the American Pizza Hut, we joyfully devoured the entire pie on top of our hotel bed, washing it down with a couple of Cokes. We always try to eat local cuisine whenever we travel, but since the citizens of St. Petersburg wouldn't allow it, we didn't feel too bad about holding up the culinary white flag.

Pat and I spent the remainder of the evening writing down a list of questions and concerns about Ben in preparation for our middle-of-the-night phone call to Dr. Aronson. As it turns out, we needn't have bothered. The "real" medical records, along with the pictures and measurements we provided, were all she needed to tell us that we needed to move on. "You can heal his body," she implored, cupping her hand over the phone as she called to one of her boys to brush his teeth. "Sorry about that. I gotta get my kids to bed. Mary, it's his brain that can't be fixed. The damage is done. That's the thing. He's got the head circumference of a two-month-old. He's twelve months."

I wanted to know if he had FAS, so I dumbly asked. "Looks that way," she said. "He does. Yeah, he definitely does. All the signs are there." Well aware of Pat's history with his own two sons, the adamancy in Dr. Aronson's voice softened somewhat as she continued. "You guys said you didn't want this. You didn't want to take on FAS. This isn't the baby for you. I'm sorry. You shouldn't do it."

Late Winter, 2009

She wouldn't budge from her position no matter how we tried to sway her otherwise. When push came to shove, she shoved, and I'm grateful for it. She must have known Pat and I needed strong handling, the telephone equivalent of a slap across the face. I believed Dr. Aronson when she told us during the adoption classes that her role is to provide information to prospective parents without making decisions for them. Thank God, in this instance, she had the humanity and decency to break her own rule.

With heart and mind aligned, Dr. Aronson attempted to knock some sense into two bewildered and grief-stricken people, who at the moment weren't particularly interested in hearing medical prognostications. She appreciated the devastating fact that we had been sent halfway across the world on false information and in futile search of a baby whose very existence was a cruel fabrication. But she also knew that the Ben we loved was a fiction and the real Ben, the baby we finally located in the hospital, was beyond the realm of our emotional and physical capacities.

I remember very little of our trip after calling Dr. Aronson, except that we held each other and made love that night, with the kind of passion that blossoms perennially from the love and intimacy that grows deeper with each shared experience, even the difficult ones. The only other thing I recall vividly is stepping onto the Delta airplane, which for me symbolized the comparative rationality of the U.S. I was so overcome with relief that I had to restrain myself from grabbing the face of the hapless flight attendant and kissing her square on the lips. Pat and I envisioned collapsing on the airplane and sleeping the entire flight home, and we quickly settled into our first-class frequent-flyer-purchased seats. But this turned out to be a naive fantasy. The plane was filled with new adoptive families, the youngest members of which were intent on screaming and complaining the entire way.

One young couple, probably in their mid-twenties, sat across from us with a baby boy about eight months old. His face was covered in angry red blotches and pinched in obvious discomfort. They thought he was allergic to the formula they brought and didn't know what to do. No one had told them to feed the baby the same diet (watered down yogurt) he was fed in the orphanage until they were safely home and within shouting distance of their pediatrician. I watched as they struggled to make the baby comfortable and listened to the escalating panic in their voices when nothing they tried worked. They seemed so young to me, probably because most people we encountered during the course of our adoption journey were older, at least in their thirties. At twenty-five, I never would have had the gumption, organizational skills, or driving desire necessary to endure the arduous, seemingly endless, high-stakes odyssey of international adoption.

At least our new friends Jackie and Sam, who we had met at the start of our trip in Moscow and who occupied the same approximate age bracket as Pat and me, were on our flight with their new five-month-old daughter. We earlier had swapped stories like irreverent, seasoned war veterans (ours, of course, trumped theirs) in an effort to while away the hours in the airport, Jackie bouncing a chubby, chortling Natalie on her knee the entire time. She was exhausted but happy, and I envied the completion so evident in her face. After a while, we left the baby in the nervous, wide-eyed care of Sam and Pat so that we could walk through the Duty-Free Shop. Staring longingly at the delicate porcelain figures behind locked glass, we eventually talked each other into buying keepsake Lladros, a baby girl for her, and despite the armor of resignation I thought I'd acquired regarding Ben, a toddling boy for me.

The figurine was bubble-wrapped and carefully stuffed beneath the seat in front of me, as there was no room overhead. I feigned interest in looking at it to avoid the imploring stares of the new mother across the aisle. She and her husband were getting nowhere with their baby, who was miserable and becoming increasingly distressed. Four hours into the flight, the woman had resigned herself to a regimen of neurotic hair twirling that eventually evolved into hair chewing and rhythmic rocking. The man cradled and shushed the baby against his chest, doing his best to comfort both the child and his quickly deteriorating wife from the cramped confines of his window seat.

At some point I dug into my satchel and pulled out the file on medical issues I had compiled for our trip. Somewhere, I knew, was a chart from Dr. Aronson explaining how to dose Benadryl in case of allergic reaction, according to the baby's weight or, if unknown, age in months. I offered the chart to the woman, who stared at the paper wild-eyed and without comprehension. After explaining that we came prepared with all kinds of instructions and medical supplies from a renowned adoption pediatrician, she hoisted the baby from her husband's arms and lifted him across the aisle into my lap. "Give him the Benadryl, please. Whatever you think'll work. Do it. Now. Will you?" And so I did. The baby slept for two hours straight and then awoke with a reinvigorated interest in screaming. The woman begged me to dose him again, but I politely refused. Pat and I put on earphones, ate the chocolate ice cream sundaes offered us by the flight attendant I almost kissed, and held hands as we pretended to sleep for the rest of the flight.

We came home to a hot, empty house. The dog was in the kennel, her bowls upside down on the counter next to the sink, right where we had left them. Sophie's room was still pristinely poised for occupation, and I smiled with the thought of the mayhem this catalog-perfect space would see once we brought her home. The nursery, small and cozy and doused with hope for Ben, echoed with the sound of whooshing air as I opened the door and peeked inside. In fading light, I stared numbly at the red baseball cap rug on the floor, the letter B adorning the lid, and the wooden BEN letters that had been meticulously painted on the kitchen island and then nailed to the wall over the crib. Taking them down was not an option that night, and neither was closing the door.

We would not call Adopt Through Us until late the next day. While Pat unpacked and listened to phone messages, I took a bath and then crawled greedily into bed, waiting for the window units to cool the steamy upstairs of our old stone house. Unable to sleep but too tired to function, I watched a *Seinfeld* marathon for three straight hours. Glad to be home and drained from our experience, Pat and I eventually fell asleep in each other's arms, pillows dampening against our heads from the quiet tears that flowed for the boy who nearly became our son.

⚜

OCTOBER 4, 2008. *Sophie, Pat, and I are at the pumpkin patch, tripping over pumpkins littered across a wide field and chasing each other through the deep-orange obstacle course. Sophie picks little pumpkins for Grandma and herself and one big one to carve a few days before Halloween. Pat and I choose a large, skinny one for Peter, who is home in his room while Lindy, his home teacher, keeps watch. We made an emergency call an hour earlier, and luckily she was able to come over and bring relief. I had to leave, get away from Peter for a while, but I had no desire to leave Pat and Sophie behind. In a sickening moment of déjà vu, I discovered Peter had thrown away my new eyeglasses, my engagement ring, my favorite watch, an engraved bracelet Pat gave me as an anniversary present, and a bracelet given to me by my sister. Recalling the incident with Sophie's birthday presents, we had come to the conclusion there was no other conclusion that didn't involve Peter, but we searched and searched for the missing jewelry nonetheless. Peter participated in the hunt. An opportunity arose to question him about it, and he finally confessed. He admitted taking my jewelry, which was on top of the vanity, and placing it at the bottom of the wicker trash can in our bedroom. My most cherished possessions went out with Monday's garbage.*

The day until then had been going so well. The kids had a soccer game in the morning, we went by the new house to check on progress, had leftover Chinese for lunch, made silly Halloween decorations, and were planning an outing to the pumpkin patch later in the afternoon. One of the happiest days I thought we'd had in a while. But now I'm numb and dazed, doing my best to feign fun for Sophie's sake. She's nervous but thrilled to have us alone. I stare at the endless vista of pumpkins and wonder whether Peter will be with us for this annual outing next year. I should be crying, I feel like crying, but the tears don't come.

Instead, I chase Sophie and let her chase me. I take pictures of Pat and Sophie as they zig and zag through the corn maze and scramble into the hay tunnel. Despite the sorrow burrowing inside, I'm having fun. As a family of three, we're happy. As a family of four, we sometimes aren't. Surely that should be enough to make me cry.

CHAPTER 12

HELLO, PETER

WE HAD BEEN home two weeks when Peter's referral information arrived. In many ways I feel our son was destined for us and we for him, as though the path leading toward him, a path fraught with hazard, detour, and impasse, was laid eons ago and in deliberate preparation for the odyssey that lay ahead.

In the intervening days after we returned from Russia, Pat and I slowly acclimated to the reality that Ben was gone. I also had surgery to remove some of the screws and the titanium plate in my lower leg and ankle. The surgery was scheduled for two days after our return but had to be postponed a week because I became so ill with giardia that I spent several hours in the emergency room hooked up to an IV. While recuperating from the double whammy of surgery and Russian-acquired gastrointestinal insult, I continued to speak with Dr. Aronson about Ben. With her urging, Pat and I also consulted another renowned physician in the field, Dana Johnson, who runs an international adoption clinic at the University of Minnesota.

I'll always remember the great compassion Dr. Johnson showed Pat and me, two complete strangers. How he dropped his busy schedule to review the information we faxed on Ben, calling back to give his opinion, free of charge, within an hour of being contacted. His conclusions, which mirrored Dr. Aronson's, extinguished once and for all the sputtering flame of our hopes. His remarks, predictable as they were unwelcome, brought necessary closure to our futile, melancholy attempts to keep hope for Beñ alight in the waning embers of our hearts.

My conversations with Denise Sowell, the executive director of Adopt Through Us, were less appreciated. I endured listening to an endless barrage of excuses and false explanations that spanned the days before my surgery and continued well into the recuperative period. They tried to call us in Russia, but Galina never gave us the messages. Our cell phone number had been misplaced. Russian orphanages are often called "hospitals." Peggy, our caseworker, was inexperienced. Lots of babies can't hold down food (my personal favorite). Even with the generous help of pain medication, I was nearing the end of my tolerance. Thankfully, Denise cracked before I resorted to violence, admitting with trembling voice that Adopt Through Us had made layer upon layer of what she apologetically claimed were unprecedented mistakes.

The Birobidzhan orphanage staff and adoption handlers had asked us to meet and consider three other boys before we left Russia. They knew that the situation with Ben was disastrous and that we were unlikely to adopt him. They also knew we had been willing to adopt two children at once. We might still be willing to relieve the state of an additional mouth to feed, they may have wagered, if even a marginally acceptable replacement could be produced. Although Pat and I had no interest in shopping for a replacement child, the staff refused to take no for an answer. Instead, they cheerfully escorted us through the orphanage halls to meet and observe three boys who I prayed were oblivious to the stakes.

The first boy we met, Andrei, was three years old and completely nonverbal. The second, Viktor, had a grossly misshapen head and unfocused eyes. The doctors tried persuading us that this poor child was keenly intelligent, despite his appearance and constant grunting, and that the shape of his head would normalize in time. The third boy, who was also three and reminded me of Christopher Robin, was tall, fair, and whisper quiet. Despite his shyness, he was verbal and able to assemble simple puzzles. Of the three, he was by far the healthiest.

At the end of the day, we told Denise that we weren't interested in another toddler and that we needed her to locate another male infant, preferably from Birobidzhan, that we could meet and adopt on our second trip to finalize Sophie's adoption. We had zero intention of taking a third trip. Despite the irregularity of our demand, we knew this was accomplishable because Pat and I had been encouraged to consider adopting one of the three boys shown us by the Russian staff in Biro.

I was nearly manic about this pursuit. Pat was in a downward spiral of grief and despair that I had never seen before. We dated for many years before marrying because of his real ambivalence and fear over having children again, something I knew I wanted and wasn't sure I could give up. Having lost two sons, along with the collateral damage of a failed marriage and a surviving daughter left fragile from the experience, it was an enormous leap of faith and love for him to find the courage necessary to give fatherhood and marriage a second chance.

But then the floor fell out from beneath him in Russia. "I'm no good for boys," I'd hear him confess to one of his friends on the phone. "First Vincent, then Joey, now Ben." Terrified of what I saw in Pat's eyes, and what the hollow sound of his voice confirmed, I felt compelled to mollify the horrible injustice of what was happening to us. Deep down, I felt his stability, and possibly our marriage, depended on it.

So I pushed. Several days later, Denise called to say there wasn't a single healthy male infant eligible for adoption in the entire country. We could wait a while longer, she explained, as long as we understood that there was a process we needed to adhere to and that too much delay might jeopardize the ability to finalize Sophie's adoption. It was an entirely false, maliciously calculated threat that Adopt Through Us would repeat more than once over the next two months.

And it had its intended effect, which is difficult for me to reconcile. I've spent a good deal of time chastising myself for allowing these kinds of bullying tactics to succeed against us. After all, I'm a lawyer who's trained and presumably inoculated against such transparent strategies. But there was so much at stake and so much had happened to shake the foundation of my more rational faculties. We had already lost one child, and after three days spent with Sophie, we were hopelessly in love with her. I had greedily indulged in the silky feel of her baby soft skin, inhaled the lush scent of her downy blond hair, and committed to memory the whorls of the cowlick that complicated the crown of her too-sparse hairline. Pat and I had heard plenty of horror stories of Russian judges refusing to finalize adoptions and of multiple agencies referring the same child to more than one couple. Whether true or complete fabrications, the very thought of her adoption being put in jeopardy sent chills down my spine. Denise was hitting below the belt when she brought Sophie into the discourse.

When I later asked about the boy we thought looked like Christopher Robin, she said we didn't want him and wouldn't say more. At the time, her silent adamancy conjured up visions of medical or social conditions too horrible to discuss, but in hindsight I doubt there was anything wrong with that child. What Denise was doing was laying the foundation for Peter, clearing all obstacles, whether newborn or preschool age, that could potentially block the way. "But we do have a child in mind," she said. "He's three, but cute as a button. He only just came available. And he's from Biro." In spite of our reluctance to consider older children, Pat and I agreed to look at the photos and medical report. Although we had been down this road so many times that elation no longer seemed possible, the pictures arrived and I smiled despite myself as I looked upon those happy, cinnamon eyes.

Quickly grabbing a blank growth chart from the stack of materials I had printed from the Internet, I plotted his measurements. His head circumference was reassuring, especially for an orphanage child, and his weight was at least on the chart, somewhere around the seventh percentile. His height was so low it couldn't be plotted.

But those eyes, the way they managed to sparkle even through the grainy blur of the low-resolution photographs. Peter's eyes are what captivated me, kept me searching and eventually longing for more positive answers that would give us the strength once more to pry open the chambers of our hearts. They were brighter than circumstances should have allowed, and I felt them draw me, nearly without volition, toward a sense of hope renewed.

The video of Peter came the next day, and we watched it in the sunroom, the soft light of late morning casting shadows across the screen and Peter's face. The film was taken in May, three months earlier. We knew this because a Happy Memorial Day banner was plastered in enormous block letters across the screen, obscuring much of the video, including the close-up footage of Peter's face. To this day, I can't figure out why anyone would think this was a good thing to do, but there it was. Peter looked great, as Dr. Aronson would later confirm, but there were certain crucial things we couldn't discern, in part because of the Memorial Day banner, but also because Peter was so happy and animated in all the photos and the video.

Second referral photo, Birobidzhan, Russia (September 2004)

For instance, we couldn't tell what, if anything, he was actually saying on the tape. Adopt Through Us claimed it had no one to translate Russian videos, and at the time, we had no access to native Russian speakers. Denise admonished that obtaining a translation was an unnecessary waste of valuable time, especially since he was obviously "talking" in the video, which she took as a very positive sign. And though delightful to see, especially given the grim orphanage environment we'd just experienced, the fact that Peter smiled so broadly in the photos and giggled throughout the video made it impossible for Dr. Aronson to tell whether he had a philtrum. "Ask for another set of photos," she told us. "No smiling, no facial expression. I need a calm, relaxed face. Front view and two-thirds profile."

Although Adopt Through Us honored this request, the second set of photos were also insufficient to allow Dr. Aronson to run the computer program that helps identify children who may have been alcohol-exposed based on dysmorphic features and growth parameters. We also weren't sure at the time, and are even more skeptical now, whether the boy in the second set of photos was even Peter.

Our request for a third set of photos, with detailed specifications, was denied. For the second time in days, Adopt Through Us reminded us not to push the envelope. If we aggravated the Russian authorities too much, Denise warned, they might deny us permission to adopt Sophie.

The unfortunate truth is that threats work when people are vulnerable because they have something valuable to lose, in our case Sophie. A lot more transpired in between, but in the end, we dropped it. We thought he looked pretty good based on the video, and so did Dr. Aronson. His healthy head circumference, though not determinative, suggested against FAS, and there was nothing dull or particularly alarming in the video about his behavior, appearance, or movements. He didn't appear developmentally like other three-year-olds we knew, but we also didn't know any children who had spent the vast majority of their day tied to a crib or sitting in a playpen, without toys and without anyone with whom to play or talk. For this reason, Dr. Aronson warns prospective parents that an orphanage child loses at least a month of development for every three months of institutionalization. Peter had been in the Baby Home since he was five months old, which meant that at the time of the video he was developmentally more like a two-year-old and maybe even younger. "Take pictures once you're there and e-mail them to me," Dr. Aronson suggested. "Meet him and get your daughter." And so that's what we did.

∾

MAY 29, 2009. *Today is a triumph, a blue-sky day in brilliant contrast to the banging, gray days that Pat and I have learned to accommodate. I lose myself in a daydream where my son enjoys a regular existence, where every day I feel like the mother I long to be rather than the commandant I have become, raising children with patience, reason, and humor, raising Sophie and Peter the way I was raised. Yesterday, Peter gouged his nose for the second time in three days and made himself vomit at breakfast. Hardly a blue-sky day. But something changed in the night. His brain is working today in a way that makes sense. Peter is trying and wants to have a good day. He announces this when he jumps into our bed for a rare snuggle before breakfast. Later he tells me in his deadpan voice that he's not going to "make bleeding" and then later still that he's not going to say "butt or stupid or kill." Peter thinks 100 percent out loud, so I am privy to hearing what should be internal monologue. He is proud of himself, and I am proud of him too. He wants to be like this every day, I know that now, but his better brain days come in unpredictable waves, in biochemical spurts that can't be summoned at will. I take my cue from Peter and treat the day as the gift that it is. My son tells me he loves me and I can feel myself beam. I waited more than a year to hear this, and it's never a phrase that rolls easily from his lips. Outside, the day is cool and rainy, but inside, for now, the sky is blue.*

CHAPTER 13

RUSSIA, PART II

WE FLEW AEROFLOT on our second trip to Russia, on October 22, 2004, and it turned out to be more comfortable and every bit as hospitable as Delta Air Lines. We also changed hotels, opting this time to stay at the President Hotel in Moscow rather than the Renaissance. We had heard from several couples that the rooms at the President were larger, more comfortable, and more accommodating of adoption families. Slowly but surely we were learning that American wasn't always preferable, at least when it came to traveling in Russia.

The little boy who so loyally thrust the picture of his future parents into my face at the orphanage was staying in Moscow, at the President Hotel, with his baby brother and new parents, Cheryl and Phil Benton. The formal adoption proceedings behind them, the Bentons still had several hoops to jump through before gaining the right to leave Russia and return to their Colorado home. But the nail-biting stage was past. With any luck, we would be jumping through the exact same hoops a week or two later, with our own two children in tow.

That night, we had dinner with the Bentons, now a family of four, in the hotel lounge. We would breakfast with them the next morning before catching our flight to Khabarovsk. Cheryl and I had become friends over the telephone and via e-mail, and it was gratifying to finally meet her in person, halfway around the world. The boys, now and forever known as Noah and Jared, were tired and pale, the stress and upheaval of the process evident in their bewildered, red-rimmed eyes. But not even exhaustion could prevent the celebratory mood that prevailed that night among both adults and children. We ate soup and sausage and watched the boys devour oatmeal, which the kitchen was happy to prepare. Noah kept asking his new father, who spoke some Russian, when Sophie was being adopted and whether they would see each other again. I felt as astonished and honored to witness this young boy's profoundly developed sense of loyalty and family as I felt the first time he approached me with the photos of his parents in Birobidzhan three months earlier.

I would see pictures of Noah and Jared a few months later and hardly recognize the undernourished, sickly boys I shared meals with in Russia, so complete was their physical transformation. People say the same, of course, about our children, whose appearance and health began improving even while we were still in Russia. But the healing power of love and good nutrition has limits. As we would soon learn, the mind is a more slippery creature than the rest of the body and can be capable of eluding even the most clever means of intervention. Cheryl and I speak frequently, often about this subject, and our families see each other when schedules and budgets allow. Her oldest son, a boy whose heart forever will be branded onto mine, has more emotional scars and difficulties from his first three and a half years with his birth family than from the neglect and deprivation experienced in the orphanage after he was removed and made a ward of the state. Like us, though milder and for different reasons, the Bentons have their challenges.

And though Cheryl and Phil knew bits and pieces of the boys' horror-filled past, concern for the future, for the health and peace of the family, was not on their minds that night. They were basking in the glow of their instant plurality, reveling in the fruition of a double adoption journey more arduous than any "How To" book would ever dare describe. And it was infectious. Bearing witness to the birth of the Benton family, I borrowed them as a kind of template for my own imagination, roughing out a vague map to mark the contours and terrain of the new family Pat and I were about to create. Though my map was still fuzzy, I felt ready. Through the labor that love imbues, I would succeed at motherhood, restoring Sophie to physical health and nurturing the spirit that even the bleakest of surroundings had failed to subdue. As for Peter? Having already seen the sparkling dance in his eyes, I felt certain I would surrender my heart completely, acknowledging with forgiveness the grief preceding him as necessary initiation into the rite of a mother-son union forged with intention from boundless love and gritty determination.

When we arrived forty hours later in Birobidzhan, after a tearful and joyous farewell with the Bentons in Moscow, we again trudged up the three flights of stairs to Galina's apartment, with four times the amount of luggage we carried on our previous trip and significantly more confidence and resolve. We were there to get our children. I packed everything they could possibly need and then some. The local pediatrician we would use once our kids were home, also an adoptive father, had emptied his entire storage closet and filled two duffle bags with sample antibiotics, vitamins, creams, and Tylenol, supplies we promised to deliver to the orphanage.

We spent a few minutes unpacking and smiling at Galina, nodding our head in appreciation while we inanely repeated "*Spasiba*," which means "Thank you." She had procured a new bed since our last trip and was excited for us to see it. Summer had given way to fall, leaving Birobidzhan even more forlorn than I remembered. Galina's apartment was quiet now that Bogdan was in school. The world outside was more hushed too, the trees having dropped their leaves in silent surrender to the coming elements weeks earlier. Later, when Pat and I walked the apartment grounds, I would listen to the crunching noise of ice splinter the brittle blades of stale grass beneath our feet. We'd leave a trail of ice shards splayed across the frozen earth like broken glass, marking our path as we marked time.

The next day, Pat and I were brought to the big sunny room in the orphanage to meet Peter. Once again, I was struck by the unnatural quiet of the place. Hundreds of young children lived in this building, yet it was as silent as a cemetery buried in snow. Despite evidence of children, such as second sets of low handrails and filthy strips of rags hanging knee-length from a string for communal nose-wiping, we heard no laughing, no babbling, not even the occasional cry or whine. We stood in muffled silence, waiting, until finally the doors on opposite sides of the room opened as if on cue. Peter raced through one door as Sophie was led by the hand through the other. In her free hand she clutched the little pink pillow with our picture in the sleeve. What joy!

First time meeting Peter, Birobidzhan, Russia (October 2004)

Wearing a red shorts outfit over red tights and a pair of plastic red fisherman sandals, Peter ran straight to Pat, leaping with short, stocky legs into open arms. Our translator Tamara looked at me and we both smiled. I walked over to look at him more closely but then moved quickly back because he screamed. The astonishing sound pierced the eerie quiet of the building like the public wail of an emergency siren. Sophie was busy with a few new toys we'd spread across the carpet, but when Peter screamed, she looked up, cocking her head in consideration of the affront, but then quickly resumed her noiseless play. She had changed surprisingly little in the eight weeks since we'd seen her last. Not knowing what to make of Peter's reaction, I inched my way toward Sophie and sat down a few feet away. Fascinated by the pretend food and shopping basket Pat and I had purchased earlier that morning at the local market, she smiled coyly and handed me a purple plastic eggplant on a plate. I thanked her, "*Spasibo*," and made gobbling noises as I pretended to eat, the whole time watching Peter and Pat from the corner of my eye.

In some ways, the lines were drawn the instant Peter loosed his deafening scream. To a certain extent, Pat and I still work to overcome the unexpected allegiances that established themselves that day. Peter, for any number of possible reasons, was drawn to Pat to the point of obsession, and Sophie, though interested in "Papa," was always more curious about me. Pat has always said that more than anything in the world, Sophie wanted a mother. And though I wish for Pat's sake that I could say the same about Peter's desire for a father, that Pat fulfills a primal need for our Russian son, I can't. Peter loves Pat, and when it surfaces, his brooding anger is less focused and intense with him than it is toward Sophie or me. But our son's dreams and wishes, the desires that dwell in the center of his heart, are often unknowable. Even in emotional moments of breakthrough, Peter's deepest desires prove too fleeting to catch and are nearly always too tangled to translate into words of healthy expression. But what is true and knowable is that Pat has forged his own lasting and meaningful relationship with Sophie while I continue to make inroads, slow and steady, toward the closely guarded chalice of Peter's hobbled heart.

In the intervening years since we first met, I've begun cultivating a quiet acceptance about Peter, as well as a growing sense of peace regarding the efforts I've shown him, that I didn't possess back then. In fact, when we first met, his reaction was so far afield from what I expected, and I was at such a loss as to how to respond, that I began a harmful, self-deprecating inquiry into my ability to mother that I still struggle daily to combat. As is the case with animals of all varieties, I've always been drawn to children and them to me. Even mean, unsociable dogs wind up licking the back of my hand and letting me scratch their ears. Until Peter taught me the danger of misplaced confidence, and the virtue of unwavering perseverance that I strive toward now instead, my "natural" gift with children was a trait in which I took pride and upon which I readily, even casually relied.

Unlike the easy bond that developed between Sophie and me, my relationship with Peter formed slowly and with deliberation. I worked for each half smile or stiff embrace my son begrudgingly offered, and the next morning we would start again from scratch, without benefit of the memory of the previous day's progress. That first day, I earned nothing. Instead,

I listened to the sound of his raspy, monotone voice and watched as he rambled around the room like a wooden soldier with sadly painted eyes, methodically gathering all the new toys and books and heaping them in a pile. Peter made a cross face at Sophie whenever she approached the growing mound but otherwise ignored her. His sole interest lay in what we had brought. He would carry with him as much as he could hold, his knuckles white from the ferocity of his tiny grip, and occasionally extend them to Pat, whom he already called Papa.

Neither the rhythm of Peter's voice nor his body language was normal, but at the time, I was more rattled by his reactions, which were robotic, repetitive, and obsessive. For instance, whenever Sophie interfered with his arrangement of toys, which she did and still does without compunction, he'd angrily rearrange them exactly as they'd been before the intrusion, while uttering something to himself that sounded like "*padushka*," which we later learned means "pillow." When he wasn't guarding his new possessions, he would pick up a toy or book, approach Pat walking backward, and then plop into his lap, legs splayed awkwardly in front of him like fallen tree trunks. I thought it a strange approach, but now I understand that Peter was trying to make physical contact without having to make face-to-face contact.

Tamara tried assuring us throughout the rest of our visit that afternoon that Peter's reactions were not uncommon and, under the circumstances, even expected. Sophie was an unusual child, she told us, gifted and wise despite her orphaned status, and we were cautioned against comparing Peter's more typical orphanage behavior with her more advanced capabilities. "He'll come around. The boys always take longer," she said. "They especially like the men. Men fascinate them. The women, not so much." After a dinner of borscht and a potato dish similar to hash browns, Pat and I talked about Peter late into the starless night, about his beautiful face and worrisome demeanor, and about the quality and shape of his mostly absent philtrum and thin upper lip.

For hours we talked about Tamara's advice, going back and forth like competitors volleying on a tennis court, regarding whether Peter's behavior and physical appearance were cause for serious concern. We never fought, but we also never agreed. As Pat would later confide, he was determined to bring Peter home, no matter what, once we had made the decision to travel back to Russia to meet him. Though worried beyond distraction that Adopt Through Us refused to obtain the additional photos that Dr. Aronson requested, Pat could not entertain the notion of leaving another son behind. It was that simple. He had buried two boys in the span of a decade and walked away from Ben only weeks before. He would not turn his back on Peter.

Unable to properly appreciate the cemented nature of Pat's resolve, his unwillingness to acknowledge my concerns frustrated me, and this, in turn, led me to second-guess my intuition and judgment. Maybe I was reacting the way I was because Peter had rejected me so blatantly in favor of Pat. Or maybe my concerns were exaggerated because they stemmed from emotional exhaustion and the inevitable letdown that occurs when expectations are beyond proportion to what circumstances should reasonably allow. As I lay awake listening to the Russian night once Pat finally fell asleep, I thought about Tamara's words: "He'll come around." It was a phrase I repeated again and again in my head as I watched the mysteriously peaceful rise and fall of Pat's chest beside me. Eventually, the delicate hope resounding in our translator's voice filtered through the firestorm of panic and doubt clouding my thoughts, and I slept alongside my husband.

I began my quest to reach Peter first thing the next morning. I planned to win his attention and trust with food. We went to the local market and bought juice, whole milk, yogurt, fruit, and cheese. While shopping with the help of our translator for the few items on the list, Pat combed the sparse shelves for sunflower seeds with the fervor of a squirrel on the eve of winter's first snow. He never found his seeds, but he did emerge triumphantly with a can of mixed nuts to quell his munchies.

Shopping in a semirural Russian grocery store is an experience not easily forgotten. For starters, there were two humorless security guards—one at the entrance and one patrolling the store—for a space much smaller than the average 7-Eleven. I was glad I'd left my green trench coat at home this time. My puffy down parka didn't seem to attract the same level of scrutiny. Also, the market was stocked much like a 7-Eleven, minus the Slurpee machine. This kind of scarcity is acceptable in a convenience store but not for a place upon which people depend to feed their families. At checkout, customers must buy the plastic bags to carry their groceries away, which is a fabulous eco-friendly idea, even if it wasn't instituted as part of a Russian green initiative.

Pat and I didn't understand that we were supposed to buy the bags, however, and Tamara had already gone back to the car. An argument almost ensued, but then the security guard took the slightest step forward and we abandoned our protest, deciding instead to resume acting like the model adoptive parents we were trying to be. We presented our rubles with open hands, let the clerk take what she would, and scurried from the market giggling like teenagers about the odd seriousness of the Russian work force.

After shopping, we picked the children up and took them to Galina's apartment. I planned to feed Peter with a spoon, as though he were an infant. I would do the same for Sophie, though she was mostly along for the ride. The adoption hearing was scheduled for the next morning and there was no time to lose. We already had been informed there was no time to take pictures of Peter, e-mail them to Dr. Aronson, and wait for her reply. The court date could not and would not be postponed. I either had to get on board with everyone else, including my husband, or stop the train that was chugging full throttle toward the station. I felt blackmailed, hoodwinked, and cornered. It wasn't just Peter on that train. Sophie was on it too. I either consented to adopt Peter, without further inquiry or opportunity to explore my concerns, or risk jeopardizing Sophie's adoption and the emotional stability of my husband. Visions resurfaced of "backup" couples hiding in the wings, waiting to snatch Sophie from our arms like a coveted prize the moment we showed the slightest chink in the armor of our commitment to complete the double adoptions.

Having the fate of your family, the child you have met and held, whose room you have decorated and whose face you have memorized, in the hands of disgruntled bureaucrats only just emerging from the collective mindset of communism, feeds anxiety the way greasy food feeds intestinal upset. I was not thinking rationally when it came to finalizing Sophie's adoption. Every insinuated threat, and every furtive glance exchanged between our handlers and the orphanage workers, sent me into a paranoid tailspin over the prospect of losing our daughter. We had rejected Ben and chastised Adopt Through Us into finding us another boy and, rightly or wrongly, had agreed to travel and meet Peter even though we were unable to obtain the additional information that Dr. Aronson requested. The rules were being bent to accommodate the misfortune with the baby, and all involved were nervous and on edge. The message was clear. Russia is not America, and when things go wrong, there is little if any recourse.

So I didn't put on the brakes and insist that we slow down, collect more information, or push the question of postponing the adoption hearing. Would the Russian officials really have revoked our opportunity to adopt Sophie if we had continued to voice concern over Peter? Probably not. But I wasn't so confident at the time. Pat already had made his decision and was turning an impassive ear against my growing and mostly unsubstantiated neuroses about the undernourished but twinkly-eyed toddler we were scheduled to adopt the following day.

And what if I was wrong? How could we return to New York without Peter? We already had turned down Ben after coming home from Russia two months earlier. What would I have said to family and friends, the hairdresser and mail carrier, the second time around? That I had a bad feeling, that something about him seemed kooky and peculiar? How could our marriage accommodate the rift that such a decision surely would have caused? I could have been wrong, and I desperately wanted to be wrong, for myself and everyone else, and for Peter most of all. I wanted two children, and I wanted Pat to have a son. I wanted Sophie to have a sibling, a brother who shared her heritage and early circumstances, if not her genetic material. And I wanted Peter to be okay. I wanted to *want* him. In the end, the uncorroborated alarm bells sounding in my head were no match for the double whammy of burning desire and nagging self-doubt.

My growing resolve to propel myself forward, to embrace Peter and make myself see what Pat saw, a precious child in need of parents, took hold as I slept. Ben was no longer a part of our family vision, and I could not allow that experience to cloud my impressions of Peter with shades of doubt that were incapable of being properly examined. And this, I told myself, is exactly what I had been doing.

So as the morning grew brighter, and the frost that spread like spiders across the windows began to melt, I allowed hope to enter my heart and mind and find purchase. Springing from bed determined to put my food plan into action, I showered, drank two cups of instant coffee, and smiled with the relief that complete surrender offers.

The orphanage officials allowed us to take the children back to Galina's apartment for a few hours that morning. As soon as we walked in the door, I unloaded our stash of food and got to work. Peter took the bait immediately, and Pat and I laughed out loud as we watched two hungry toddlers gobble up every morsel offered. They loved having someone feed them and opened their mouths like newly hatched chicks. Peter's eyes stretched so widely I thought he was in shock from the novel abundance of the experience. After ample servings of fruit and yogurt that would later cause minor intestinal distress to their underdeveloped digestive tracts, Pat and I introduced the kids to sippy cups.

Neither of them had any sucking instinct left, as they had been drinking from cups since babyhood. Although drinking from a regular cup works the muscles in the mouth needed for proper language development, using them as toddlers can be a messy endeavor, especially while traveling. Pat and I were aware of how thirsty the children were, and we wanted them to have unlimited access to water and milk, whether in the car, at the orphanage, or on the airplane. We demonstrated the use of the sippy cups and watched as they struggled to get the contents into their mouths. When they gave up on water and milk, we tried white grape juice. The sugary flavor did the trick, enticing them both to keep working the cups until they figured out how to use them.

I would continue the strategy of building trust and intimacy through the medium of food for several weeks. Though Peter would quickly learn to use food, particularly the refusal of meals, as an expression of defiance, frustration, and sensory overload, his basic fear of not having enough to eat was a powerful motivator in the first few months he was with us. During the rest of our stay in Birobidzhan, Pat and I fell into a mini-routine of playing with the kids in Galina's cramped apartment, taking a break for our feeding/bonding session, and then venturing out in the cold to take walks or kick a ball around the deserted grounds. Pat mostly played with Peter, and I mostly played with Sophie. The few people we passed on our walks seemed dumbfounded by the image of the strange Americans strolling the grounds with two Russian toddlers in near freezing temperatures. Most Russians we encountered believed that babies and young children should not be subjected to the cold unless absolutely necessary, and they at least should be bundled so that no skin is exposed. After the second or third cockeyed glance or indecipherable insult, we'd give up and take the children back inside.

The books fascinated Peter, while Sophie focused on scribbling with the studied intensity of someone writing a dissertation. Later, we tried on their new clothes and let the kids wear them around the apartment until it was time to go back to the orphanage for their whopping three-hour naps. We were told not to send them back with anything we intended to keep, because an orphanage is a communal place that lacks the luxury of individual ownership. Although Peter continued to scowl and sometimes scream whenever I tried to play or read with him, he happily let me dress him in new clothes and shoes. Like his insatiable craving for food, the instant rush associated with the act of acquisition, in this case clothing, overrode his other impulses. A faint warning bell rang inside my head as I noticed the possible connection, but I quickly dismissed it. I was done looking for signs of trouble, at least for the time being.

⁊

JULY 11, 2009. *Yesterday Pat and I took the kids to Hancock, Massachusetts, to visit the Shaker Village that once bustled to the peaceful, insulated rhythms of more than three hundred souls. As we strolled the grounds, stopping to explore buildings or speak with the costumed gardeners, woodworkers, and other caretakers, I couldn't help but think of Peter. I could almost see him there, transported to the early nineteenth century, a young adult working in the fields, wearing rolled-up sleeves and a straw hat, his sinewy muscles rippling in his deeply tanned forearms. Peter seemed at home there, darting quietly between the slats of the magnificent circular barn and walking between the apple trees, their fruit still tart and green. Somehow his strange body language became exaggerated in this place, almost as though the environment didn't require any accommodation. It was as though he sensed this and gave himself permission to be free. I watched as he skipped along the planked walkways with an oddly irregular gait, his form shimmering in the heat like a lonely mirage as the distance between us increased. I knew he felt peace in this place, a religious compound that closed its doors a half century ago. Although his brain often failed to make the connections that most of us take for granted, he understood implicitly the harmony that still permeated this village.*

Dr. Federici once told us that he knew of several couples who had "given" their troubled FAS adolescents to the Mennonites over the years. Funny how strange but absolutely logical that sounds. Peter would no doubt flourish in such a protected, insulated, simple environment, where members were expected to contribute to the extent of their abilities, no more or no less. Choices were greatly limited, but so were temptations—an ideal template for those living with the crippling consequences of prenatal alcohol exposure. Not only could a youth like Peter be safe and remain safe, he could be productive and experience genuine fulfillment. The very notion would be entirely intoxicating except for one serious, sobering drawback: the parents must agree forever to relinquish custody, guardianship, and any future relationship with their child.

Although I can envision Peter living contentedly among the Mennonites, and I glimpsed as much in a hazy dream during our visit to the Shaker Village yesterday, I cannot envision living without Peter. In the last declining decades of the Shakers, most of the men had left the movement, leaving the remaining women no choice but to hire male laborers to work and live among them. If only Peter could reach across the time-space continuum, he might find refuge there in the fast-approaching decade of his own adolescence. Pat and I might find peace too, peace in knowing that we found a place where our Russian son could live safely, in pursuit of a purposeful existence, and where simplicity was a gift, not a hindrance.

Chapter 14

Adoption Day

My parents were married on October 25, 1948, in St. Petersburg, Florida. They remained for the most part happy and in love for the next forty-six years. On October 25, 1994, the first wedding anniversary my mother spent as a widow, my niece Haley was born. A day destined to aggravate an open, grieving wound transformed into a celebration of family and possibility restored. The fact that this squawking baby resembled my mother and would later become the apple of her eye was another blessing that with time would joyfully reveal itself. On October 25, 2004, three and a half years after my mother's death, Pat and I began our family in a colorless courtroom in Birobidzhan, Russia. For my family, this date has always resonated with hope, celebration, and new beginnings. I never thought that it would be different for Pat and me, so despite being halfway around the world, I awoke that morning feeling the enveloping presence of family, the knowledge of their warmth, comfort, and companionship a welcoming contrast to the bleakness of our surroundings.

My greatest hope was that we could in turn bestow this gift, this sense of belonging and place in line, to Peter and Sophie. So as I dressed that morning, rehearsing answers in my mind to questions about my suitability or desire to parent, a sense of calm emerged. I realized that Peter and Sophie were already a part of our family and just waiting to go home. They felt as much a part of me as the memories of my brother singing "White Wedding" at our reception (to the shock of a few and with riotous laughter from the rest), or the churning sensation of riding in the backward-facing seat of my mother's station wagon, or even the autumn afternoon in Tallahassee that I learned my father had terminal lung cancer. These children were already woven into the fabric of who I was, and who I might one day become.

I clung to this realization like a rudder to help steady me through the next several hours. At the appointed time, Tamara arrived and drove us a mile or two down the main road to the courthouse, which was distinguishable from any other building in Birobidzhan only in that it enjoyed a more official-looking façade and a clearly marked entryway. As with other buildings we encountered, official or otherwise, the concrete on the stairs was disintegrating and the handrails offered a minefield of splinters just waiting for uninitiated palms. Inside, a number of blown-out light bulbs created a dappled glow in the otherwise décor-less halls. Tamara led us around two or three corners and then asked us to take a seat on a bench next to the courtroom door. She was clearly not worried about the impending hearing. Despite what I had read and watched about the topsy-turvy nature of Russian adoption proceedings—how judges can and do make unexpected, even arbitrary and devastating decisions—the vibe that day was matter-of-fact and therefore reassuring. We eventually were invited in and took our seats on either side of Tamara in the front of the courtroom. Two female doctors wearing white coats and one other orphanage staff member sat directly behind us. A stenographer was present too. We recognized one doctor because she was the woman who had taken us around to meet the three boys at the end of our first trip. Through the whole torturous process, she had treated us with kindness and compassion. It felt good to have her there.

Unlike the rest of the building, the courtroom was sparkling clean and brightly lit. Except for the peculiar jail cell to the left of the judge's bench, I found it completely ordinary. Tamara explained that defendants must sit in locked cages during their trials. In Russia, it seems the presumption of guilt is a difficult hurdle to overcome. The lawyer in me was still contemplating the obvious differences in our legal systems when the bailiff walked in and directed us in Russian to stand for the judge as she walked in and took her seat behind the bench. She was a plain and sturdily built woman in her fifties, and it was clear she could orchestrate these proceedings in her sleep. With an unceremonious rap of her gavel, the hearing was underway.

Peter next to woman squatting, Baby Home (October 2004)

The orphanage representative read into the record the case histories of Sophie and then Peter: their birth histories, their social circumstances, and the reasons they became wards of the state and were unsuitable for domestic adoption. Even though I knew this was part of the Russian adoption proceedings, the whispered translation of these dire reports, the extent of poverty and deprivation that our children had endured, the defects of mind or body officially alleged, was difficult to endure. This was true even though I knew that the sole reason the speaker was making the case—that Peter and Sophie were of no value to the Russian people—was so they might lead the kind of hopeful lives she dared not wish even for her own children.

The judge then asked Pat to stand and approach the bench. Pat soberly responded to a number of questions, then I stood and repeated the process. How could we give two needy children the individual attention they each required? What was the state of our finances, our views on education? Did we have proper support to help us through what would undoubtedly be a difficult transition?

After that, the judge asked me to describe Sophie in my own words. Amazing, inquisitive, beautiful, mischievous, headstrong, smart, funny, and enthralling. I said all these things and more. "And Peter?" she asked. I held my breath for a moment and stared at my shoes. The moment of truth had arrived. I didn't know whether the judge was aware of the circumstances that brought us to Peter or was on board with the relaxation of procedures that was clearly occurring on our behalf, but I didn't want to lie. I didn't want the start of our family to begin with fabrication and deceit. "I don't know him too well, yet," I said. "We came to Russia the first time to meet Sophie and another baby who turned out to be very ill. We had to say no to him, and after we got home, our agency told us about Peter. I hope you already know this." My heart thumped inside my chest, and I couldn't bear to meet Pat's gaze. I could see the judge riffling through paperwork, and I was afraid to keep on speaking. After a torturous minute, the judge looked up, nodded gravely, and waved at me to continue. "He won't come near me unless I'm feeding him. He seems to like my husband. I think he's afraid, which I understand. He'll come around. He's beautiful and we want him. I want him."

And then she asked me to sit down. I was shaky but holding my own until I felt Pat's physical presence, and then the tears began. He has this profoundly kind way of absorbing my pain, taking it wordlessly as his own, without fanfare or complaint, so that my burden is lessened. To this day, I honestly don't know whether those tears came from the enormity of the moment or the awareness of how precious my life with Pat is. Tears of worry and relief soon turned into tears of cautious laughter when the three orphanage women stood up at the judge's request and began describing Sophie's personality. "There is no one else like her," Tamara translated. "She is naughty, very naughty," one of them said. "The mama and papa must not be afraid to discipline her!" And with that, suppressed waves of giggles spilled forth from all three women, their hands reflexively and in unison rising to cover their mouths. "We are sorry," they sputtered in tandem. "There is something special about this child. She's a good girl. A very good girl."

The hearing part of the proceedings ended on that note, and the judge excused herself for deliberations. The mood in the courtroom remained light. I was curious about why the judge hadn't asked the orphanage staff about Peter, but having already said more than what was prudent, I kept my mouth shut. Tamara occupied us during the ten minutes or so that we waited by discussing our afternoon plans with the children and how we intended to celebrate. Because Sophie and Peter were too young to participate in the adoption decision, they had stayed behind at the orphanage. She knew we would be anxious to see them.

The three of us spoke in hushed tones, Pat and I instinctively assuming Tamara's quiet manner. She reassured me that my honesty about Peter had not been a mistake and that all was well. I took comfort in her words despite the fact that the emotion in her eyes betrayed her soothing tone. Early during our first visit, Pat and I had guessed there was a deep and penetrating sorrow inside Tamara that her eyes could never quite conceal and that had nothing to do with us. Though I barely understood it, I came to recognize this melancholic trait in the faces and expressions of many Russians, Peter included. A communal, inherited sadness.

Before long, the bailiff reappeared and we were anxiously on our feet again, watching the judge as she briskly walked, head bowed, toward her place behind the bench. The stenographer shuffled some papers and then gave a slight nod toward the judge, which must have been her cue to proceed.

"Mary Evelyn Greene and Patrick John LoBrutto," she said, in halting but clear English. "The married couple residing in Kingston, New York, and who are citizens of the United States of America? You are now the legal parents and guardians of the minors known as Peter Thomas and Sophia Katherine LoBrutto." And with that, the judge stood up, walked around the bench and over to where we were standing, and gave me what may have been the most hearty, memorable, and unanticipated hug of my life.

Our quest to adopt two orphaned children was finally over, but my journey toward becoming a mother had only just begun.

AUGUST 17, 2009. *Today is Peter's second day of art camp at a wonderful space housed in an old chocolate factory called Imagination Station. Yesterday he was very excited, though nervous, to begin this new adventure, but he becomes verbally assaultive as soon as Sophie and I walk into the room to pick him up. "The juice is rotten!" he hisses. "I had nothing to drink at snack." I know what he's talking about because we've gone through this before. The design of his favorite juice box changed a few months back and its new packaging is something with which he just can't cope. Really, I understand. Peter struggles through so many changes—they're all so difficult for him, and yet some are so minuscule that they're nearly invisible to the rest of us. If he has to put his foot down about a manufacturer's audacity to change its packaging without first consulting him, if that's where he decides to draw the line, then I want to be sympathetic. But at the same time, I don't want his obstinacy, his perseverative tendencies, to overtake all reason. In truth, I also don't want to throw away a perfectly good case of his favorite juice—a flavor Sophie won't even touch—because he's dug his heels in over something nonsensical. "Let's read the expiration date together," I begin, pointing to the stamped "use by" date that clearly says May 2010. "No, it's rotten—you want to poison me, you bad mother person!" I desperately want to avoid a meltdown in this sanctuary dedicated to creative exploration, so I steer him out and mumble something over my shoulder to Norine, the saintly woman who runs the program.*

Once outside, away from the other children, he regains some semblance of composure, and we head toward home. Over lunch, the underlying cause for the assault reveals itself: Peter had first-day jitters, and it seems that some of the "older kids" (all of whom are younger than he) were staring and making fun of, among other things, the way he speaks. Teasing is a cruel reality when it comes to a child like Peter, and constant vigilance is required to combat it. "I cried in my head, Mom, but not on my face." He can be so brave, our young son. He wanted to cry—he felt like crying, but he held it in. How many times has this happened without our knowledge? For the handful of episodes about which I know, there are bound to be dozens more, little acts of unkindness, left unacknowledged and unrevealed, in the clandestine recesses of Peter's fragile psyche.

    After lunch, I speak with Norine, who listens carefully and promises to help ensure tomorrow's a better Peter day. Sleep doesn't lessen his anxiety, however. He spends breakfast laughing uncontrollably, without provocation, partially chewed biscuit crumbling from his mouth as Pat struggles to corral him. "You can't go to art camp if you keep this up," I interject. "I don't want to go," he says, laughing. A staccato half squeal, half moan accompanies every physical movement. And this is where I trip up: I shouldn't have brought up the possibility of not going unless I was ready to not send him. I need the break, I really do—it's only three hours, and Peter needs the opportunity to work on his social skills, hopefully learning a little something about art in the process. Never mind the fact that we've already paid in full.

    "Peter," I try reasoning. "You can do this. You love art. You just have to calm yourself down. Everybody gets nervous when they start something new." But he keeps insisting that the other kids stare at him and make faces. He doesn't know why, he says, but he insists they don't like him. "Did you stare at anyone yesterday?" I ask. "No way, Mom. I didn't. I swear!" And that's when I know I've hooked him, the faintest hint of a smile betraying his plaintive voice. Peter and I spend countless hours working on his unsettling habit of staring at people—he can bore a hole right through a person's skull—so I know he's just made a little joke on himself. "Okay, Mom," he says, smiling shyly. "I'll try." When we arrive at camp, I walk him inside where Norine asks Peter where he prefers to sit for table work. He chooses to sit with the younger group, some of whom are just four, and I nod my head in agreement. He's more comfortable with children this age, and

that's okay. Yesterday he told me he preferred to sit with the younger kids, and together we agreed he'd make a wonderful "helper."

I linger near the exit for a moment, sensing his insecurity, but Norine clearly wants me to leave, her body language signaling that it's okay, that she's attuned to the situation. I'm becoming more adept at recognizing early on whether a new adult in Peter's life will help or hinder. This kind woman exudes helpfulness, so without further hesitation, I say a quick goodbye and walk away. My hope is that when I pick Peter up three hours from now, he'll be full of chatter about papier-mâché and drawing, and will have forgotten yesterday's difficulties . . . maybe even to the point of forgiving the crime of changing the juice box design!

CHAPTER 15

WE'RE HOME (ALMOST)

LUNCH, HOMEMADE CAKE, and a beaming Galina awaited our new family when we arrived back at the apartment after the hearing. But despite the festivities, including picking up the children and holding them for the first time as their parents, I remember that afternoon as quiet and peaceful. Sophie had claimed every fiber of my being the instant our eyes met in August, and though my commitment to Peter was more recent, he was mine too. I had made a resolute decision about my new son, having sealed our fates together during a restive night less than forty-eight hours earlier. Turning back was neither an option nor desire. Pat and I were happy, certainly, but we were mostly relieved. We had many more hoops to jump through before going home, including several days in Moscow, but from this point forward none of our decisions, fears, misplaced words, or misunderstood actions could in any meaningful way jeopardize the formation of our family. We had reached the finish line. Peter and Sophie were ours.

But it didn't quite *feel* that way at first. For one thing, there was no room for the children to stay at Galina's, so they remained at the orphanage and on the same strict schedule until the morning that we picked them up before the sun rose for the drive to the Khabarovsk Airport. The night of the adoptions, I was keenly aware of how incorrect it felt to lie in bed with Pat knowing our children were still sleeping amid more than a dozen other toddlers, most of whom, Peter and Sophie included, had never known the comfort of being kissed goodnight.

The authorities waived the post-adoption ten-day residency requirement, which enabled us to leave Birobidzhan once the children's Russian passports, new birth certificates, and adoption certificates were ready. Ten days in the region were suddenly compressed into two, forcing us into a flurry of activity. We wanted to make a contribution to the orphanage and had intended to donate cash, but the women in the white coats told us that money had to be declared and that most would be eroded by taxes and "less-official" fees. So they instead suggested that we buy snowsuits, jackets, mittens, boots, and hats because these items could not be easily tracked. Tamara took us to the store, and we bought more than we could afford. We nearly emptied out the entire children's section, which was smaller than our kitchen. We also bought brightly painted, locally made chairs, which we'd seen in abundance at the orphanage, as keepsakes for Peter and Sophie. Other than the grocery, it was the only store in town and therefore the only place to buy clothes, shoes, books, toys, bedding, household appliances, cosmetics, and baby supplies. Even though more than 200,000 people live in Birobidzhan, we were its only customers that day.

Our next stop was the farmer's market, which was busy and boisterous. Pat kept whispering for me to keep a firm hold on my purse because he didn't like the vibe coming from a scattering of young men who patrolled the aisles with heads bent and arms shoved deep into heavy canvas jackets. He needn't have told me. His body language changes so abruptly in these instances, reverting with a flash to his Brooklyn-bred street smarts, that I read his thoughts with a single glance. We quickly bought a bushel of bananas big enough for King Kong to enjoy, at least eighty bananas, and as much other fruit as the three of us could carry. When we returned to the orphanage, we took great pleasure in distributing our bounty to the mostly nonverbal toddlers who nonetheless had mastered how to say "Mama" and "Papa" and who still clamored for our touch and attention. It was both wonderful and profoundly sad to watch these children's faces light up and their mouths water over the prospect of something as simple as a piece of fruit. There was nothing they took for granted.

It was also funny and wonderful to marvel over the way Sophie began exhibiting proprietary behavior in our presence. To this day, we don't know exactly what she was saying, but whenever any of the children in her group showed us more than casual interest, she would furrow her brow and wag her finger in the direction of the diminutive offender. She would then fire off a salvo of verbal warnings so caustic that any children brave enough to have remained in the wings scattered in retreat, immediately. With clenched fist and steadfast determination, she also had no trouble establishing ownership over the little pink gingham pillow with our picture in the sleeve. She carried it everywhere she went, and according to her caregivers, whose eyes sparkled with the telling, refused to relinquish possession no matter what the circumstances, including using the potty. She behaved like a crazed old babushka rather than a barely two-year-old child. We loved her for it, and still do. Immensely.

That night, we sat in the easy company of Galina, Bogdan, and Sergei, another grandson who stopped in frequently, and watched their favorite Russian soap opera, which had become our custom. There was nothing else to do. We couldn't visit the children, and roaming the pitch-black streets of Birobidzhan after dark, which by late October was sometime around 3:00 p.m., was not a safe option. We had brought books and a portable chess set, but we were too exhausted and mentally depleted at this juncture of our trip to focus on anything that required even minimal mental acuity. The wardrobe in the soap reminded Pat of 1974 Staten Island on a Saturday night. We knew it was time to leave when we earnestly began looking forward to the next episode, checking our watches to make sure we didn't miss the kickoff.

Peter stopped screaming at me about the time we were ready to say goodbye to Tamara, Galina, and the orphanage staff. He even grudgingly allowed me to sit near him and interact with the blocks and plastic truck we bought at the store and left behind for the orphanage. But our contacts were still brief and tenuous. If I picked him up and sat him near me, he'd bounce up and run over to Pat, his short little legs moving faster than what seemed anatomically possible. But he didn't scream. He merely grunted. I interpreted this transition as progress and cheerfully continued my strategy of inching my way toward intimacy, or at least more sustained contact, often with food in hand as collateral.

Sophie too began loosening up around this time. Galina's living room could be closed off with French doors, and we took advantage of this design to contain our new cubs. They had never been in a home before, and for

Sophie, everything was worthy of exploration: the furniture, the kitchen, the television, Galina's fish tank, her knickknacks, the light sockets. The toilet topped the list of curiosities, though, as she had never seen one. The orphanage used pots lined up in rows for toileting, one child next to the other. The entire contraption, especially the flushing mechanism, fascinated her, and it wasn't long before we realized she didn't really have to go *peesit* every fifteen minutes.

But even confined to a single room, Sophie was a challenge. What became obvious quickly was that she had long ago mastered the art of playful yet clear defiance. She understood the limits we had imposed, she just didn't agree with them. And the mischief in her eyes, the twinkling intelligence that belied her tender age, was difficult to ignore and even more difficult to curtail. We would soon learn that we weren't the only ones under her spell. People fell victim to her charms wherever we went.

What wasn't so obvious at the time, but now stands out as clearly as fireflies in the night sky, was Peter's complete lack of curiosity about his new environment. I was chasing Sophie around like a madwoman, convinced her frenetic activity would result in instant and tragic death before we ever got home, but Peter barely budged. All he wanted to do was sit with his blocks or look at a book with Pat. But this behavior didn't strike us as necessarily strange back then. After all, we were strangers, we didn't speak Russian, and we were planning to whisk him away from the only home he ever knew. We thought he was scared and tentative, which I'm sure he was. Though we've seen vast improvement, we understand now that Peter tends to behave this way no matter what the circumstance or environment. He's uncomfortable navigating the contours of new experience. Rather than struggle to integrate, he retreats into the comforting spaces of his own thoughts or the rituals of repetitive play. It took years of intensive intervention to coax him from this mindset, and, even today, constant vigilance is required to keep him from withdrawing.

When it was time to leave Birobidzhan, we thanked and hugged Galina, promising to send pictures and updates once we were home. I don't remember whether we went to bed that night, but I'm guessing we didn't. At 4:30 a.m., Tamara took us to the orphanage, where the children were already bundled in their new clothes and jackets, standing with two women beneath the shelter and the dim light of the entryway's concrete overhang. Because we were leaving before dawn, we had said our emotional goodbyes to the women at the orphanage the night before. Two of Sophie's caregivers had rattled off instructions for us to keep Sophie on schedule and content, tears overflowing while they competed to stroke her tiny back. One of the doctors insisted we take a tube of cream to ease Peter's itchy skin. They were decent, basically kind people who were forced to look after Russia's discarded babies under conditions of extreme poverty. Although I was moved by their affection, I also was invigorated by the knowledge that Peter and Sophie were finished with orphanage life. Peter had spent all but five of his thirty-nine months in an institution, and Sophie, who was twenty-seven months old, had joined him before her first birthday. They had served their time and now were forever pardoned.

Both children were dazed, confused, and exhausted the entire bumpy trip to Khabarovsk. Our driver dropped Tamara at her apartment on the way out of town, and I watched her wave to us as we began our journey home. Our translator, who in the process became our friend, was gone. Until we reached Moscow, where Sergei awaited, we were on our own, relying on gestures and the few Russian words we had committed to memory as our only means of communication. Sophie sat on my lap, and Pat held Peter. There was no room for car seats, much less our luggage, which was tied to the roof with lengths of scratchy twine. When he wasn't dozing, Peter repeated his Russian name the entire ride, while Sophie stared, unmoving, out the window. Listening to this eerie cadence, the rise and fall of "*Gera Gera Gera*" against the clanging backdrop of the car, I worried whether our new son was trying to hold on, somehow, to his former life, even his very identity. The idea made me shudder.

The plane ride from Khabarovsk to Moscow was uneventful, thanks to a young Russian girl who appropriated Peter, drawing pictures and otherwise entertaining him for most of the flight. Sophie stayed content as long as I kept the Goldfish and Cheerios flowing her way. Neither of them slept during any portion of the ten-hour flight, and by the time we arrived in Moscow, they'd been awake, except for momentary catnaps, for almost twenty-four hours. Their bellies were full, and they had their first lollipops—for takeoff and landing. They found the airplane ride exciting and were uncharacteristically compliant for children their age. But they also were dead on their feet.

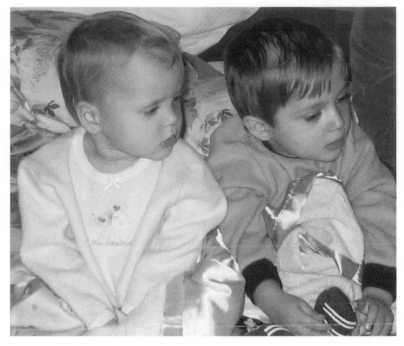

Our first night as a family, Moscow (October 2004)

The four days we spent in Moscow were exciting, scary, and in every way novel. The President Hotel is more than accommodating of newly adoptive parents, and we were happy to find two cribs set up and ready to go when we opened the door to our room, which was really a suite. It was the first night we would spend together as a family, and I had a raging yeast infection, which for me, was a first. I had ignored the mild symptoms that started to develop our last day in Birobidzhan. With so many important things on my mind, and having no idea how bad this kind of problem could get, I simply dismissed the warning signs as an aggravating nuisance. Boy, was I wrong. The culprit turned out to be the powerful antibiotics our doctor had us taking throughout the second trip to stave off a giardia relapse and prevent other pestilences. By the time we reached the hotel room in Moscow, sleep-deprived and with two bewildered and exhausted toddlers in tow, I was desperate for intervention. Pat was uneasy about me venturing into the Moscow night by myself, but there was no reasonable alternative. Every passing second was torture.

Trying to explain to the women at the front desk the nature of my problem was about the funniest and most exasperating experience of my life. The word *yeast* in Russian has no meaning unrelated to bread-making. After many rounds of passing the dictionary and using gestures not suitable for polite company, a eureka moment finally occurred, and they understood what I needed. These otherwise stone-faced women giggled like schoolgirls as they wrote down the address of the nearest pharmacy and showed me on a map how to get there. It was past midnight, I hadn't slept in God knows how long, Pat was no doubt panicking in the hotel room by himself with the kids, and I had no choice but to venture into the Moscow night in search of over-the-counter feminine relief.

Luckily, the directions were good and I arrived at the pharmacy after a fifteen-minute walk. Then I encountered the next hurdle: the pharmacist also didn't understand what I needed, and unlike American drugstores, customers in Russia do not have direct access to nonprescription drugs. Products are locked up and out of view. So I started my ridiculous pantomime routine all over again. Eventually a tall, elegantly dressed businessman walked in, saw me gesticulating like a crazed woman, and asked in fluent English if he could help. Ordinarily I would not have pulled an innocent into such a private matter, but I was desperate.

"I need something for a yeast infection," I said. Luckily I was too exhausted and uncomfortable to worry too much about his embarrassment.

"Uh-oh. Well, yes, of course. I can help with that." I thanked him for his kindness and apologized for the awkwardness of the situation. He took my place at the counter and explained to the pharmacist what I needed.

I might have emerged from the store with some semblance of dignity intact if the humorless pharmacist hadn't then decided to ask the man to translate the package directions. He really was managing well until that point, but this taxed his Samaritan attitude well beyond the tipping point. Bowing his head to review the instructions, he slowly looked up at me with what can only be described as horror.

"I simply cannot do this, miss. I am quite sorry. I cannot read these words to you out loud. I just cannot." His face was beet red and his eyes implored me to release him from this unbearable situation. He continued,

"You can manage from here on, right, miss? I'm sorry. Good night and good luck." With a slight bow and what I thought might be the click of his heels, he disappeared into the welcoming anonymity of the Moscow night.

When I entered the hotel lobby with white paper bag in hand, I was greeted by the sounds of the reserved but jubilant desk clerks cheering my success. I thanked them hastily and then raced to my room and waiting family. It was now the middle of the night, and Peter and Sophie were still ambulating like zombies on parade. I was still working off the adrenaline boost fueled by the pharmacy adventure, but Pat was out of juice. I found him slumped like a rag doll in an armchair, supervising our children in a semiconscious, unshaven, and close to delirious state.

We spent the rest of that night with all the lights on and Peter thrashing between us in the king-sized bed. He had screamed with terror every time we put him in the crib or attempted to dim a light, so we thought bringing him into bed with us would help. We were wrong. Sophie fell asleep in the crib after methodically rocking herself for forty-five minutes in spite of the considerable racket. Pat and I watched helplessly as she lay flat on her back with arms stretched toward the ceiling and rhythmically swung her body from left to right, the muscles in her neck taut and twisted. She was not ready or willing to receive our comfort.

Despite how exhausted we were the next morning, the prospect of eating breakfast as a family held great appeal. We watched in amazement as Sophie and Peter, regardless of the fatigue and trauma of the last thirty-six hours, ran with abandon down the long hall of our floor, falling, rolling, and generally howling with delight. From their expressions, we realized they had never experienced any real sense of personal freedom before. In fact, just like that first morning in the hall, Sophie and Peter would continue to react with complete and utter delight in response to the simplest pleasures for the entire first year they were home. The gift of a balloon, for instance, brought shrieks of joy, as did the sight of hamburgers, balls, television, bananas, frogs, honey, open spaces, milk, grass, and even their double stroller.

The breakfast buffet at the President provoked a truly unforgettable feeding frenzy. Eggs, crepes, bacon, sausage, milk, orange juice, oatmeal, fruit, breakfast potatoes, and French toast. They devoured everything in sight and then lifted their plates for more. Sophie ate three times as much as Peter, which is saying something, because he ate more that morning than he's ever eaten since.

The rest of our time in Moscow was spent getting perfunctory but mandatory medical exams for the children at a Russian clinic, making sure the U.S. Embassy processed their visas correctly, and generally tagging along with Sergei as he skillfully navigated the remaining post-adoption paper chase. Between appointments, we did some sightseeing and bought some incredibly expensive clothes for the children. The clothes I picked out prior to the adoptions, mostly 3Ts and 2Ts, hung from Peter and Sophie as loosely as potato sacks. We wound up buying Peter a few outfits in size twelve months. Sophie easily fit into size nine-month clothes.

Three other memorable events happened while we were in Moscow. The first had to do with bathing. Russians shower, even their babies, because they feel bathing in a tub full of water is an unclean practice. Sophie and Peter were so terrified of the water when we first put them in the tub, screaming like teenage victims in a horror flick, that I'm surprised someone on our floor didn't call security. But in a last-ditch effort to salvage the experiment, I splashed my hand in the water and gently splashed their bodies. Sophie paused for one second, considering the implications of this act, and then we watched with amazement as her features transformed and she surrendered, completely, to childhood instinct. Attack! The ensuing water fight was a moment that forever will be imprinted on my memory. Peals of laughter replaced blood-curdling screams, leaving Pat and me drenched and covered in bubbles. Bath time was never a problem again.

The next unforgettable moment occurred at a Moscow McDonald's, where Sophie caused a considerable crowd to gather. For some reason, Sergei assumed we'd want to go there, and we were too tired to protest. We ordered Happy Meals for the kids, but they didn't know what to do with them. They ate their apples, but their hamburgers went untouched. Sergei tried to coax them into eating, but they just stared blankly. We finally gave up and began eating ourselves. As soon as Pat lifted his burger to his mouth, Sophie picked hers up, staring at it curiously. It then occurred to us that they had never had a sandwich before. They either didn't know it was food or they didn't know how to approach it. So Pat picked up Sophie's cheeseburger and helped her position her infant-sized hands on either side. Then all three of us illustrated the chomping procedure, looking ridiculous, I'm sure. And that's all it took, at least for Sophie. Squeezing both sides of her cheeseburger so hard that bits of crumbly meat squished between her fingers, she took a single bite and paused. Her eyes moved back and forth with measured deliberation, and then an elfish grin, one of her hallmark characteristics, slowly emerged. She ate the rest of her burger, which was nearly the size of her head, with such gusto and intensity that people began gathering around us in amazement. Half act, half genuine enjoyment, she played to her audience like a seasoned professional, relishing the glow of the spotlight. Though we never convinced Peter to eat anything else that day, Sophie had seen the face of God, and her name was American Cheeseburger.

To this day, Pat and I refer to the last noteworthy event as simply The Fight, which occurred in the late afternoon of our second full day in Moscow. We were taking a well-deserved break in our room's big, over-stuffed chairs, watching contentedly as the children played and continued to explore their new environment. Sophie played kitchen with her doll and the plastic food, dishes, and pots we bought for her while clothes shopping in the fancy Moscow department store. Peter spent his time stuffing everything he could into his new backpack: Duplo blocks, books, cars and trucks, hotel magazines, water bottles, action figures, and even washcloths. Nothing was too banal for inclusion. When finished, he'd hoist it onto his back, circle the room, dump the contents out, and then start the process anew.

Although Pat and I exchanged worried glances over Peter's repetitive, ritualistic play, neither of us had the energy to intervene. Instead, I asked whether Pat would get me a pillow from the couch to prop behind my back, which had begun to ache. Both of us were unprepared for what happened next. Peter stopped what he was doing, went over to the couch, and brought me the pillow. He understood what we were saying! What a remarkable moment!

Our joy and surprise over this revelation was soon dwarfed, however, by what began as a simple breach of toddler territory. While we were praising Peter for his brilliance, Sophie seized the opportunity to snatch what had become a prized book from his otherwise closely guarded backpack. Until that point, neither of them had paid the slightest attention to the other. But all that changed when Peter discovered the missing item in Sophie's hand. The boy who we'd begun to worry was completely passive suddenly exploded with a litany of verbal outbursts. Sophie followed suit. With her brow knit in consternation as she shook her fist savagely in Peter's direction, she came back with a barrage of her own. The indecipherable argument continued, with both of them charging the other, fists clenched and chests puffed, for a considerable length of time. Pat and I watched in stunned silence as this drama unfolded. To this day, I don't know whether we chose not to intervene because the fight wasn't physical or because we were simply in shock. Regardless, the chaos stopped as suddenly as it began. Sophie and Peter had reached some sort of understanding. Although far from Camelot, they no longer ignored each other and, in ways small and large, began acting like the siblings their adoption papers declared them to be.

Overall, our last days in Moscow were lovely. The days were crisp and clear, and we could see the children's health improve on an almost hourly basis. Sophie's skin became less translucent, Peter's angry red rashes began to subside, and the dark blue bags under their eyes diminished by the minute. Breakfast continued to be a show worthy of charging admission, and running the length of the long halls became a favorite daytime activity. At night we'd read to them in the king-sized bed or let them watch a Russian cartoon with the lights dimmed ever so slightly. Peter never slept well in Moscow, but at least the screaming lessened.

In fact, the only really troubling part of our stay revolved around our children's intestinal health. Although we first thought the change in diet was to blame, the frequency, volume, and room-clearing odor made us rethink our diagnosis. I frankly had never smelled anything so foul in my life, and it was coming from both of them. But without additional symptoms, such as nausea, cramping, fever, or any other kind of distress, we decided the problem could wait until we got home. Having already obtained their medical clearances, we didn't want to jeopardize our departure date.

With Sergei serving as our guide, translator, and companion, we spent our last afternoon in Moscow exploring the city, which was both exciting and sad. Moscow is every bit as alive and vibrant as New York City, Los Angeles, or Boston, with all the noises, energy, and pulsations, but there is a crucial difference. The disparity between the wealthy Muscovites and the other residents, not to mention the rest of the Russian citizenry, is abundantly apparent. The ostentatious displays of wealth in Moscow make American vanities seem modest by comparison. I found it difficult to reconcile the abject poverty my children had experienced with the incredible brand of nouveau riche consumerism on constant exhibit in the streets of Moscow. I truly hope the country one day settles on an economic and social model that allows capitalism to flourish and wealth to accumulate, but in the presence of a healthy middle class and without so much graft that basic human rights are so casually overlooked.

I was never more aware of the depths of Russia's troubles than when I stepped on the plane that would take us home. Sophie and Peter had experienced unimaginable hardship in their first, most crucial years, and theirs were the faces I saw when I reflected on the failures of their birthplace. Pat and I were confident we could change their health and living circumstances for the better. What was less certain was the impact we'd have on their psyches, our ability to heal the damage to their developing brains and hearts, damage that was the result of neglect, abuse, and deprivation—the hopelessness and, in some ways, indifferences, of an entire people.

I said goodbye that morning to Russia, grateful for our children and poised for the adventures and struggles ahead. I was ready to go home. And I would not be looking back.

❧

NOVEMBER 9, 2009. *"Annie's not real?" Peter asks. I don't quite know how to explain; my previous thousand attempts haven't done the job. "No, honey, she's acting. It's pretend. Like when Sophie was in her play over the summer. She was pretending, right?" We watched the first part of the movie Annie last night, and Miss Flanagan's rendition of "Little Girls" gave Peter nightmares. "So Annie's a robot?" he continues, undeterred. The inflexibility of his thinking frustrates me, and I struggle to remain patient as I think of ways to help him understand. Peter at eight still is unclear about the distinction between fantasy and reality, fiction and fact, film versus life. If someone on television, or even on stage, is a real, live human being, rather than a cartoon character or puppet, he stolidly clings to his belief that the characters are "real" and therefore, in many instances, an immediate trigger for his countless fears. Carol Burnett's rendition of Miss Flanagan might have hit too close to home for Peter's fragile sensibilities to assimilate. We don't really know what our children consciously remember of orphanage life, if anything, but the preverbal memories are undoubtedly there, lurking in the corners, ready to spring at the slightest provocation.*

Peter later tells me, on the way to the public library, that he wants to watch the rest of the movie tonight, if there's time, and that he's not afraid anymore. "Why not?" I ask. "Because that bad lady only gets mean to girls," he answers. It's a valid point, and I tell him so. "Plus," he adds, looking at me over the top of his glasses like a mini-version of his father, "she don't talk Russian." That's when I realize I'm not reading too much into our son's distress. He really did make the connection between his past and the movie. Despite Annie being my favorite Broadway show when I was eleven, perhaps it isn't the best choice for our family right now. I try distracting him with chitchat about which of his newly borrowed books we're going to read first. He's dead set on reading a Magic Tree House book that's well beyond his ability, so we agree to read it out loud, together. I don't hold much hope for making it through the book—Peter's not one to read (or listen) to a chapter or two a night and then continue the next day where he left off, but we'll give it a try nonetheless. Pat's in the city today, and I want to make sure I have a quiet, snuggly evening with the kids.

On the way home from the library, Peter comments how Pippin, our little terrier mutt, loves to sit on my lap while I drive, preferably with my left arm draped around him. Then he exclaims, "Mommy, I wish I was Pippin's size!" When I ask him why, he says because then he'd be little enough to sit on my lap all the time and be carried around. "Wouldn't that be nice, Mom?" I'm so struck by the pronouncement that I have to fight back tears as our eyes meet in the rearview mirror. Not so many years ago, that mirror was the only medium through which Peter could tolerate eye contact. I used to catch him staring at me in the car, his head whipping around, his gaze growing vacant, the instant our eyes met. Then slowly, slowly, and with the mirror to cut the intensity, he began risking a brief moment of eye-to-eye contact. Today, nearly six years our son, Peter not only looks at us directly, without the crutch of a mirror, he pines for those intimate moments—particularly with me, moments he either never had or was never able to tolerate. There was a time I pined for them too, but not anymore. Today I look at Peter and see my son, a loving, beautiful boy who greets the world with an easy smile and ready heart. I never allowed myself to even dream that he would get to this point, that he and I would make the kind of progress, as mother and son, that we've made.

So it's true. I don't mourn the loss of the orphaned infant I was never able to hold, nourish, and protect. That child is gone. The boy in the car, the one wishing to be small again, that boy is my son, my Peter. So tonight I plan to hold him tight, for as long as he can bear, so that together with his sister, he'll know that intimacy, protection, and a mother's embrace isn't just for baby boys and furry friends. They're for Peter, too.

CHAPTER 16

We're Home!

BEFORE WE ADOPTED, most of my career was spent working as an enforcement attorney for the U. S. Environmental Protection Agency. Eight years in Atlanta and almost four in New York City. Pat playfully still refers to two of the attorneys in my division, Carl Garvey and Tom Lieber, as my "office husbands." Carl was a fellow staff attorney and Tom was our supervisor. Both are exceptionally kind and generous people, and kidding aside, they and their families are among our most cherished friends.

When we finally made it through customs at JFK, where a bewildered Sophie and Peter were welcomed as U.S. citizens for the first time, Tom and Carl were waiting for us, cheerfully waving a stuffed horse for Peter and a blue elephant for Sophie. They had picked up our car, which had been left at the Liebers' home in Oyster Bay, and driven it to the airport during rush hour so that we could leave directly for upstate. I was so happy to see our friends, with their goofy grins and bouncy steps, that I audibly gasped with relief. We had gone through so much, our new family of four, in such a short time, and the finish line was now within sight. Exhausted, scared, disoriented, and excited, we were in one piece and, thanks to our friends, would be home for good in just a few more hours.

I don't know how Pat managed to drive the hundred miles in his comatose condition, but we arrived home in one piece. It was about 8 p.m. in New

York, and we decided to put the children to bed in their new rooms without fuss or fanfare. There would be plenty of time for exploration in the days and weeks to come. Sleep was priority number one. We changed them into pajamas and Pull-Ups, brushed their teeth, and tucked them gently into their new beds. I remember them staring up at us, confused and disoriented but too exhausted to complain. Bending down to kiss the downy soft skin of their foreheads, I consciously marked the memory of this occasion in the quiet refuge of my heart.

I was shocked to wake up that next morning and find the children still sleeping. I had listened for the better part of the night to the hushed sounds of the house, napping in brief snatches in case Sophie or Peter woke. I had every right to be dead on my feet, but instead I felt exhilarated, ready to plunge into the life and role I'd been longing for since Pat and I first met. I'm not sure what I expected—pouncing, screaming, general chaos certainly—but what I found that early morning was a stillness that belied my newfound status. With Pat still sleeping too, I decided to tiptoe downstairs and survey our depleted breakfast stocks. It felt strange being in the house without our dog, Scout, whom we would board for another two weeks. Normally she shadowed my every move. Though the size of our family had doubled, I felt oddly alone as I rummaged through the pantry, finding nothing to eat except cereal with Parmalat milk and instant oatmeal. In the stillness of the kitchen, I noticed the sky-blue booster seats already strapped onto our kitchen chairs, standing empty but ready for action. As with the car seats, we had installed and tested them before leaving for Russia. I smiled a little nervously with the knowledge that our quiet home was about to come alive with the clamor of children.

Before we became the owners, a ninety-three-year-old spinster, the last of her line, had died in the old stone house. She had been born and raised there, and her death ended two hundred fifty years of continuous residency by one or more members of the same Dutch farming family. How many decades, I wondered, had it been since the old plank floors shook with the patter of little feet, the high-pitched squeals of laughing children reverberating off the thick plastered walls? Too long, I guessed.

But change was coming. There was no misinterpreting the sound of heavy thumping I soon heard upstairs. Merely twenty-six pounds, Peter walked with the weight of a lumberjack. Thud. My son was up. Our life as a family was beginning in earnest.

Marbletown, NY (Summer 2004)

My sister, Patty, was due to arrive from Atlanta in four hours. Since our own mother had died a few years earlier, she would be filling the expanded role of mother, sister, friend and all-important crutch. Sophie and Peter adore Patty because of the way she treats and loves them, but also because children are programmed to intuit from their parents who is good, who is dangerous, who will protect, and who is trustworthy. Patty exudes goodness and quiet confidence. Although some might say we're more different than similar, I do believe we bring out the best in each other, and I'm certain Peter and Sophie sense our closeness. When we're together, we have this way of filling the spaces around us with laughter, happily retreating into the center of our shared, occasionally secret, and always silly sister experiences. I desperately wanted her to meet Sophie, and to watch and study Peter, without the benefit of Pat's and my concerns or preconceptions. I suppose I was looking for her reassurance that our fledgling family would be okay; whole, healthy, and in possession of all of the ingredients needed to grow and thrive.

By the time I ran upstairs to check on Peter, the whole house was awake. Pat was wrestling into sweats, greedy for a cup of non-instant, fresh-ground coffee. I gave him a quick kiss and hug, and then followed the noise across the hall. I found Peter in Sophie's room, touching her new possessions one by one with wide-eyed wonderment. Sophie stroked her pink-and-yellow quilt with one hand as she clutched the blue elephant given to her by Carl and Tom in the other, and I watched as she studied, mouth agape, Peter's near reverent explorations. Furniture, rugs, rocking chair, wallpaper, books, closets, clothes, stuffed animals, drawers, and hampers—items commonly found in children's bedrooms around the world but notably absent from Russian institutions for orphans.

After having them use the potty, Pat and I tried carrying the children downstairs, but both insisted on walking. Sophie was particularly unsteady on her feet and was already covered in bruises from the effects of her new-found freedom. She didn't want me to hold her hand on the stairs, but I insisted. I counted one, two, three as we slowly stepped down, Peter's footsteps pounding heavily behind us.

"Gera, Gera, Gera . . ." he repeated.

"Peter-Gera," Pat suggested.

Since Peter had not stopped repeating his name, Pat cleverly decided to use this preoccupation to introduce the American name we had chosen for him. After the adoptions, we began calling them "Gera-Peter" and "Katya-Sophie," but once home, we reversed the order in an effort to gradually drop the Russian familiar. At the time, I was convinced of the correctness of our decision to change their names, especially since German LoBrutto and Ekaterina LoBrutto don't roll easily off the tongue. However, in the name of rescue and new family beginnings, we wound up stripping our children of every ounce of their former, tenuous identities. There's no doubt they are forever Peter and Sophie now, their names imbued with our love just as if we had named them at birth. But still, I wonder whether it may have been an unwise choice. Their Russian names were the one part of their former lives we could have kept intact.

Pat managed to make pancakes for breakfast thanks to a squirreled-away box of Bisquick, and the children gobbled up every bite. I remember Pat staring at the two of them, happily belted into their new boosters at our breakfast bar, and I noticed that the bags under his eyes were deeper than they should have been.

He was so tired. At fifty-six, he was no longer a young man, and we had committed to an incredible, life-altering undertaking. Sophie and Peter were needy, not necessarily healthy, and undoubtedly carrying emotional and developmental scars that had yet to reveal themselves. They were also virtual strangers. I could see the self-doubt in Pat's face but there was nothing to be done, at least not then. This was Sophie and Peter's first morning home, and they needed us.

I needed them too. I was desperate to interact with Peter and excited to strengthen the fledgling bond I was cultivating with Sophie. Because we had read so many books about adoption and attended Dr. Aronson's adoptive parenting classes, we were careful not to overload the children's sensory systems with too many new toys. So I took out the same few Duplo blocks from Peter's backpack and the doll and kitchen toys from Sophie's, and placed them on the floor in front of the fireplace. Then I patted the rug to entice them to come toward me. My efforts were interrupted, though, because the kitchen door swung open and I found myself staring at my brother Mark, who stood smiling in the doorway with a small duffle bag in hand.

"Facial!" he roared, addressing me by one of several inexplicable nicknames he's devised over the years. "Are these the kids?" I nearly broke down in tears when I saw him. Not only was Patty on her way, but Mark was there too. The older brother who terrorized me daily throughout my childhood was at that moment, in my eyes, the sweetest, most welcome sight in the world. While we were still in Moscow, he figured out a way to finagle his impossibly busy trial schedule so that he could spend thirty-two hours with the kids and us. Grabbing Pat and me brusquely by the shoulders, he pulled us to him like a quarterback preparing to huddle.

"So what are we doing today?" he laughed. Peter and Sophie hadn't moved a muscle since their new uncle appeared, but they knew enough to stare, transfixed. In the way that big men can be surprisingly gentle, Mark untangled himself from us and made his way toward the children, bending down to their level and ever so carefully lifting first Peter, then Sophie into his arms. Any faint doubts I had concerning whether my family would be able to fully embrace our Russian children disappeared in that instant. The tears I'd been holding back flowed freely, and with quivering voice I managed to yell "Shut up!" to both Pat and Mark as they teased me about the waterworks.

Although I admit I've been known to sob without warning over milk-carton photos of missing children, these tears were fully justified and personal. I was tired and running on nothing but nervous energy. Pat was near shock too and showing signs of becoming seriously overwhelmed. Even though I clung to the belief that my brothers and sister, all of whom live in the Deep South, would hop on a plane at a moment's notice if I ever truly needed them, the theory had never been tested. The surprise of watching my brother walk through our door made me realize how wonderfully important it is to be loved, truly loved, to be part of a family and circle of friends larger and stronger than yourself. Mark was standing in our kitchen, grinning like a kid at Christmas, and Patty was on her way. Pat and I could have survived those first few days on our own, but it was a great relief knowing we weren't alone. The gift of family is one I hope Peter and Sophie will always cherish and appreciate.

Patty pulled into the driveway in a Ford rental a few hours later, ushering in a second wave of energy and a necessary call to action. She was the only one in the house who had more than a week's worth of bona fide mothering experience, so she naturally assumed a commanding role. Groceries had to be bought, clothes and shoes that actually fit needed to be secured, and for some reason, the four of us decided that Sophie and Peter needed to have tricycles, immediately.

Patty and I would shop later that afternoon, once Sophie and Peter were napping. I remember being so proud of my children as I watched them interact with my sister and brother. Despite the complete upheaval they'd been made to endure, their resilience, with some notable exceptions, shined through in those first days and weeks at home. Sophie examined every square inch of Patty, looking in her mouth, her ears, her nose, even pulling apart strands of hair to study her roots and scalp. She had done the same to me in Russia, and I was tickled to see the routine repeated on my living room couch.

Peter was indifferent toward my sister but mesmerized by Mark, whom he followed with great devotion. I watched as they built Duplo towers together and laughed when he showed Peter how to make them crash, causing my new son to scream at the top of his lungs and wag an angry finger in Mark's direction. It was the loudest noise Peter had made since that first night in Moscow, and it caused all of us to stop and take stock. It was also an early clue as to his absolute need for external order and predictability.

One of my favorite memories of those first days home happened on the same night that Patty and Mark arrived. After putting the children to bed, which was shockingly easy as they showed no inkling of being afraid as well as no inclination to wander, we set about unpacking the large Fisher-Price tricycle boxes that Patty and I had purchased at Toys "R" Us earlier that day. We planned to spend no more than forty minutes on assembly so that we could devote the rest of the evening to talking about our trip and just enjoying each other's company. What we didn't take into account was the fact that my siblings and I are lawyers and Pat is a fiction editor, which means the four of us are largely devoid of everyday, useful skills. It didn't help that the directions were the size of a hymnal and each box came with six bags of plastic nuts, bolts, and other mysterious parts. Not even the pedals came preassembled.

In no time at all, forty minutes became four hours, and the living room was still strewn with plastic parts whose bright colors flickered ominously from the glow of the fireplace. For reasons that remain unclear, I decided that s'mores might improve our chances of success, so I searched for the necessary ingredients and a few spare coat hangers. I don't know if it was the s'mores that did it, but eventually we finished, a few beer bottles littering the coffee table, somewhere around midnight. We were exhausted, stiff, and punch drunk, but we stood united and humbled in the presence of our awesome, sticky accomplishment.

I awoke smiling the next morning with the memory of the previous night's escapades. I'll never know why we decided tricycles were necessary for Sophie and Peter to begin their new lives, especially since their legs were too weak to even pedal. But the trikes were downstairs, ready and waiting to be used, and hopefully without serious defects in assemblage. The thought of taking our children to the emergency room on our second whole day home was not one I savored.

Pat was the first to greet Peter that morning and therefore was the first to witness the scene. In the months and years to come, we would grow accustomed to the ritual, though never the shock. Pat found Peter sitting squarely in the middle of his bed, wearing his pajamas and peering serenely about the room. He had defecated on one end of the bed and urinated on the other. His caregivers had told us that at three years and three months, Peter was completely potty trained, day and night. True to their word, he had not had a single accident since becoming ours. That morning was no exception. Upon inspection, Pat discovered that his pajamas and Pull-Ups were dry and completely unsoiled. The quest to unravel the mystery of our son, his mind, his motives, his fears, and his damaged heart, was officially underway.

❦

FEBRUARY 22, 2010. *The school nurse and Peter's special education teacher greet me as I pick Sophie and Peter up from school. Having navigated the special education system for four battle-scarred years, I know the dual nature of their presence is not a good omen. Today's topic revolves around the apparent districtwide angst caused by the fact that Peter wets his pants at school. Never mind that Peter has been wetting his pants at school, as well as at home, in the car, while sleeping, at the movies, and while eating ice cream, with unpredictable regularity for close to four years. In the school's mind, the issue at last has reached a fulminating level of crisis that must be addressed. For the last few years, Pat and I have taken a hands-off approach to this problem, deciding mostly to ignore it. None of the experts seem to be able to tell us why Peter comes in and out of incontinence—though overstimulation and stress do seem to play a role—or what we should do about it. It doesn't help that Peter repeatedly reveals that he likes the feel of hot urine washing across his skin. Is the problem developmental, medication-related, sensory, mitochondrial, psychological, structural, emotional, social, or, my bet, a medley of them all? Since it's anyone's guess, Pat and I eventually settled on a low-key approach.*

However, Peter usually doesn't alert anyone to the fact that he's wet his pants, preferring instead to continue with his day as though nothing has occurred. Complicating the problem is the fact that he often doesn't empty a full bladder, he just piddles here and there, which makes it hard to detect—by us as well as his teachers—because usually he's not so soaked that he's dripping. What happens is that we find wet spots all over our home and cars, our lives constantly permeated with the smell of stale urine. And so we devised a containment plan about eighteen months ago, and this is what it is: when he's in a wetting cycle, like the one he's been in for the last four months, he wears Pull-Ups during the day; when and if he can stay dry for three days, he goes back to underwear. For the record, he hasn't had a three-day streak of daytime dryness since before Halloween, and though we presently don't address this issue at all, he hasn't been dry at night, even once, since he was six years old.

For whatever reason, however, Peter more or less has begun alerting his teacher when he pees at school. Personally, I think he liked the attention he recently received at the urologist's office, which no doubt precipitated the change in his reporting behavior. Before then, he would pee in his Pull-Ups stealthily and without acknowledgment. Because he usually wears jeans and most of his shirts reach below mid-hip, his accidents went largely unnoticed at school. Pat and I constantly tried talking to his teachers and the rest of the IEP team about this problem (just as we had last year and the year before that and the year before that), but no one seemed too concerned or interested. Almost like they didn't believe us. But things have changed now that Peter has decided to tell his teachers about his daily wetness.

After school today, the nurse asks that I obtain a letter from the urologist stating that Peter is required to wear Pull-Ups to third grade. She could suffer an official reprimand, she suggests, if our Pull-Ups-until-three-dry-days parenting approach is not officially endorsed by the medical community and filed in her records. The very idea is ridiculous! I also have the nauseating feeling that the nurse is being used as a puppet, that this newest directive comes from one of the school psychologists, who is obsessed with Peter and determined to prove me wrong at every possible turn. This school won't, the previous school wouldn't . . . perhaps no school ever will accept the fluidity and complexity of Peter's medical, social, emotional, psychological, and psychiatric status. The fact that they have him on a toileting schedule exonerates them, in their minds, from any contributory liability for the problem. And that, of course, leaves Pat and me as the sole culprits. The obvious implication is that if it were not for the Pull-Ups, Peter would be dry. Therefore, the school's logic goes, it's appropriate for Peter's "team" to impose their will upon what is and should remain a parenting issue. It's just one of countless implications we've faced over and over when it comes to Peter's more perplexing behaviors. With the school, it seems, Peter's successes are theirs, but his failures? They belong to us.

CHAPTER 17

THE PARADE MARCHES BY

PAT AND I decided not to tell Patty or Mark about that first bed-soiling incident. We were horrified of course, and worried that something was terribly wrong, but we were also confused. I wanted Patty's take on Peter's behaviors, but this discovery was in a different category altogether. My siblings knew even less than we did about the complicated psychosocial issues involved in international adoption, and we didn't want to set off alarm bells incapable of being unrung. But why would a child do that? What did it signify? What was Peter trying to tell us? None of it made sense. If he needed to relieve himself, why didn't he just go in the Pull-Ups he wore for safe measure or, better yet, use the toilet? There was not a speck of mess on either his pajamas or Pull-Ups. Whatever the reason, one thing was clear: his actions were deliberate.

After Pat and I cleaned what we could and stripped the bed, we tried talking to him, which was an exercise in futility, of course. Peter didn't speak English and we didn't speak Russian. But we did know a few key words: *nyet* (no), *da* (yes), *peesit* (pee), and *kakut* (poop), which enabled us to say something along the lines of "*nyet peesit, nyet kakut, nyet* in bed" (and then we pointed to the bed). Peter just stared at us blankly, picked up a familiar book, and walked out, repeating "*nyet, nyet*" as he began clomping down the stairs. I walked him back up and into the bathroom, where I pointed at the toilet and implored, *"Da peesit, da kakut."* He nodded. *Da, da.*

Christmas 2004

Mark left that afternoon, and Patty flew back to Atlanta two days later. Although I couldn't have imagined asking any of my siblings to keep their distance, I know now it was a mistake to have visitors, especially as many as we welcomed, those first months home. Having Patty and Mark with us at the beginning was a tremendous comfort, especially for me, but it wasn't best for Sophie and Peter. They needed time to adjust to their new environment—language, diet, smells, routines, clothes, weather, and home. They also needed time to become accustomed to us, their new parents. They'd been taught in the orphanage to call us Mama and Papa, but they had no reference from which to attach meaning to those words. They were coveted prizes we had yet to earn.

Over the next two months, we ran a bed and breakfast for an impressive number of family and friends. After my sister left, my brother's wife, Paula, arrived to take over the helm. She wasn't working at the time and was able to stay five or six days. Her presence was incredibly welcomed and helpful. She taught me about cutting grapes in half, as well as how to introduce new foods, clip the nails of wiggly toes and fingers, buy shoes for toddler feet, cut juice with water, and even assemble an outdoor Little Tikes jungle gym. Like Patty and Mark, she also has an amazing sense of humor, an ability to bring levity and laughter into the mix of genuine challenge.

In fact, Paula's the one who devised the unit system, to which we all still fondly refer. Somewhere around ten days into the adoptions, Pat and I began looking terribly ragged, primarily because we were losing the battle for control of the premises. The children's needs and activity levels were eons beyond what we anticipated; not only were we struggling to keep pace, we were losing ground. It's not that we didn't count on their being busy—we knew they were toddlers—we just failed to estimate the extent of their frenzy. Russian orphanages may be called Baby Homes, but they don't look like homes, and they aren't run like homes. Consequently, Sophie and Peter arrived with no understanding of what family meant and with no experience to help them safely navigate the hidden or overt dangers present in a real home. For instance, neither of them knew that stoves are hot, couches are for sitting, electrical outlets are dangerous, fireplaces aren't for hiding, refrigerators are cold, washing machines make noise but aren't dangerous, bookshelves aren't ladders, toilets aren't just for flushing, drawers pop out when tugged, and most knobs and dials turn something on.

They were blank slates on greased-up wheels. Thank goodness Paula suggested the unit system to help us through the day. One thing we were successful in doing right off the bat was establishing a wake/sleep schedule. I'm not sure how we did this, but I do know our will to succeed was fueled by some brand of instinctual desperation. We were exhausted and would not survive without rest. So the children went to bed at 7 p.m. and woke, most mornings, by 7 a.m. That meant there were twelve waking child hours per day, and Paula suggested we divide the time into half-hour units, which equates to twenty-four units a day. One unit was taken up with breakfast, one with lunch, three to four with nap, one with bath time, and so on. Not only was this incremental approach great fun—"One more unit to go," or "Hey, if you keep the kids up late, you're gonna owe me a unit tomorrow"— it also helped preserve our shrinking sanity.

Buoyed by the help of my siblings and sister-in-law, and armed with the unit system to fool us into thinking what we'd done to our lives was survivable, Pat and I began to fall into some semblance of a schedule. Except, that is, until our next round of visitors arrived, with presents, cakes, hugs, kisses, and loads of heartfelt enthusiasm. Then we'd have to start from scratch again. My other brother, Lee, friends from Atlanta, Pat's daughter Jenny and her husband, Patty again with her teenage children, Mark again with the rest of his family, my grown nephew and his wife, and then, en masse, the rest of Pat's family. It was wonderful, exciting, and comforting for Pat and I to be showered with so much love and support, and yet this extended period of celebration really did nothing more than prolong what was already a difficult adjustment period for Sophie and Peter.

I remember when Pat's entire family came to visit. At least I had the presence of mind to know that eight or so strangers showing up at the house at once would overwhelm the kids, but there was nothing I could do. They were excited to meet Sophie and Peter, and we were anxious for the visit to go well, to prove that our decision to adopt was correct and that our decision to start what for Pat was a second family was not destined for failure, heartache, or division. His family is fiercely protective of him and they'd always been reticent about our decision to adopt. After countless years of being lost in his own grief over the death of his two sons and the failure of his marriage, and almost paralyzed with fear over how those events would shape his surviving daughter, he had emerged into life again. He and I were so happy when we first met and throughout our first childless years of marriage. I understand now that his family was worried, if not terrified, that we had gone too far, had moved too fast, and mostly, had taken on more, in terms of the children, than he ever should have been made to handle. Just as Pat was getting his footing back, we decided to bring home two busy and demanding toddlers capable of shaking the Earth off its very axis.

But I believed in Pat, and still do, with the cocky confidence of the newcomer who, unlike the people standing in our doorway, never had to shoulder the burden of walking beside him through those dark, lonely years. I believed him when he said he wanted to give fatherhood another try, and I clung to this belief in the days and weeks after we first brought the children home. I especially clung to this construct as I welcomed Pat's family into our home on that late autumn afternoon. I remember thinking the first snow was near, because I could feel the heavy air as it swirled around our property, plucking without apology the last few remaining leaves from their branches.

They were all smiles and hugs as Peter jumped into arms and laps as casually as if he had spent every day of his life with my husband's family. It was a worrisome pattern Pat and I had begun to recognize but rarely voiced beyond the privacy of our bedroom, and one that we would combat for years. Peter was displaying indiscriminate friendliness, meaning he'd seek affection, when he needed it, with casual adroitness. The boy who screamed if I tried holding him more than a minute, who would tilt his head away from my body as though we were opposing magnets, nonetheless knew how to charm and win the affection of Pat's family, and all the other visitors who filed through our door those first months home. His overfriendliness toward people he barely knew really was like that of an addict willing to trade actual happiness for momentary, fleeting euphoria. For a long time, Peter favored the quick fix of a stranger's praise or affection over lasting intimacy and closeness.

Pat and I barely understood what we were witnessing during this critical time, but we knew something was wrong. In my mind, the visit by Pat's family cemented my concern. Sophie was so overwhelmed by the number of good-intentioned family members fawning over her that she retreated to the bathroom and refused to come out. She didn't speak the language, people she didn't know were asking for hugs and kisses, and she became overwhelmed. In fact, she would not come out of the bathroom until everyone left, two hours later. Although I was disappointed that Pat's family would have to meet the "real Sophie" another time, her behavior was understandable, and developmentally normal. But Peter was holding court, and not in a happy, healthy way, either. He bounced from lap to lap, briefly hugging and squeezing necks and repeating *"padushka"* as he worked his way around the room like a spinning top.

But with the exception of the bed-soiling incident, which would evolve into a chronic problem, and the dichotomy of Peter's overaffection toward visitors but underresponsiveness with us, our initial transition was easy. Sophie delighted in every way and with every move, her spunk, cognitive prowess, and resiliency evident to all who met her. And Peter was compliant. Other than the bizarre soiling behavior, he was incredibly easy. Though we didn't understand it, Pat and I weren't even sure the bed soiling was deliberate conduct. This was partly because Peter never did anything else wrong. He was a picky eater and aloof, he repeated the few words he knew, whether in Russian or English, with annoying consistency, and he was still stiff and robotic in his manner and physical gait, but he also was obedient. Completely. He never tested a single boundary we established and would become visibly upset whenever Sophie did, which was often.

Even so, it was also like he was a ghost, an empty shell. One night when the units were up and we lay exhausted in bed, Pat and I confessed that neither of us had any idea who Peter was. He was our son, he was living in our house, we were meeting his needs, but he either lacked or would not reveal any of the personal traits, habits, or preferences that distinguish a person, even a three-year-old person, as an individual. It was an uneasy, hollow feeling we shared, and we talked at great length about the reasons we felt that way. Were we doing something wrong? Letting Sophie steal too much of the show? Our questions were as endless as they were unanswerable. We only knew we had no inkling into the heart or soul of the little boy we named Peter, a child who needed and deserved parents, and whom we had committed to love and nurture the rest of our lives.

Other than the hundreds of mistakes we made during those first weeks home, and the uneasy feelings we'd begun to accumulate about Peter's odd behavior and almost surreal submission, the visit into the city to see Dr. Aronson also remains prominent in my memory. We had taken the children to our local pediatrician in the first days we were home so that he could make sure we weren't overlooking any urgent problems. Knowing we planned to have the children fully evaluated by Dr. Aronson, he graciously agreed to wait for her work-ups and reports and then implement any care or interventions she recommended.

Although the pediatrician, who also is an adoptive parent, withheld his initial impressions at the time, he later shared that when he first met the children, his immediate reaction was that Sophie was in dire shape. Grossly underweight, nearly bald, and the size of a ten-month-old, he considered her more medically fragile than Peter, who despite his short stature, had a certain robust quality.

We would eventually exchange knowing smiles over the irony of those first impressions as Sophie grew stronger and livelier with every passing month while Peter's clinical and psychosocial presentation grew exponentially more troubling. I couldn't help but recall, and in many ways recoil over, what Dr. Aronson said to Pat and me during the days we agonized over the baby Ben: you can heal the body, but the brain's a whole different ballgame.

In fact, when we brought the children to see Dr. Aronson, she repeated this mantra, but in the context of reassurance. Sophie would heal. We would make her well and strong with the basic ingredients of parenting: food, love, nurture, and attention. Her head circumference was good, and she showed no signs of alcohol exposure, either physical or via cognitive patterns. Peter did have telltale signs of FAS, as her hands-on examination would reveal, but as she would write in her report, "only time will tell." His weight was good and so was his head circumference. He was incredibly short, a finding she labeled "psychosocial dwarfism," but she felt this would resolve in time, and it did. Blood work revealed that they both suffered from rickets, which is caused by a lack of vitamin D (found in both milk and sunlight), they were both infected with giardia, and they both tested positive for tuberculosis.

We weren't exactly happy with the news, but we weren't shocked either. Lots of orphanage kids have these diagnoses, and as for the TB, a lung X-ray would hopefully reveal they had been exposed but not infected. I filed the possible FAS news away in the same part of my brain as I had filed the apprehensions I'd felt upon first meeting Peter in Russia. We were moving forward, he was ours, and there was no going back. We spent the rest of our time in Dr. Aronson's office relishing the excitement of being new parents, of having taken this journey with her for nearly a year, and the triumph and excitement of having her meet our children face to face, in flesh and blood. She had helped us weather many storms during our tumultuous passage toward parenthood, and she would continue to guide us in the years to come. "They're here," I felt like saying. "They're real and they're ours!"

Even though I knew she met parents with their newly adopted children on a frequent if not daily basis, she shared our joy and excitement genuinely, with open heart and reverent respect for the incredible milestone our visit represented. As we left her office, with Sophie and Peter irritable and still howling over having been probed and stuck with needles, she yelled to us over the din, her wild gray hair flying as she sped to catch us. "Don't forget their vaccination schedules!"

❧

MARCH 18, 2010. *I'm accosted again today at parent pickup. This time by a middle-aged woman who has appointed herself Peter's protector and guardian. I'm really considering putting the kids on the bus. That way, at least, I wouldn't have to dodge insults and poorly disguised accusations by certain members of Peter's special education "team" as I try to corral my children and their belongings toward the car. Today's guest appearance is the school psychologist, a person without children and apparently no familiarity whatsoever with either FAS or attachment issues. This person has been second-guessing our parenting decisions (thus the reference to having no children) and criticizing our choices regarding our son's educational program since we had the displeasure of meeting in late 2007. When we entered the world of special education, I had no idea we'd be opening our home, our values, our every decision to suspicion and judgment by educators who have never stepped inside our house, who don't know us outside of school, and who have no business interfering with our privacy.*

Today's accusation revolves around the fact that Peter peed in class this morning. For the last few weeks, since the urologist confirmed no physical problem, and with this doctor's urging, we began giving Peter a consequence when he wets during the day. Essentially, he needs to pay for his own daytime diapers. If he goes through his $2.00-per-week allowance, he does chores to earn the money. We've been having him do everything from sweeping the mudroom floor to picking up dog poop in the yard, now that the snow's melted. The dog poop chore is naturally the least preferred and, not shockingly, has had the greatest effect. He's been dry three days in a row (for two consecutive times) after he's had to do this. When he stays dry, he earns time on his Nintendo DS, or the Wii, or he can watch television. It's working.

He's been dry more days in the last few weeks than he's been in the last six months. But the ever-vigilant school psychologist needs to inform me this afternoon that Peter is devastated by his latest accident, so much so that this person had to have a "double session" with him.

Now I love my son, and I also know him. When he finds sympathy in the path of one of his missteps, he grabs hold as tightly as a tick on a dog. While the other parents file out, I'm informed that the psychologist knows about the poop chore and can't help but question the wisdom and compassion of our approach. "You have one devastated, sad little boy who is afraid, ashamed, and mortified of what's going to happen to him. You can't think this is helping." The reality is we hate making Peter do this, but it's next to impossible to get him to accept responsibility for his decisions unless the consequence is something he truly loathes. At dinner, Peter tells us that this person (oh, how I want to use a name!) said that he must feel like we're "beating him" when we make him do chores for wetting. Yes, that's right. Beating him. I know Peter makes things up, and it's possible the psychologist didn't say these exact words, but what was said was close enough—this person just about said as much to my face this afternoon. How can we possibly deal with Peter's attachment issues, the stealing, destruction, toileting misuse, and aggressiveness, when people at school are reinforcing for him that we are bad, that we are hurting him, and that he shouldn't trust us?

This woman isn't just interfering with our ability to heal and parent our son, she's actively sabotaging our efforts. She has no right! She refuses to even consider that we have well-considered reasons for making some of the tough decisions we've made. We're trying to make Peter understand cause and effect, action and consequence, and assume at least an iota of personal accountability. Maybe it's time Pat and I start interjecting ourselves into certain "team" members' private lives. I must admit, the thought does make me smile.

CHAPTER 18

IS THAT YOU, SANTA CLAUS?

I NEVER THINK back to our first six months home without ambivalence, confusion, joy, and relief, a mixed bag of feelings that don't typically complement each other. On the one hand, the children were home, they were ours, and we were a family whose members were learning to adjust to the cadences and demands of one another. I was quickly becoming a competent parent, and Pat was rediscovering some tricks of the fatherhood trade he had shelved more than a decade earlier. We were on the path toward becoming a whole, healthy family and should have been content and satiated with the bounty of our blessings.

And there were blessings. When Sophie first got home, her legs were so spindly and weak she couldn't climb the stairs or pull herself onto the couch. If she tried walking without assistance on a path with even a slight slope, she'd wobble and fall, exhibiting what Dr. Aronson called "poor motor planning." Pat and I called it "poor bruise prevention," often joking that Sophie's skin tone, especially during those first months home, was a mottled black and blue. All elbows and knees, our precious bundle of occupational hazard doled out as many bruises as she suffered.

Dr. Aronson strongly encouraged us to have her evaluated through our county's Early Intervention Program, reminding us that institutionalized children lose one month of development for every three months they spend in an orphanage. Sophie's motor skills were so delayed, and her rickets so severe, that she didn't think we should risk waiting. However, in the three weeks it took to arrange for the therapists to come to our home, her health and ambulation improved tenfold. In fact, she'd caught up. She didn't qualify for occupational or physical therapy services, and, astonishingly, her English language skills, both in terms of what she was able to speak and understand, had become age appropriate.

At the time, Dr. Aronson suggested that we have Peter evaluated too, but because his motor skills were more developed than Sophie's, she thought there was benefit in giving him time to adjust. She felt the bed-soiling incidents likely were attributable to stress, including stress that was possibly derived from fear over leaving his room to use the bathroom. She suggested that we put a potty near his bed and let the issue resolve itself, without giving the unwanted behavior negative attention. This was important, she advised, because orphanage children, even those as young as Peter, quickly learn that certain unacceptable behaviors will cause even the most immune and indifferent caregiver to perk up and pay attention. In adoption speak, these are called maladaptive behaviors, maladaptive because they may help a child survive in an institutional environment, but they interfere with bonding and general integration into normal family life.

Her line of reasoning made sense to us, and it helped assuage our worries over what we considered super-disturbing behavior. Plus, as pleased as we were with Sophie's progress, we were also encouraged by the positive changes in Peter. To begin with, he grew so quickly that I had to replace clothes and shoes every month. By the end of our first year home, he had grown ten inches and gained twelve pounds. During a checkup, I remember the nurse apologizing for the "mistake" in his chart when she wrote his new measurements down. After listening to me explain that he really had grown that much, that it was "catch-up growth" and not an error in transcription, she just stared at me, mouth agape.

During this time, he learned how to pedal his tricycle like a champ, discovered the simplistic beauty of Thomas the Tank Engine, experienced the joy of sledding, and pored with devotion over endless picture books. He used the potty (*peesit!*) regularly and never had any accidents, although we still struggled with the bed-soiling trick. The bald patches on his head started to fill as his wispy hair began to thicken and grow with regular haircuts and plenty of healthy food. Physically, he was thriving.

But in other ways, he wasn't. Week after endless week Pat and I waited for Peter's personality to emerge, for the memory of the adoption trauma to subside enough so he could show us who he was. That's what we thought and what we told ourselves for a very long time: that he was traumatized, shell-shocked, but with enough patience, love, and understanding, he would learn to trust and become less guarded, less inhibited.

As weeks turned into months, though, our largely unspoken fears failed to subside, while the nervous glances Pat and I exchanged over breakfast began to increase. We could never quite put our finger on it, but there was no doubt we felt the oddity, the inherent lack of synchronicity, settling like fog over our new young son. We kept waiting for the hidden boy inside to emerge, but he hadn't, at least not yet. There was a distant, detached, almost hollow quality about his demeanor, as though the boy we saw, the one we called Peter, was shielding someone else entirely—a child who was darker, more complicated, and definitely hurt.

And there was more than just uneasy, hard-to-define feelings. His overt behaviors were odd too. For example, he wouldn't look us directly in the eye, though he happily smiled for the camera. Whenever he sat, he kept his legs straight out in front, just as he had in Russia, and he had this way of stomping across the floor, knees locked. He was as rigid and inflexible as the action figures we encouraged him to play with; he only seemed to bend in a few key places. He also wasn't speaking much, though this was lower on our list of concerns because I'd read online that international adoptees must first lose their native language before their brain can acclimate to learning a new one.

Play was another cause for worry. Peter could occupy himself for hours with a solitary car or wooden block. At first this seemed like a good thing because I could get all kinds of chores done around the house, but it wasn't. He wasn't exploring his environment the way Sophie was, or interacting with his toys in any purposeful way. Early on, Pat coined the phrase "the crashing, screaming, falling game" to describe Peter's favorite activity then and, to some extent, even today. No matter what's at hand, whether it's a car, penny, or cereal bowl, he'll lift it over his head, look at the object with growing trepidation, then lower it quickly in a simulated crash, all the while screaming, "Awwwwwgh." Although there's nothing unusual about a boy

amusing himself this way, Peter will do it all day long until someone interrupts the ritual and makes him stop. *That's* the unusual part.

Spring 2005

We understand that now, but at the time, we gave this strange fixation,
along with all the other odd behaviors, the benefit of the doubt. Peter didn't
know how to play, he was living in the shadow of Sophie's big personality, he was a naturally wistful child, or maybe he was reacting negatively to
the potent mix of medications he took on a daily basis. Both Sophie and
Peter needed to take Isoniazid (INH) for nine months to kill their latent
TB infections, as well as multiple rounds of medications to eradicate giardia
from their intestinal tracts. Perhaps, we told ourselves, the combination of
these powerful drugs was causing side effects that impacted his behavior
and mood.

When we began confessing some of our concerns to Peter's pediatrician,
at least the more objective ones, he suggested we enroll him in preschool.
"He needs socialization," he told us. "He doesn't know how to interact in
a normal environment; he's going to have to be taught." So that's what we
did. After a week or two spent researching our options, we enrolled him in
a wonderful little nursery school whose teachers and administrators were
thrilled to have him. Peter wasn't their first internationally adopted pre-

schooler, but he was their "freshest" in the sense that he hadn't been home very long. He would start in January, right after the holidays. As for Sophie, I enrolled us in a Mommy and Me class that met at the same school every Tuesday morning. She would get to meet and socialize with other two-year-olds, and I would get to know their moms.

Having made that decision, Pat and I did our best to shelve our worries and resume the business of becoming a family as well as adjusting to our new relationship as married parents. Pat had an easier time with this than I did, because my list of worries rose as high as a mountain, where his resembled more of a hill. But I tried, and in large part I succeeded. Bringing home two toddlers at once from an orphanage in Russia is a formidable undertaking, one that we clearly hadn't appreciated sufficiently at the time, but that was becoming abundantly clear with each new day. Pat and I were exhausted. As in dead tired, asleep on our feet, is today Tuesday or could it be Friday, and how many years before they leave for college tired.

But when the units were nearly up, the children bathed and cozy in their fleece pajamas and perched on our bed watching their *Corduroy* DVD or listening to us read *Goodnight Moon*, I allowed my thoughts to drift toward Pat. Childless for many years, we had long ago discovered a beautiful rhythm to our relationship that could be sustained, I imagined, indefinitely. Although becoming parents to Sophie and Peter hasn't challenged the depth of our commitment, it definitely has altered its composition. For instance, patience, a quality rarely called upon before the kids, has become a key player in our successful alliance, as has perseverance and humility.

Once we recovered from the first exhausting month or two, when we'd fall into bed, flat on our backs and still fully clothed, approximately three minutes after we kissed the children goodnight, Pat and I in earnest began reclaiming ourselves and our marriage, at least partially. By three months into the adoptions, we were capable of staying awake long enough, on most nights, to watch a movie or participate in a conversation lasting more than five minutes. Little by little we became less like deer in the headlights and more like the human beings we once resembled.

Although our waistlines suffered, our grammar deteriorated, our love life cooled, my cooking abilities declined, and we both sloughed a good ten points off our IQs, we were adjusting. Our first Thanksgiving came and went without much fanfare because we opted not to travel to the mountain house in North Carolina where my siblings meet for the holiday. We had a quiet dinner at home, just the four of us, but with all the usual trimmings. Afterward, we watched the geese practice their landings on the fallow cornfield across the road. Sophie and Peter had no real sense of the holiday, but like every other day, they absorbed the experience eagerly, each in their own way. Sophie made a place for her Cabbage Patch doll at the table, carefully removing a booster seat in the kitchen to help prop her up, while Peter greedily inhaled the luxurious smells of Thanksgiving dinner, making sure to stay nearby so as not to miss out.

Our first Christmas was memorable for all the reasons first Christmases are always memorable. Sophie and Peter whizzed through the holidays with wide-eyed stares and disbelief, their innocent joy and unaffected sense of wonderment spreading like a contagion to anyone lucky enough to have mingled with them. Everything they saw, everything they touched, heard, or tasted was so new and captivating that they became wholly mesmerized: Christmas lights, the tree, jolly music, sparkly decorations, scores of sugary treats. Nothing was too small or insignificant to explore and appreciate. A bowl of candy canes at the dry cleaner's produced the same level of enchanted euphoria as the grand spectacle of Santa and his elves at the mall. We made batch after messy batch of holiday cookies with overnight guests while dancing in a floury, sprinkle-strewn mess to Chipmunk Christmas music.

Between gifts and books we bought ourselves, we must have acquired 90 percent of all the children's holiday books ever written, from *Corduroy's Christmas* and *Madeleine's Christmas* to *Father Frost* and *Twas the Night Before Christmas*. We read them religiously every night, even though we knew the children couldn't decipher most of what they were hearing. But as Christmas drew near, Sophie could sing a good many of the words to "Rudolph the Red-Nosed Reindeer" and was able to ask Santa, when the opportunity arose, for a brand new *kukla* (doll).

Peter participated actively in most of the festivities, and I smiled with relief to see his normally doleful eyes sparkle in a way I hadn't seen before. Pat, who was always willing to yield to the deceiving caress of Peter's apparent wellness, was more convinced than ever that time and love would heal. Christmas came and went that year without snow on the ground. Pat gave me a Lladro figure of a little girl to match the figurine of the boy I'd bought in Moscow. He catches me by surprise sometimes, that husband of mine, and that Christmas morning I found myself crying, tears of joy and blessing mixed with fading melancholy for Ben, the baby I had begun allowing myself to forget. But it was okay, and surely Pat knew that. The Lladro figurine wasn't Ben, it was Peter, and after I opened my present and felt the cool, delicate porcelain against my skin, Pat lifted it gently and placed it next to the other on our shelf. Our family was complete.

I look back on the thousands of photos I took of Sophie and Peter over the course of our first holiday season and wonder where that bright-eyed boy is now. Peter was at his best then, as though he'd been granted a temporary reprieve from the demons and disasters that play havoc with his mind. He loved the presents, adored the attention, and had his hand in a plate of cookies every time I turned around. As Pat and I watched our sleepy children play in front of the crackling fire toward sundown, I began to trust, really trust, that Peter would emerge from whatever protective cloak he had constructed and that one day soon he would be okay.

Slumped with Sophie against the nylon wall of their new play tent, talking into a play phone, his new cowboy hat perched cockeyed over one brow, Peter seemed a beautifully typical three-year-old boy. As usual, Sophie controlled the scene, barking colorful instructions to her new brother with what had become their secret, indecipherable language, some sort of toddler-styled Russian with a sprinkling of mispronounced English words. Not only was he listening, he was interacting, even playing. Not with Sophie's characteristic display of complex thought and imagination, but he was holding his own.

Pat and I fell asleep that night to the gravelly sounds of an old Judy Garland Christmas special aired on PBS. Her voice strained from years of alcohol abuse, she floated around her living room with Mel Torme and her three children singing carols and reminiscing in black and white about Christmases past. As nutty as it seems, I found myself searching our television screen for glimpses of her children's philtrums, including Liza Minnelli's. Did she drink while she was pregnant? Could her children be alcohol-exposed? I don't know. I never caught a good glimpse because the film was grainy and I was too tired to keep pursuing such a pointless objective. But what I did notice was Judy Garland's eyes, the ever-searching, soulful way they could seduce you into believing even the gayest Christmas carol was meant to induce melancholy.

I had seen the same look in the eyes of our new son, who was asleep down the hall and who had been momentarily distracted by the gaiety of Christmas. But Judy Garland's life can be dissected and studied on the Internet, and I knew nothing about the past of the little boy whose dark, plaintive stare can convey a life's worth of sadness, hurt, and disappointment.

❦

MARCH 23, 2010. *Today is an all-time low. This on the heels of coming back from my sister's surprise fiftieth birthday party in Atlanta, which was one of the most enjoyable weekends I've had in years. The festivities were a bit much for Peter, but my family and sister's friends rallied around him and found ways to give him space and quiet without causing undue and unhappy isolation. There are times when it's okay to bring the party to Peter, just as there are times Pat and I need to work to bring Peter to the party, to the table, to the playground, and hopefully, ultimately, to life. It was a wonderful lesson, and I returned home full of new memories and a little wiser, at least when it comes to my challenging son.*

But today is entirely different. Today I spend the better part of the afternoon and evening vacillating between uncontrolled sobs and searing anger. Pat and I meet with Peter's principal after lunch to discuss the poop chore and "beating" comments made by the school psychologist last Thursday. We talk about building trust and the need to have this person removed from our son's "team" so that we can focus on helping him improve his cognitive skills rather than constantly having to defend ourselves against callous, unfounded, and harmful allegations. We've been making this request since Peter started first grade. But this time he hears us loud and clear and assures us that this individual won't be interacting with our son anymore. Pat and I leave thinking we've finally put our long-standing problem with this particular person to rest.

The kids are happy when I pick them up from school, and I have an unusually pleasant conversation with Peter's teacher, who is often reticent with Pat and me. There's a car in our driveway when we get home. I soon learn that someone from the school—and the school psychologist is the prime suspect—has filed a complaint with Child Protective Services. Yep. The school, or at least a representative thereof, has now officially accused us of child abuse. Apparently, giving Peter the consequence of doing chores to deter his daytime penchant for wetting, including picking up dog poop in the yard with plastic covering his hands, equates to "excessive corporal punishment" in the eyes of our accuser. Also, my forgetting to send a change of clothes in case Peter wets at school on a day he's wearing underpants, a request made by his teacher the day before we left for Atlanta, has been transformed into a "refusal to send extra clothes in an attempt to embarrass." I don't think the principal was aware of any of this when we met earlier, but trust has been destroyed, so I can't be sure.

Before the CPS investigator came to our home, which is where I learned of these spurious allegations, he pulled Sophie and Peter out of their classrooms and interviewed them. I have no choice but to send the kids to the playroom in the basement to deal with the investigator and this manufactured situation. Sophie is crying and worried about what's happening, but I can't console her. I'm sure the whole school knows by now and half the town to boot. Ours is a small, tight-knit community where news spreads fast but where I pray judgment takes a slower, more reasoned course. The very polite investigator speaks to Pat, Lindy, and me for about an hour and says he needs to call Peter's pediatrician and psychiatrist to make sure they've never noticed anything unusual or untoward.

I can't go into this any further, we're under investigation after all, but I do find certain parts of this saga ironic. To our knowledge, no one at the school has ever picked up a book or read an article we've suggested regarding FAS or attachment issues, though we've distributed plenty. These people know little to nothing about a very complex, deceiving set of disabilities, yet they feel empowered, even obligated, to interject their "expertise" into our personal lives and private decisions. If I had to bring my car to an airplane mechanic, I'd expect him to study auto repair before disassembling the engine. A pediatrician has no qualms about admitting she knows almost squat about prostate cancer. But apparently certain educators, by right and title, know everything there is to know about all children, all disabilities, and all psychosocial issues. And if you're so bold as to question this absolute authority and supreme knowledge? If you're so bold as to fight for your child's future, for your family's stability, by pointing out when these folks are out of their league and causing more harm than good? They get hurt, offended, even outraged. And guess what? They can call CPS, and there's nothing you can do. Yes, this person is making us suffer, surely. But mostly this person is hurting Peter, the very child purported to be in need of protection. Where do we go from here? Home schooling? Do we move again? I don't know the answer, but I do know this: the experiment of full disclosure and presumption of good will has failed. Miserably.

Chapter 19

Something's Not Right

Somewhere around the six-month mark, Pat and I realized denial was no longer a rational pursuit. By this time, Peter was attending preschool three mornings a week, and I was grateful for the break. It gave me the opportunity to focus on Sophie without the distraction of Peter's increasingly difficult presence. During this time, we still clung unsteadily to the "give it time" theory, continuing to hope that Peter's odd behaviors would eventually resolve. Clinging to this possibility made about as much sense as running a marathon with one shoe, but we weren't yet ready to face reality. It didn't help that everyone we turned to—whether doctors, preschool teachers, family, or friends—kept urging us to practice patience. He needed time to heal, acquire language, and discover a sense of self. It was a mantra we repeated over and over, well beyond what turned out to be a prudent time frame.

Another reason we didn't move sooner was that although his puzzling behaviors and social interactions were worrisome, they didn't scream out for attention. The bed soiling hadn't stopped, but it hadn't escalated either. He was acquiring language, but at a slower rate than Sophie, who was chattering happily and nonstop. Peter still only had a few dozen words, but, more importantly, he had a habit of stringing them together in a way that didn't quite seem right. For instance, he called the bathtub "bath tonight" and referred to the sink as a "drink of water." It was easy, though, to dismiss these language mistakes, especially since he was still transitioning from Russian to English.

His preschool teachers were happy to have him, even though, when pressed, they confessed that he kept to himself and wouldn't join in with the other children. He also didn't follow directions, even simple ones. I remember these kind-hearted women almost whispering these confessions, as though it was impolite to discuss a recently adopted child's lack of progress. "But he's no problem," they'd say, grabbing my hand warmly. "And he's cute as a button . . . those eyes!"

Blowing Rock, NC (July 4, 2005)

Then there was the sitting-down behavior, a precursor to the tantrums and rages that still pepper our daily lives. Whenever Peter was upset because he didn't want to do something that was asked of him, like stop a preferred activity or leave before he was ready, he'd drop to the floor. It was the strangest thing. He'd sit with his legs straight out and his hands resting rigidly in his lap, silent as the night and staring blankly ahead. And he wouldn't budge. One of us would have to hoist him, one-armed, and carry him like an unwieldy mannequin.

These were warning signs, certainly, but except for the bed soiling, they felt manageable. Peter was a little boy who was obviously having trouble adjusting and who was withdrawn and reliant on maladaptive behaviors to express his needs and frustrations. We accepted this and tried our best to embrace the adage that patience and love were the greatest of all healers.

But then the other shoe fell off. About six months after the adoptions, Peter abruptly abandoned his passive approach to living in our house. Almost as though an alarm bell sounded inside the deepest recesses of his brain, our son awoke to the sounds of his own primal screams. His demons became loosed, and consequently our family's course, laid from hopes, dreams, and a pinch of folly, took a turn toward a future we never expected or imagined.

One early Sunday morning when the bulbs had bloomed but the grass was still brown, Peter ran into our room and uncharacteristically jumped in bed. Despite the darkness that still blanketed the day, the house was awake from the rumbling of a springtime storm. Sophie had already beaten him to the punch and was lodged deep under the covers, hiding from both the thunder and the high-pitched howl of the wind whistling through the newly leaved trees. Peter wiggled his way between us in search of a spot where he too could disappear. Despite the children's fear, I was grateful for the banging storm, for the intimate opportunity it offered.

Because it was still mostly dark, I didn't notice anything unusual when Peter stretched his arm out from under the quilt. But I quickly smelled the odor. "What the . . . ," I gasped as Pat fumbled for the lamp switch. To our horror, the light revealed what we already suspected. Poop, coming from Peter. And it wasn't a simple accident. He was covered in feces. He had taken his own waste and smeared it all over his body and pajamas and into his hair. He was completely covered in poop.

Sophie started crying as soon as she realized what happened, and this caused Peter to run screaming from the room. The place on the bed where he lay was fouled, and so were Sophie and I. Because Pat was unaffected, he sprung into action while I remained stunned and on the verge of getting sick. "Get him," I groaned as I fought back the urge to vomit. Lifting Sophie gingerly from the bed, as if she were injured, I carried her into the bathroom.

Stripping her pajamas in the tub, I scrubbed her delicate skin under water as hot as she could stand until the germs fell off and her sobs subsided. After wrapping her in a towel, I handed her over to Pat as he long-armed Peter toward me.

It was a morning I'll never forget. By early afternoon the house was sanitized, as were the human occupants. I remember sitting at the breakfast bar, sipping strong coffee while I stared numbly at the rivulets forming and reforming on the windowpanes. I couldn't manage much more. Peter was busy riffling through our junk mail, stacking the flyers and advertisements into a big messy pile, and Sophie was engrossed with her Little People Farm. Every once in a while, the blare of "cock-a-doodle-doo" would rouse me from my thoughts, and I'd turn and smile toward our daughter. Surfing the Internet from his perch on the couch, Pat too would look up and smile briefly. We had so much to talk about and were biding time until we had some privacy.

Before we put Peter down for his nap, we explained very simply that he would be spanked if he ever did that again. Unsure whether he knew the English word, we gently but firmly demonstrated the spanking process. "Peter know," he said, nodding solemnly. "Peter know." I don't know whether he knew or not, but two days later he delivered an encore performance. Enough was enough. We'd been tolerating the "poop on one end and pee on the other" bed routine for six months. Every possible solution we tried to stop the behavior, including putting a potty in his room, either backfired or didn't help. Not charts, not rewards, not consequences. And he had upped the ante substantially.

So as promised, the second time around we spanked him. It felt like a defeat, certainly. During all the years I dreamed of becoming a mother, my imagination never took me to a place where I resorted to spanking a toddler I'd brought home from Russia only six months earlier. But I also never dreamed of parenting a child who willingly covered himself in feces. I was at a loss, and so was Pat.

It's not that I think children should never be spanked or that any parent who chooses to spank is a borderline abuser. But spanking our kids? That was different. Sophie and Peter had been neglected and half-starved and who's to say they hadn't been physically or even sexually abused? We just didn't know. But we also felt like we had no other choice. Perhaps the worst part of all is that the spanking worked. He never did it again. As we would soon discover, Peter experiences some kind of psychic release when he's thoroughly punished, whether spanked or disciplined in some other way, which by far is the more usual scenario. It's almost as though he's hit rock bottom but doesn't realize it until a strong punishment intercedes to alert him. Only then can he pull himself together and resurface.

Looking back on this phase of our lives, I now understand that Peter wasn't able to hold himself together, that the strain of keeping his behavior and impulses in check was too great for him to bear any longer. The honeymoon was over. Maybe by that point he felt secure enough in our home to shed the perfect robot routine. Conversely, maybe the sudden change in course signaled his inability to cope with the demands and nuances of family life. To this day, I'm unsure which is the more probable explanation or whether there's even a third or fourth consideration that would shed light on the shift that occurred with ominous abruptness.

Unfortunately, the feces-smearing incidents, though perhaps the most shocking acts of his rapid descent, weren't the only issues we faced. During this period he also became destructive, ripping wallpaper from the walls in the middle of the night and pulling toys apart piece by piece. "Truck broke," he'd complain, showing me the various pieces he plucked apart. "Garbage time." Whenever Pat or I tried making him acknowledge his role, so that he understood his actions caused the toy to break rather than random fate, he would scream, red-faced, "Peter no break. Truck broke!"

It was in this manner that I gradually came to understand that Peter had trouble making logical connections. For a long time I thought he was just being stubborn, that like most young children he didn't want to admit his mistakes or role in a particular misdeed. But over a period of time I realized that Peter constantly overlooked, even angrily denied, the most obvious cause-and-effect relationships. Twisting the arms of sunglasses will cause them to break. Ripping the wallpaper will bring about a consequence. There's no dessert when dinner is left uneaten. The doorbell always signals a visitor at the front door (as opposed to another door). Dishes will break when dropped. Peter simply didn't register these kinds of unshakable facts.

Not only was his inability to make logical connections a serious source of concern, it made disciplining difficult because Peter didn't learn from his mistakes. More likely than not, he's destined to repeat tomorrow and the next day the mistake he made today. Maybe on some level he understood this, or at least sensed that he lacked the tools to navigate the complex world of family and expectations. Maybe that's why he opted to take no risks or make even the simplest of choices during those first months home.

In the orphanage there were no choices. Peter was never left alone or unattended, not even at night. Fifteen other children slept with him, and a caregiver stood watch, or at least remained minimally conscious, throughout the night. Meals were eaten in groups with caregivers combing the aisles to help or maintain order. Toys were kept high on shelves, and when they were brought down, they weren't scattered across the floor so children could pick and choose. Children were given one toy at a time. Use it or lose it. In the orphanage Peter was told when to potty, when to play, when to go outside, when to eat, when to shower, when to sleep, when to be quiet, and when it was okay to make noise. It's the kind of system where independent thought is not encouraged and certainly not required, and where a lack of independence or self-regulation might actually make yielding to the rules easier.

But in a home, he was free, at least relatively. Free to explore his environment, free to make certain choices, such as what he wanted for snack, and free to express his thoughts. The same held true for Sophie, but the difference was that where Sophie learned from her environment and adapted, Peter became more bewildered and frightened. He didn't have the tools.

Once he began showing his frustration, whether by smearing feces, ripping wallpaper, or launching rocks at Sophie's head, other telltale signs emerged. For instance, once he realized there was plenty to eat, always, and that he would never go hungry, he began using food as a weapon. He often refused to eat dinner. Keeping a single piece of food in his mouth, whether a pea or a bite of chicken, he would chew and chew but never swallow. Over time, his refusal of food evolved into a more active assault where he made himself throw up at the table, especially in restaurants. Logical consequences had zero effect. He either never made the connection or he didn't care. Sometimes Pat and I still catch ourselves uselessly debating which is the more prevalent of Peter's states of mind, can't or won't. It's impossible to say because the two are inextricably intertwined.

The behavioral regression we began witnessing during this time was further complicated by what seemed like developmental backtracking. His rate of language acquisition reached a sort of plateau, and he began exhibiting unusual physical movements. He repeated himself constantly, particularly his name, and always in a loud, monotone voice. Busily engaged in the "crashing, screaming, falling game," he might for example, hear someone ask for the time. Without awareness he'd parrot the question, "Is it 6 yet?" He also could spin on the middle of the living room rug for thirty minutes straight, oblivious to any action around him. He regularly walked on his toes and flapped his hands. Sometimes he rolled his head so violently he looked like a rag doll drunk on a roller coaster.

By May, we knew something was seriously wrong. Despite varied opinions and our own desire to wish them away, Peter's behaviors could no longer be ignored or casually explained. Instead of lying awake wondering who Peter was and how spooky it felt to live with a child we barely knew, our sleep soon became interrupted by an entirely new brand of torment. Namely, whether our son was missing a few key ingredients, components essential for normal childhood development. Afraid to waste any more time, I made appointments to have his hearing and speech evaluated and have him seen by occupational and physical therapists.

The wait-and-see game was officially over. Peter had let us know, loud and clear, that time would not heal his wounds. Frightened as we were, at least we didn't miss this last desperate scream for help.

❦

APRIL 7, 2010. *The temperature soars to a sizzling 91 degrees to-day, which feels more like 191 because winter is just barely over, it could still snow yet, and no one in this area is the least bit acclimated to temperatures worthy of mid-August. Spring soccer season begins today, and I dutifully deliver Sophie and Peter to the fields for their first practice. For us, spring soccer marks the recommencement of the season after a prolonged winter break. So the kids are happy to be reunited with their teammates, some of whom they haven't seen since late October, and I'm just as happy spending time again with many of my parent chums. As we loosen up around each other after our long hiatus of not having to stand around a soccer field in either boiling or freezing weather, depending on the season, the jokes and gibes begin to fly. "Be nice to me or I'll call CPS!" someone warns. When Peter drains his water bottle, I joke that I better refill it quickly in case CPS is watching.*

It feels good to be joking about something that only two weeks ago wracked me with tears and robbed me of that all-important sense of control over my family, over my own destiny. The ordeal's not yet officially over, but we've been assured by the investigator that the case is being dismissed. It also feels good to know that our friends, fellow parents, and townspeople seem to be as outraged over this woman's retributive act as we are. As we huddle in the heat discussing my son's future, and the school's inability to address his needs, he darts away from whatever practice activity is occurring because he has an urgent question for me. "Am I nine year old yet, Mom? Has my birthday for nine already come to me?" Poor guy. He can't remember how old he is (he's eight and a half) but the school puts him through the charade of doing fractions and discussing geometrical concepts such as "lines of symmetry." Thankfully unaware of the controversy surrounding him, he rejoins his team once I remind him of his age and his birthdate, and I smile as I watch him zig and zag across the still mostly brown field. Peter's having a good day and for that I'm grateful. Pat desperately needs to work late tonight, so the kids and I go to the town diner after practice for grilled cheese sandwiches. We sit at the counter, something we never do when Daddy's with us, and I let the kids take their stools for a few glorious, squeaky spins. Once settled, Sophie draws until our sandwiches arrive, a bumblebee pollinating a tulip, and Peter works on drawing a beautiful Chinese dragon. All cylinders are firing today, it seems.

As the kids color, the waitress, a lovely divorcee, shares tales of spending spring break with her teenage son and four of his friends as she breathlessly works the tiny but bustling restaurant. While we walk toward the car, I click the unlock button on my key chain and Peter asks, "How you always know the car's locked, Mom?" I tell him I know because I'm the one who locked it. "Wow, Mom," he replies. "You can remember that long?" It's a dose of reality that stops me dead in my tracks. I don't want to embarrass him, so I quickly shake off the chill and pat his newly trimmed hair as his smile meets mine. As I buckle the seatbelt, I remind myself to practice more patience and love. Forget about fractions and centimeters and electrons and telling time and identifying verbs. What Peter needs is patience and love.

CHAPTER 20

WIDENING THE CIRCLE

ONE SUNNY MORNING in May, my sister walked in to find the kids and me playing on the floor. All three of us looked up when the door opened, but only my face registered shock and surprise. As much as I love the idea of Patty being able to drop in, it's impossible because she lives in Atlanta. But there she was, broadly smiling in her quiet way, bracing for the noise and ruckus that her arrival was about to cause. Surprise!

She had come for my fortieth birthday, which was only two days away. Pat's mother was turning eighty, and, with my encouragement, he and his brother had flown to West Palm Beach the night before to surprise her. I knew I wouldn't feel alone on my birthday, because I had Sophie and Peter. Despite growing concern for our son, I still reveled daily in the bounty of their presence and felt content and fulfilled with our children by my side. But it seems Pat and Patty had conspired to make sure the kids and I had company for the weekend. I couldn't have been more thrilled.

"What should we do?" Patty asked, once the hoopla settled. "I mean, after we go to Albany. . . ."

So Pat had told her. Thank goodness. Within the hour, I needed to be in the car, heading to Albany for our appointment with a pediatric infectious disease specialist named Dr. Martha Lepow. Peter's pediatrician had called three days ago to inform us that an X-ray of his chest showed a lesion on his lung, an indication of active tuberculosis that could not be ignored. His preschool was not thrilled, though the director took the news fairly well. Although we agreed Peter should stay home, she would wait until she heard from us to inform the other parents. We had called Dr. Aronson about the X-ray findings, and she urged us to stay calm and wait for the specialist's opinion. "In all my years of practice," she said, "I've never seen an active case of TB in any of my kids."

When Dr. Lepow, a short, commanding woman with a gray pixie and tortoise-shell glasses, walked into the examining room, she took one look at Peter and proclaimed that he didn't have TB. "So you've looked at the X-ray?" I asked. "No, not yet," she admitted. "I can tell just by looking at him. He's got other problems—we'll talk about those—but let's get this TB thing over with."

Sure enough, she examined the films and confirmed that Peter didn't have active TB. The "lesion" on the X-ray was his arm. I was so relieved that I couldn't even get angry with the radiologist who obviously had been asleep at the wheel. Even I could pick out the outline of the tiny elbow once Dr. Lepow showed us the film. Clearly he had moved during the procedure. I'm sure Peter wasn't the first three-year-old to squirm during an X-ray, either. How was this overlooked? Still, he was okay, and that's what mattered. There would be no mass hysteria at the preschool, and we wouldn't have to embark on some awful, long ordeal that may or may not have restored his health.

It's amazing how much a word like "tuberculosis" can hang over your head, clouding your thoughts and feeding your very worst fears. Our perplexing son was physically healthy, at least relatively, and I felt free to enjoy Patty's company and my impending fortieth birthday with an unburdened mind. Like other doctors who had met our son, Dr. Lepow was worried about what she saw, and, perhaps more to the point, what she didn't see, but I naively downplayed her observations. After all, he didn't have TB, and wasn't that the take-home message?

But she did point out a few things that I dutifully committed to memory. His range of motion was abnormal, there were prominent and dark circles under his eyes, and, despite his being much sturdier than Sophie, Dr. Lepow said he needed to gain weight. She suggested we supplement his diet with PediaSure and keep a close eye on his growth. If his height didn't make the chart in three months, she said, we should take him to a pediatric endocrinologist.

"He's not catching up like you'd expect," she said. "It doesn't mean he won't, he may just need a jump-start. His gait's off too—this little fellow's got low muscle tone."

Patty and I discussed the doctor's concerns on the way home, and by the time we'd driven the sixty miles back home, we agreed that Peter's odd behaviors were of greater concern than his unimpressive growth. My sister hadn't seen Peter since January, and she felt his strange affect and behaviors were every bit as peculiar as they'd been last winter and maybe even more pronounced. She also gently pointed out that Sophie, who was a year younger, was running developmental circles around her brother. I assured her that I'd speak with Pat when he returned from Florida about getting some additional assessments done.

Thanks to the eradication of the TB scare, the rest of the weekend was remarkable in that it was unremarkable. That is, until Sunday, which was my birthday. I don't remember what we did that morning, but when we came back home after lunch, Patty insisted we go shopping, even though her plane was leaving later that afternoon. She said she wanted to see the new outdoor adventure store at the mall, which I did think was an unusual request (my sister's not really a mall person), but I was happy to oblige. I was just glad she was there. So we left again and walked around the big retail space, complete with camping equipment, kayaks, fishing poles, and hunting gear. Stuffed bear, deer, and bobcat heads hung from the walls, and we quickly made for the exit sign once Peter noticed the taxidermy displays and began screaming inconsolably. On the way home, we stopped for milkshakes at Stewart's and laughed at the sight of Peter and Sophie trying in vain to suck the thick contents through their flimsy straws.

By the time we got home, the kids' clothes were covered in milkshake, and the four of us were hot and sticky and smelled like melted ice cream. When I walked in the door, I was instantly bombarded with "SURPRISE!" and the sight of Pat's smiling face. He and my sister had fooled me, and fooled me well. Our living room was stuffed with family and friends, many of whom had driven from the city to celebrate. I had no idea how Pat arranged to come back from Florida early or how he managed to throw the party together in the short time we'd been away from the house that day.

But somehow he managed it, so I kissed him, my face turning flush as the guests cheered.

It would have been a great party too. As it turned out, though, I never even got the chance to say hello to anyone. In fact, I was still standing in the doorway when Sophie came barreling around the kitchen island, tripped over a bar stool, and suddenly became airborne. I saw the coming catastrophe clearly in the split second it took before she landed face first on the corner of the counter and then bounced toward the floor where Scout, our child-loathing dog, stood waiting. I lunged to catch her, but it was too late. Sophie landed on top of Scout, and the only thing I remember after that was a horrible yelping, screaming noise. I one-armed Sophie from the snarling mayhem and held her to my chest as I dashed around the corner into the mudroom, which was unoccupied. I held her tightly for a moment and then gently lifted her quivering chin to assess the damage. I could hear Pat gasp, "Oh my God!" behind me. Sophie's face and my shirt were covered in blood. "Get a towel," I yelled. My voice shook with fear and my body began trembling. "I'll be in the car."

Pat drove to the hospital like Robin Williams on speed while I sat in the back seat and cradled Sophie, whose screams by then had dwindled to the occasional muffled sob. By the time we got to the emergency room, she'd stopped crying altogether. The gash responsible for the copious outpouring of blood was less than a half-inch long and ran perpendicular to the right side of her upper lip. We tried to keep her still in the waiting room, but it was nearly impossible. Holding the towel to her face, she played peek-a-boo with a young man who was also waiting to be seen. "*Koo-Koo*," she smiled, wincing in pain.

The only blessing that came out of the whole ordeal was that the ER doctor assured us that Sophie's injury was not a result of a dog bite. Scout caught her lip with her toenail, which is not good, but the news was a relief because it meant we didn't have to consider finding another home for our beloved old dog. If she didn't bite Sophie in that kind of situation, we felt confident she never would. There was no plastic surgeon available, but after waiting over two hours, an ENT finally showed up to stitch the wound. The ER doctors felt an ENT was the next best thing to a plastic surgeon because they do so much facial work. Because of Sophie's age, they had to sedate her, which was no fun, but I was allowed to hold her the entire time, even while the surgeon sewed her bruised and broken lip.

As we were leaving the ER, a nurse approached us with a wonderful ink drawing the young man in the waiting room drew for Sophie. He too was obviously struck by our daughter's amazing resiliency and charisma. By the time we got home, the party was over. Pat's cousins stayed to watch Peter and clean up. My sister's plane had left two hours earlier. The cake was eaten, the food and drinks were decimated, and the couch was littered with unopened presents and cards. Pat had periodically called home to check on Peter and our guests, so everyone knew that despite the horrific amount of blood, Sophie's injuries were minor. It seems our guests were so relieved that Sophie was not seriously hurt that they decided to party in earnest. We later heard that Pat threw the best party we never attended.

Because Sophie still clung to many of her orphanage ways, she insisted on wobbling up the stairs from the garage into the house on her own drunken volition. Her lip was twice its normal size, and the right side of her face and eye, where she bounced off the corner of the kitchen island, was grotesquely swollen and purple. "Where the peoples?" she asked, in the most pitifully small voice. "I want cake."

We quickly explained that cake would have to wait and shuffled her upstairs, where I took off her blood-soaked clothes and changed her into pajamas. She was asleep midway through the process, and I fought back tears as I tucked her in and lightly kissed what I prayed was only her temporarily misshapen face. After changing my own clothes and throwing the entire bloody pile in the garbage, I sat on the floor next to Sophie's bed and watched her sleep. The rhythmic sound of her breathing had a calming effect, and after a while, I too relaxed.

While Sophie healed over the next week, I forgot all about the Big Four-Oh. After all, any trauma I might have been willing to entertain regarding my fortieth birthday had been snuffed out instantly in the wake of our daughter's accident. However, once it became clear that Sophie would not be permanently disfigured, and that we wouldn't even need a plastic surgeon to improve the scar, our worries migrated back toward our son and his unshakably troubling traits.

As we grew to understand Sophie's moods, including some new twists because she was cranky and sore in a way we hadn't yet experienced, the continuing sense of not *knowing* our son grew increasingly intolerable. Pat and I could ramble on about Sophie, her likes and dislikes, her funny and annoying habits, as amiably and confidently as any other set of parents. But Peter was an enigma, and as his behaviors began escalating, he seemed less like a cuddly toddler and more like an explosive device waiting for the last tick-tock before detonation.

Poet's Walk, Annandale-on-Hudson, NY (Fall 2006)

The floodgates finally burst open in earnest just as we began taking some proactive steps, making appointments for various evaluations despite our pediatrician urging us to wait. Peter began rubbing feces on himself and his belongs again, peeing everywhere and on everything, ripping wallpaper, raging, hurting Sophie, biting, spitting, refusing to eat, vomiting at the table, bolting from us in crowded places, and destroying his toys. It was as though he had been in a trance, and all of a sudden he went into some frenzied overdrive. Looking back, it seems that one minute we had an oddly robotic child who was nonetheless generally compliant, and then we blinked and found ourselves staring at a feral child who could neither be consoled nor contained.

As we waited for the appointment dates to arrive, and the written reports of the evaluations that followed, Pat and I did our best to support each other. Leaving the kids with a baby sitter simply was not an option. How do we explain Peter's behaviors to a teenage girl or grandmotherly woman? That she needs to wrap duct tape snugly around our son's diaper at bedtime so he doesn't pull it off and cover himself and his bedroom with unspeakable filth? Or not to pay any attention if he vomits his meal at the dinner table? Just clean it up and offer him another plate of food! I just could never play out these conversations in my mind. So we stayed home, always.

But at least we had our evenings, thanks to our rigidly imposed 7:00 p.m. bedtime for all those under the age of thirty, and on weekends we'd take the kids hiking, do our best to wear them out, and then take a long, leisurely drive afterward. On the days when all went according to plan, the kids would nod off from exhaustion and boredom and Pat and I would escape into our own private revelry as we cruised the back roads in search of yet-undiscovered treasure. Every once in a while we'd come upon a fantastic barn or homemade road sign, even an interestingly posed cow, and I'd swat at Pat's arm to pull over so I could take a picture.

Also, our virtually symbiotic ability to read each other's signals, to jump to the rescue with a silly joke or a supportive squeeze or maybe even something as small as a knowing smile, is what kept us afloat, as parents, partners, and individuals. I suppose we've always had this kind of relationship—we certainly had our share of hardship as a couple before adopting the kids—but combating and coping with Peter's problems made us consciously aware of it. I'm not sure I possess the strength or resolve to parent our son without Pat by my side; I shudder to think what it would be like, so I pray each night that our health remains intact for at least a year or two beyond Peter's undoubtedly prolonged adolescence. We are one of the few couples I know where adversities, sometimes the size of land mines, have failed to corrode the seams of our marriage. I truly look forward to that time when Pat and I can go out to dinner again, maybe even catch a late night movie, or take an exotic trip. So what if he's eighty-one and I'm sixty-four?

I was engaged in just this sort of daydream, renting a house for a year in Ireland, to be exact, when Pat walked in with the mail, which turned out to contain the key to unlocking Peter's access to special education and preschool intervention services. Peter's speech and language evaluation indicated significant delays in both receptive and expressive language skills, as well as profound difficulty processing auditory information. In light of his normal hearing test, these results more than supported the need for preschool-based speech/language intervention. The occupational therapy evaluation was no different. Peter was significantly delayed in both gross and fine motor skills and demonstrated great difficulty with motor planning and oral manipulation.

Within a few weeks, the county had arranged for therapists to work with Peter twice a week at home. Having professionals in our living room, their bags of therapy toys in tow, felt wonderfully productive. Peter's new therapists were confident and knowledgeable about child development and their respective disciplines. In no time they had him blowing bubbles, crawling through nylon tunnels, stringing beads, working on single-step directions, pronouncing the letters of the alphabet, and matching pictures to their corresponding words. We were assigned a case manager whose job was to oversee Peter's therapies, assess his overall improvement, and make any changes or recommendations to services based upon observed progress or newly identified need.

Overall, we couldn't have been more pleased. After months of waiting and hoping for Peter to turn the corner, it felt good to be taking action. In my heart, I'd always known something was askew with Peter, and the escalating turmoil our family had endured over the last several weeks solidified my resolve to seek help. When I confessed to our new case manager, a can-do woman with curly red hair who was also an adoptive mother, that I thought we were struggling with attachment issues, she immediately wrote down the name and number of Sue d'Aversa. "Contact her," she said. "You won't be disappointed. People up there," she said, laughing warmly, "they call her the Adoption Whisperer."

"Up there" turned out to be Albany, sixty miles north of where we live. After what seemed like months of Pat dragging his feet when it came to facing Peter's problems, it was a relief to hear him agree so readily to yet another intervention. Although I've since lost a good deal of my naiveté, there was a time when I greeted each newly identified specialist, therapist, or intervention with great anticipation, as if well-being and normalcy for our son was only a single appointment, drive, or office door away.

So on that cool, sunny morning in June when Pat and I discussed making the appointment as we pushed the kids on the swings of their newly installed jungle gym, I felt hopeful. Sophie was thriving, growing stronger, wittier, and sharper every day, Peter finally was getting help, and I was certain the therapist named Sue was about to throw Pat and me a priceless lifeline.

By the time our appointment rolled around, the children looked healthier than we ever imagined possible. They no longer had translucent complexions; their skin now radiated health thanks to nutritious food and plenty of sunshine. Their hair had thickened and grown shiny too, though Sophie still didn't have enough for pigtails and had to settle instead for a Pebbles bow on top of her head. Although Peter's growth would not sky-rocket for a few more months, Sophie was growing by leaps and bounds. By that summer, she was still tiny for her age but had outgrown four sizes of clothes and just as many, if not more, shoe sizes.

We went together as a family the first time we met Sue, a woman with a well-known reputation for healing adopted children and their beleaguered parents. She shared office space with other counselors on the floor, and there was a large cabinet in the waiting room that Sophie soon discovered was filled with books, toys, and puzzles. For whatever reason, I felt the need to dress the children as though this were a semiformal affair, and I felt a little self-conscious about their dress as they plunged into the heap of well-used toys in their nifty new outfits.

Within a few minutes, Sue opened her door and beckoned us inside. She introduced herself, and I liked her immediately. It was clear she was a no-frills, middle-aged woman with an open face and an interesting, hopefully insightful perspective. I also would soon learn that she possessed a great sense of humor and loved to laugh as much as I do. Her office was arranged like a comfortable living room, with a sofa on one side and two chairs with a table on the other. Multiple toy boxes were placed against the walls, and Kleenex boxes adorned every table. Either someone had bad allergies or there were a lot of tears shed in that room. Still conflicted and confused about my feelings for Peter, I hoped and prayed that she had an unusually allergic clientele.

After we sat down and she spent a few minutes talking to the kids, she said, "So, tell me why you're here." Pat and I just stared at each other, dumbfounded. We were at a loss when it came to discussing our feelings toward our son. We could barely express our complicated feelings to each other, much less to a stranger we'd met only five minutes earlier. When it became clear we needed to be walked through this initial process, Sue suggested we tell her about our adoption story, how Sophie and Peter came into our lives, and what our initial impressions were of each. That we could handle, barely.

We gulped, almost in unison, as we wordlessly determined which of us would speak first. Our year of intensive attachment therapy had begun.

⟳

April 11, 2010. *News broke over the weekend about a Tennessee woman who put her seven-year-old adopted son on a one-way United Airlines flight to Moscow, with a note directing a prearranged driver to take him back to his orphanage. A single mother, she had adopted the boy only six months earlier. She claims the child is psychopathic and dangerous, that he tried to burn her house down and threatened to kill other family members. He's telling Russian authorities that she was cruel and physically abusive. It's impossible to say what's true and what isn't, but one fact is undisputed: the boy was removed from his Russian home and put in an orphanage because his birth mother was a serious alcoholic. I can't help but wonder what that boy would be like today if he had been adopted when he was three, like Peter was, or even younger? Would he be outside playing tag right now, after a breakfast of pancakes, fresh fruit, and cold milk, with his sister and best buddy from school, which is what Peter's doing? Our son had his first sleepover last night, and he's happy as a clam. I too am overjoyed because the experience has been completely positive, another impressive milestone that we weren't sure developmentally he'd ever reach. I shudder to think what shape Peter would be in, or if he'd even still be alive, if he'd been made to endure several more years in a Russian orphanage.*

When I first read the Tennessee story, I thought the boy's degree of FASD—for surely he was alcohol-exposed—must be far worse than Peter's, but after some consideration, now I'm not so sure. We've poured heart, soul, sweat, tears, and considerable financial resources into rehabilitating our son, who still struggles but has made tremendous progress. Putting aside the multitude of nonessential achievements, such as learning to ride a bike, swim, or play soccer, Peter's learned to love, and trust. It's taken years, and, though imperfect, we're there. He now knows, and I can sense this as readily as I can sense the sun breaking through the clouds, that we'll catch him when he falls but that we also expect him to stand on his own two feet whenever he's able. Peter knows our dreams for him extend as far as his dreams for himself, that we'll be happy if he's happy, when he's as independent as he can be, and as accomplished as his spirit and talents allow.

I doubt the woman in Tennessee saw any viable future at all, either for herself or her adopted son, when she desperately, and by that juncture irrationally, sent him back like a mail-ordered outfit that didn't quite fit. Is it her fault? Yes, but I can appreciate the despair, the isolation, the hopelessness that might seed such poisonous rumination. The child, however, was her legal (and moral) responsibility and no rational person would send a seven-year-old on a plane halfway around the world with nothing more than a note. Is it the boy's fault? No. Does Russia bear any responsibility? Of course! International adoption is a two-way street. Russia should not be allowed to pawn off its undesirables, no matter how blameless the children, without properly disclosing to potential adoptive parents their complete files, including medical records, psychosocial histories, prenatal records, orphanage caretaker notes, and all court documents, including transcripts, related to the relinquishment of parental rights. Further, all children over a certain age with pending adoptions should receive counseling in the orphanage to better prepare them for what's ahead and to help them integrate, heal from, and cope with their prior life circumstances.

Likewise, Americans have to stop thinking that a trip to Disney World and a heaping bowl of Cheerios are reasonable approaches to healing a neglected, undernourished, likely drug- or alcohol-exposed, and quite possibly sexually and/or physically abused child who may have a family history of psychiatric disorders. Pat and I took pre-adoptive parenting courses, read every book available on international adoption, consulted not one but two renowned adoption pediatricians, and still wound up parenting a very troubled, permanently compromised little boy. We love him, but his country's shortfalls have irreversibly altered the course and quality of the remainder of our lives. Russia has turned a blind eye to its love affair with vodka. Its foolish choice to withhold birth control, the rampant unemployment that's created a permanent underclass, and a still closely held Soviet-era belief that the state is responsible for individual's well-being are three compounding factors, in my view, that explain why Russia's orphanage system is still alive and well. This is true despite the fact that something like 80 percent of children raised in them will end up dead, drug addicted, or incarcerated by the age of twenty-five. Never mind that close to 90 percent of these children are not even true "orphans" in that they have at least one living birth parent.

So what do I think about the woman in Tennessee? I think she should be held accountable for endangering the life and welfare of her child. I'll leave the judging to others. The little boy? He may be beyond help, but I hope not. I hope someone in Russia comes to his rescue, though this may be wishful thinking. I know I don't have the strength to handle him. I can barely handle our son. Here's the irony, though: the boy on the news very well could have been Peter, or any number of other troubled youngsters turned over to Americans eager for parenthood in exchange for significant sums of money that may or may not be earmarked for the scores of children left behind. I hesitate to speak like a lawyer, but what began in Tennessee and ended in Russia was a travesty for which there definitely should be "joint and several" liability.

Chapter 21

Attachment 101

One of the first things that Sue made clear was that attachment work was serious, all-encompassing business. Because Peter was institutionalized from the age of five months until almost three and a half years, he was deprived of certain crucial developmental steps that permanently affect his psychological and social functioning. Children attach to a caregiver when their needs are met on a continuous and predictable basis. A baby cries when he's wet and he gets a clean diaper. The same holds true for hunger, thirst, temperature control, tiredness, and boredom. At birth, any baby will seek comfort from any person as a matter of survival, but as early as two months, all normally developing babies start to discriminate, relying on familiar caretakers to meet their immediate needs and provide a sense of security.

Most of us take this cause-and-effect relationship for granted because someone—a mother, father, grandmother, aunt, or foster parent—routinely responded to our cries and subtle signals when we were infants. Our primary caregiver's consistent, loving, and nurturing responses provided the essential sustenance our brains required to develop normal, healthy abilities to process and cope with feelings, thoughts, and complex relationships. These interactions are as essential to normal brain development as nutrition, sleep, and physical safety. Children deprived of early attachments risk lasting neurological impacts that interrupt not only their abilities to relate socially and emotionally, but also their cognitive capacities.

During World War II, babies and young children were sent away in droves from London to avoid the bombings. When they returned, sometimes years later, parents were shocked to discover that their formerly happy, well-adjusted youngsters had regressed, both socially and intellectually. The disruptions in attachments were responsible. In the 1960s, researchers studied a group of babies and toddlers ranging in age from seven to thirty-six months who were moved from an orphanage to an institution for retarded adults because of overcrowded conditions. The retarded people cared for, played with, and loved the youngsters on a consistent and regular basis. When these same children were returned to the orphanage several months later, their IQs had improved 27.5 points on average. The children who remained in the orphanage during the trial period, however, continued their downward spiral.

There are plenty of other studies as well. One of the most heart-wrenching was conducted by a researcher named Harry Harlow from the late 1950s through the early 1960s. Taking day-old monkeys away from their mothers, he put them in separate cages where they could see other monkeys but had no physical contact. He then placed these monkeys in a room with man-made "mother" dolls. One was made of wire but offered milk through a bottle secured between the slats. The other was furry and warm, but offered no nourishment. The newborn monkeys without fail chose the security of the "living" doll over the nourishment offered by the wire doll. The monkeys permitted to receive comfort from the warm, furry doll, though feeding occurred elsewhere and antiseptically, fared far better than their counterparts in both cognitive and psychosocial development. Those monkeys who were exposed only to the wire doll and who had no physical contact with other monkeys became highly disturbed and incapable of rehabilitation. Though controversial for a number of reasons, including the ethics of animal research, these studies were responsible in part for the birth of the foster care system and the demise of orphanages throughout the United States, Canada, and Western Europe. The profound damage in these monkeys caused by the lack of physical touch and maternal bond simply could not be ignored.

This was weighty stuff to consider in a cozy office in upstate New York as we watched our disorganized, hyperactive child bounce from corner to corner making quick work of destroying the room. I hated to think our son, and maybe even to some extent Sophie, had been treated like one of those horribly deprived monkeys in the black-and-white films.

"Peter," Sue said. "Come here." He looked up from whatever he was pulling apart and obediently walked over. "Now look at me." He wouldn't. With eyes diverted toward his shoes, he simply smiled and grunted as she attempted to grab him lightly by the wrist. Once he shook free, he quickly returned to his corner where he resumed his purposeless activity.

I found Peter's reaction to Sue very curious because usually when he met someone new he happily ran to them, often plopping himself backward into their laps. He would kiss and hug and say, "Hi, I Peter" to countless strangers' delight. In fact, he was much more social and affectionate to people he didn't know, or at least didn't know well, than he ever was with us. But with Sue, it was as though he sensed something different about her. His body language was pensive, his eyes wary. He seemed to understand, somehow, that this benign-looking woman knew what he was all about. Pat felt the same way. I realize we were assigning a lot of credit to a very damaged, troubled little boy, but it's the feeling we had all the same.

I remember watching with fascination as Sue attentively followed our son's every odd move, his back to her almost the entire time. After a few minutes she pulled out a bin of Lincoln Logs and asked whether he would help build a house. "Peter no build. No thank you," he mumbled, returning to the puppet he was manhandling. Sophie, of course, immediately dropped what she was doing and joined the activity. When Sue finally coaxed him into joining them, Pat and I realized he had no idea how to follow her lead. She'd put one piece down, show him where the next went, and then ask him to follow suit. But he wouldn't. Or couldn't. It was a paradox with which we were already familiar. He didn't know how to interact with her, or Sophie, and he certainly didn't know how to play—at all. Left to his own devices, he began throwing one Lincoln Log at a time into the air, watching with awe and horror as each came crashing back toward the floor.

He repeated the pattern over and over as Sue mostly ignored the behavior and spoke directly to Pat and me. She didn't seem to mind that Peter was fixated on throwing toys at the ceiling, though she did at one point redirect him toward the softer stuffed animals. "This is what you need to do," she said. "You have to start from scratch. I've seen this over and over with internationally adopted kids. He doesn't know how to play, think, organize, or take direction. He's confused and scared and completely inside himself. He's missing a lot. He doesn't trust. It's not your fault, but you're the ones who've got to deal with it."

She sent us home that first week with instructions to nurture and treat Peter like a baby. The idea was that he needed to experience the developmental stages he missed so that his brain might make new connections and fill in the gaps. I was to cradle him several times a day, rock him before bed, sing lullabies, devise tricks to engage eye contact, even give him warm milk with a bottle while I held him in my arms. We were never to look him directly in the eye when we were correcting his behavior or if we lost our cool; eye contact from this point forward was reserved solely for bonding and making up for three years of lost parenting.

We also were instructed not to let him jump into other people's arms or otherwise monopolize their attention. "You just need to explain ahead of time," Sue said. "Or when it happens, just politely remove him and tell the person that hugs and snuggles are for parents only right now." Easier said than done. Some people understood, but others would look at us as if we had Medusa heads as we bent down and removed our soon-to-be-screaming son from the joyful contentment of their laps.

But other than committing social suicide in public places near and far, the approach seemed to be working, at least somewhat. If Peter could receive physical comfort only from us, then he would have no choice but to allow us to meet his needs, both physical and emotional. We played peek-a-boo (still "koo-koo" in our house) to encourage eye contact. After dinner we sang and softly drummed our hands on the table to a song we dubbed "Abu De Abu Da," which was something of a rhythmic chant. Peter couldn't sing— he can't to this day—because he can't process the words and the music at the same time. But he could, with practice, manage the four sounds of our LoBrutto after-dinner jam fest.

In the ensuing weeks and months, I dutifully drove Peter the sixty miles to Albany once a week to see Sue. Sometimes I took Sophie, occasionally we went as a family, but mostly Pat took a half day off each week from his business to stay home with our daughter. During our sessions, Sue would interact with Peter, trying to engage him in purposeful play while she and I rehashed the previous week's progress, or, in many instances, regression. I found her incredibly helpful and understanding when it came to expressing my worries and frustrations, as well as celebrating our small but significant strides forward. She understood what Pat and I were going through in a way I hadn't previously experienced, and it was tremendously comforting to let my pent-up concerns pour out without fear of judgment.

After our very first meeting, Sue suggested it would take about six to nine months of intensive work both at home and in her office for Peter to become more securely attached to us and for us to notice measurable change. A lofty goal, for sure, and one I dreamed longingly about as the endless days continued. During the times Sophie was with us, she'd bounce around Sue's office like a kangaroo, often refusing to take direction or calm down. I could see the unspoken worry in Sue's eyes, but because she always returned to me once her blitzes had run their course, I felt we were okay, that we were bonded. In short, I believed that Sophie's problems were fixable. It turns out I was a little naive in this regard too, but at least not entirely off the mark. But I couldn't say the same about Peter, not even remotely. I believed in the work Sue was doing with our son—maybe, more significantly, I *needed* to believe in it—but secretly I struggled to see an end in sight.

"That's okay," Sue would laugh, whenever I confessed my reservations, usually when Peter was taking one of his lengthy bathroom breaks. "As long as you keep doing what we talk about." So every week I would leave recharged, ready to give the bottle another try, which never did work, and stay committed to practicing our other assignments, which did seem to produce some improvement. For whatever reason, Peter could not tolerate either Pat or me trying to give him milk (including chocolate milk) from a bottle. He would squirm and giggle maniacally. Any milk that made it into his mouth would come out in a bubbling, spurting mess that would then invoke another wave of hysterical laughter. He simply couldn't handle intimate, physical contact.

One thing I realized early on, though, was that Peter would look at me using the rearview mirror from his car seat. At first I thought it was merely a coincidence, but then I started noticing how he'd stare at me in the car more and more. It was as though the mirror was a go-between, a metallic medium that made the interaction for Peter somehow less intense. When I shared this theory with Sue, she was thrilled, and not particularly surprised. She said it wasn't that different from sending an e-mail to someone you're afraid or unwilling to confront face to face. So this was progress, I learned, though of a variety I hadn't expected. Just one more reminder that improvement for a child like Peter must be measured in minuscule, sometimes barely perceptible increments that nonetheless add up, slowly but surely, over the course of a month, a year, or, in some cases, a lifetime.

But in other ways he wasn't improving at all. Peter still smeared feces and sometimes hurt himself. The worst self- injury he ever inflicted was on the day before his and Sophie's joint birthday party, which was our first as a family. Sophie turned three on July 22, 2005, and Peter turned four two weeks later, on August 4. He had been screaming and stamping his feet about something, and Pat and I had sent him to his room. When he began slamming the door with such ferocity that we were afraid he would hurt himself, Pat closed it, sending Peter into some kind of frenzy. As best we can tell, he leapt from the bed directly at the door, the left side of his face slamming into the doorknob.

Pat was still upstairs when the screams began, and by the time I turned the corner at the landing, tears were streaming down my gentle husband's face. "I did it to him," he sobbed. "It's my fault. I closed the door. This is no good. I just can't do this. I can't."

The blood pooling beneath Peter's skin and along his cheekbone and brow formed an exact replica of the doorknob, including the push lock. Ice was not an option, as Peter couldn't tolerate it, but I did manage to get some Tylenol into him. By morning, his face looked monstrous. Pat had deep circles etched beneath his eyes from sorrow and regret on a day that should have been filled with happiness and celebration. It was no fun explaining what happened to the other parents as they watched Peter flit from present to present with obsessive, bug-eyed interest. I remember some of the parents nervously laughing, doing their best to reassure me that all kids do that kind of thing on occasion. I couldn't help but wonder whether they were referring to the doorknob impression on my son's face or his compulsive interest in the birthday presents to the exclusion of everything else around him.

Although there were no more incidents that severe, he was still banging his head, throwing his body against doors and walls, and occasionally hitting himself several months into our therapy. We also weren't making much headway with the attachment parenting except for the small gains with eye contact. Peter routinely cringed whenever I tried to hold him. He became so stiff that his joints locked. My feeble attempts at reenacting his lost infancy felt more like snuggling with a tire iron than a child. But I kept trying. And so did Pat.

Self-inflicted injuries obvious during Peter's gymnastics

During our rare times alone we would discuss how things were progressing with Peter, sometimes fooling ourselves, sometimes not. By then I had taken a post as a visiting professor at Bard College, teaching graduate-level environmental law and policy. It was an exciting and terribly welcome change to be able to channel at least a portion of my nervous "Peter" energy into an intellectually stimulating pursuit. The only problem, which any first year teacher knows, is that my course load was more time-consuming than I anticipated. I was a part-time faculty member, earning a part-time salary, but easily working fifty or more hours per week. Each two-and-a-half-hour lecture had to be prepared from scratch, using a textbook and other materials with which I was wholly unfamiliar. I also found myself often covering for our program's director, who is a dear and important person in my life, but whose substantial expertise in international environmental policy was far beyond the realm of my legal background.

So, in short, I was busy, very busy. I often started grading papers and working on upcoming lectures at 7 p.m., after we put the children to bed, and continued well past midnight. I did this so that I could spend every possible minute with our children. This was especially important for Peter, but Sophie needed me too. Pat and I didn't travel halfway around the world on two separate occasions to turn our children over to someone else. It just wasn't going to happen. My only concession, which was unavoidable, was that on the two afternoons a week that I was physically teaching, the kids stayed for both the morning and afternoon preschool sessions.

But despite my fatigue and the welcome distraction that teaching provided, I was never able to shake the feeling that our situation with Peter wasn't really improving. He was still unengaged with us, he still didn't interact with other children, and he could alternate between screaming over the simplest injury, such as a slightly torn fingernail, to not reacting at all upon being stung by a wasp. He laughed when others hurt themselves, and sat down like a wooden puppet, refusing to move, whenever he became irritated or angry. And most alarmingly of all, he began directing more and more of his hostility toward Sophie.

After a while, Sue began suggesting that we double our sessions, which we did. She and I would do our best to engage Peter in meaningful, organized play, but to little avail. She also had me read to him in her office, cuddled on a couch and wrapped cozily in a blanket. They were always books that addressed attachment, whether directly or indirectly, such as *Llama Llama Red Pajama* or *Twitchy*. Although Peter still struggles to read, he's always been drawn to picture books, a characteristic very much in his favor and one that certainly endears him to his book-loving parents. At the time, books were one of the few and easy inroads into our son's troubled and heavily cloaked heart.

But not all our sessions were about books, snuggling, and play. Often Peter was very angry in Sue's office; he didn't like what she was doing and let us know loud and clear. He would throw toys and stuffed animals across the room and dig his nails into the walls. Sometimes, when I was trying to cradle or otherwise physically comfort him, he'd bite me.

When he wouldn't calm down in her office after one or two verbal warnings, Sue made him practice "strong sitting," a technique we still use with Peter and, on occasion, even Sophie. It entails having your child sit cross-legged (something Peter physically cannot do, so we relax this requirement) with hands in lap, back straight, and head held high. The psychological point of the exercise is to allow the child to regain the strength and self-control that obviously was lost as a result of the outburst. "You need to get strong again," Sue would whisper softly but with authority. Peter would face a wall and practice his strong sitting until she thought he had regained his composure enough to rejoin us. In the meantime, she and I would talk as though he weren't present.

Although Sue hinted about the possibility that Peter was alcohol-exposed, and definitely thought he exhibited attachment problems, she never addressed the concern head-on. But she did acknowledge he had trouble with impulse control, distractibility, organization, problem-solving, and self-regulation, all telltale signs of executive dysfunction. Not a good thing. The executive function center of the brain, which is located in the frontal lobe, is responsible for working memory, cognitive flexibility, abstract thinking, rule acquisition, initiating appropriate actions (and inhibiting inappropriate actions), and selecting relevant sensory information. In short, although Sue was a social worker and not a diagnostician, she sensed that for Peter, the wiring in the area of the brain that makes us uniquely human was riddled with short-circuits, missing links, and faulty pathways.

"He can't organize his play," she commented one afternoon. "He moves around so quickly from one thing to the next. And he never chooses people to play with. Only things. He won't let me in. It's as though we're not even in the room with him." I hadn't heard this level of frustration in the six or so months we'd been coming to see her, so my ears, as well as my heartbeat, naturally perked up. "Mary," she said, her hands dropping heavily in her lap, "I would have hoped to have made more progress by now."

So there it was. Pat and I weren't the only ones at our wits' ends. The "Adoption Whisperer" was frustrated too. "I'm thinking you and Pat should consider a short-term round of medication," Sue offered. "Just to see whether there's something that might help lower his resistance a bit." I hadn't thought of medication—Peter was only four, and the very idea terrified me. Pat didn't receive the suggestion any better than I; in fact, he was even more opposed to the idea.

But another month or two elapsed, the conversations continued, and Peter's behavior and development were at best stagnating and at worst deteriorating. Pat and I also were becoming more and more exhausted. Any unsuspecting baby sitters we cajoled into our home fled quickly upon our return, with fear in their eyes and ponytails flying. The only young woman who ever came back more than once was the twenty-year-old daughter of our friend and house cleaner. She worked as an aide at the Children's Annex, a local day school for autistic children, so we thought she might have the training and stamina to handle our kids, especially Peter. But we later found out she would call her mom for survival advice several times during the three hours we were away. We couldn't keep doing this to either our friend or our daughter, especially knowing they were operating an emergency hotline just to make it through the evening.

Finally, the proverbial shit hit the fan. Pat went out of state later that winter for one of his writers conferences, which are absolutely necessary to maintain business and attract new clients, and the director of my teaching program left for China at the same time. It was a double whammy that left me with twice the teaching responsibilities and zero help at home. Although I'm not the type to fall apart when my husband leaves town, I have to say this particular trip was a cathartic experience. Peter never does well with change, and certainly didn't then, but what happened over those three or four days cemented my decision to medicate our son. The strangest part is that I can't even tease from my mind a single event. I do recall, however, that I endured a constant onslaught of unrelenting attacks, tantrums, and waves of nonsensical laughter that caused chills to run up and down my arms.

As I gradually came upon the little love notes that Pat leaves me when he travels—an "I love you" in the medicine cabinet or an "I can't wait to be back in our bed" on my nightstand—I tried to survive being bitten, spit on, kicked, hissed at, and vomited upon by Peter. Sophie was so overwhelmed by his behavior, as well as the anxiety oozing from my pores, that she began putting forks in her eyes and jamming crayons in her ears. Despite my efforts to keep my composure, I found myself sobbing on the phone almost every time Pat called, which I knew was a horrible thing to do to him. I don't know what's worse: being in the middle of a blitz or knowing the one you love is fighting for her life and there's nothing you can do.

We were both miserable, and we knew it. As hard as it is to admit, we decided then and there to medicate Peter, if not for him, then for us. Within two weeks we obtained a prescription for the antipsychotic drug Risperdal, prescribed by a psychiatric nurse practitioner with whom Sue worked. That night we gave him the tiny terra cotta-colored pill and kissed both our children goodnight. We had been warned that the drug would need to be in his system for a few days before we could hope to notice any changes. That night Pat and I stayed up watching dopey horror movies, neither of us able to sleep. The decision had seemed so huge, and it weighed heavily on our hearts and consciences.

But at some point I obviously did fall asleep, because I woke to the familiar plop of a small body at the foot of the bed. I opened my eyes expecting to see Sophie, who loved to burrow under the covers and snuggle in the morning. But instead I saw Peter, who had never, not even once, come into our room to say good morning or seek comfort because of a nightmare or thunderstorm. "I love you, Mama!" he announced, his eyes shy, his voice monotone, and the smallest of smiles creeping across his face. "I love you too," I whispered. Within seconds, the tears gushed unchecked down my face and neck and onto my silly flannel nightgown. I opened my arms to receive him, but he couldn't move any closer, and that was okay. "I love you too, my Peter boy." I could barely choke out the words. I had waited more than a year to hear that phrase from my son, and it was the most melodic, beautiful, and divine declaration I'm ever likely to experience.

❧

May 4, 2010. *Today we filed our second due process hearing request in fourteen months. Thirty pages long with twenty-seven attachments, it tells our educational story in painstakingly grueling detail. At the very least, the school district will have to spend significant money on attorney fees to prepare and file its answer. But that's not why our document is so lengthy. Because the school has put us through a haunted house filled with trick mirrors and smoke screens, we have no choice but to lay it all out, gory incident by gory incident. The school simply doesn't appreciate our handouts, our books, our statistics, our experts, and generally what has become our doctorate-level knowledge regarding educating and rehabilitating children with FAS, attachment issues, and the other countless disabilities that plague post-institutionalized kids like Peter. I get it. They want and need to be the experts. We've offended their sensibilities, their pride, maybe even rattled their confidences, all in the name of helping our son.*

Perhaps it really is arrogant of us to acquire such specialized knowledge about these matters; after all, it's not our careers or professional reputations that are at stake, just our lives, our family, our children's welfare, and our marriage. Through a system derived from blood, sweat, and tears, we send Peter to school more or less well-regulated every day, but we face a completely unregulated child once school is dismissed. Our hope is that the hearing officer, after reading our voluminous and woeful tale, might declare that the LoBrutto family has endured enough, that their most troubled member, Peter, deserves an appropriately tailored educational opportunity that will concurrently allow his family to recuperate. With a special education program designed to keep Peter regulated throughout the day, we just might be in a position to reclaim some semblance of manage-

able home life. Domestic tranquility is not the goal or even a dream. Hysteria, screaming, self-hitting, defiance, anger-driven urination, and mood swings so extreme that they make the Jim Carreys of the world seem sedate—these are what plague our daily lives and from which we seek relief.

Yesterday, I noticed a familiar odor, so I asked Peter whether he had peed his pants at school. The perfunctory answer, of course, was no, that he was dry, but then I looked more closely at his stained shorts and his tune quickly changed. "I peed a little, Mom, not so much. I was dry, but then I weren't." I had no choice but to feel his clothing, which had dried just enough so that the urine no longer dripped. When I asked when he did it, he eventually replied "a little at reading, then some more at recess, and then just yesterday [meaning a little while ago] in the playroom." This morning his teacher e-mails that he peed at 9:40 a.m. So just like I did yesterday, Lindy marches him upstairs to take a shower. "We pee in toilets to be clean, to keep germs off our bodies. When we pee on ourselves, we need to wash." This is what she tells him. I hear him vacillate between screams and maniacal laughter as the echo of the shower sounds above me.

An incredibly fierce but brief thunderstorm rolls through our patch of land shortly after the water stops. Sophie is ready for horseback riding but wants me to call her instructor and cancel. She's terrified of thunder. Despite the rustling wind, I'm about to persuade her to go when a pinging chorus of hailstones interrupts the effort. A few minutes later, Peter and Lindy rush downstairs, and the four of us sit on the kitchen window seats and watch as the hail bounces off the grass like rubber gumballs. It's strange to admit, but this is the best part of my day. The fierce but localized storm rages outside while I huddle with my terrified children and our loyal, talented Lindy. I can protect my children against thunderstorms, at least for the most part. It irks me no end that I can't protect our son against a school district more intent on acting like peacocks in a parade than helping a little boy that they must realize, once the pageantry of public education is past, will at best flounder through life, but at worst will suffer the consequences of a series of damnable decisions. I can protect Peter from the dangers of springtime thunderstorms, Sophie too. But I'm not at all sure I can protect him from the storms raging inside his head, from the inevitable consequences he'll face one day because his actions were driven by an impulsive, unremediated, and highly dysregulated mind.

This future, this reality that keeps Pat and I rubbing our foreheads forebodingly while the rest of the world sleeps, is the reason we've filed for hearing again. We can't keep this pace up indefinitely; it's too draining and not nearly entertaining enough to hold our interest. We've been wrestling with the issue of Peter's schooling for the last four years, more or less. It's time to forget the skirmishes and call out the brigade to fight the big fight once and for all. We need to do it for ourselves, for our daughter, and, last but not least, for our son, Peter, who in the eyes of God, if not man, will always be an innocent who deserves protection against all storms, whether natural or, in this case, man-made.

CHAPTER 22

FROM ALBANY TO VIRGINIA

OUR WORK WITH Sue continued over the next few months. Peter's transformation on Risperdal was nothing short of miraculous. Although the medication was not a magic bullet, the tantrums, the toileting escapades, and many of the other unmanageable behaviors either diminished significantly or disappeared. Each night I drifted off silently thanking the pharmaceutical company that manufactured those tiny round pills so that parents like Pat and me might occasionally sleep with both eyes closed.

The other noticeable difference had to do with Peter's speech. Despite speech and language therapy twice weekly, which had begun six months or so earlier, we hadn't noticed much improvement before Risperdal. I don't know why the medication helps so many autistic kids and other children with developmental disorders, but there's no doubt it works. The medicine didn't bring him out of his fog entirely, but the change was like the difference between a fog so thick you can't see your hand in front of your face and one in which visibility is low but it's still safe, let's say, to drive. To us, it felt like a clear, crisp fall day, the kind of day when a steady breeze purifies the air. Without warning, pronouns began to show up, as did plurals and even a few conjunctions.

He was becoming a different child, at least for a while. Sue began making small but noteworthy inroads, optimism returned, and I found myself eagerly awaiting each Tuesday so that Peter and I could make the trek to Albany and learn something new that I could then take home and practice. But then something happened, and the medicine seemed to stop working—not all at once, but slowly, like a retreating storm. Over a period of weeks the aggressive edginess returned, the dizzying mood swings, the rages that seemed to last for hours. They left Pat and me feeling as if a rabid forest animal was dismembering us, slowly, of all the hope we thought had been restored.

This unexpected downturn led to more drugs, and sometimes different drugs, though nothing brought back the window of opportunity Peter experienced during those first virgin weeks on Risperdal. We gave Ritalin a try, but stopped after watching our son sob uncontrollably for three days. Then we added Risperdal back but at a higher dosage. The unwanted behaviors only escalated. We've since learned that the Risperdal dose that works best for Peter is an extremely low one, .5 mg twice a day. So far, age and growth have not altered this fact, though we have tinkered with dosages now and again, just to make sure.

Pat and I knew that yielding to the temptation offered by medication would be a tricky proposition, but we had no idea of the emotional roller coaster it entailed, both for our child and us. We were confused, frustrated, and angry. We weren't happy with the prescribing nurse practitioner because every time we went to see her she asked the same solitary question: "What behaviors are you trying to control?" She barely ever spoke to Peter and she certainly didn't interact with him or make any effort to evaluate or understand his problems. To us, she seemed nothing more than a dispensary. She also was not accessible by telephone. Every single fiddle with medication, every little report of a possible side effect or change of dose required a $75 cash-only, five- to seven-minute office visit, with Peter in tow. I found myself making the trip to Albany two or three times a week. It was ridiculous, expensive, time-consuming, and entirely unfair to Peter, who, once we arrived, was completely ignored.

Sue was sympathetic when we shared our complaints, but she also offered a gentle reality check. There are very few child psychiatrists within a ninety-mile radius of where we live, and waiting lists can reach well into the following year. Second, medicating children for psychological disorders is an unpredictable business, even more so than with adults. This was especially true in Peter's case because we had no family history and no confirmed diagnoses from which to make at least a few educated guesses.

So we kept plugging along, returning eventually to our original dose of Risperdal, but without much progress. For instance, during one session, I shared with Sue that Peter once again threw a sizable rock directly at Sophie's head, so then he and Sue reenacted the incident using rubber frogs on the floor of her office. Although she did her best to tease from our son a rudimentary sense of empathy, responsibility, and cause and effect, in the end, her efforts proved largely fruitless. Peter showed no understanding or interest in what she was trying to accomplish, and he often behaved sarcastically, certainly passive-aggressively, toward her. Before long, it was clear we had reached another stalemate, and Sue finally said as much one afternoon. I knew it too, but our sessions, though frustrating in terms of Peter's progress, benefited me tremendously. I wasn't ready to give her up, even if she knew it was time to turn Peter over to someone more specialized. In many ways, over the course of our year together, I had become the patient.

I remember Sue smiling sagely when I brought this to her attention. She implicitly understood my struggles in a way no one else besides Pat ever could have imagined. But we weren't there for me, at least not officially. Helping Peter was the goal and primary purpose. "I think his problems are organic," Sue said. "I think there's some physical damage. Neurological. His responses are the same no matter what we do. It just doesn't add up." I knew in my mind, if not my heart, that I was hearing the truth, so I nodded slightly. "It's beyond what I can do," she whispered. "Let me make some calls and see what I can come up with."

When we left that afternoon, I hugged Sue goodbye and ambled out of her office with Peter's hand firmly gripped in mine. When I let go, he ran to push the button on the elevator, something he still enjoys doing, and my stomach sank as we descended to the ground floor, knowing full well the two of us were on our own again, flung lovingly, but undeniably, from the comfort of Sue's nest.

While I waited for Sue to make her calls, I began making some of my own. My first was to Jane Aronson, our trusted ally in what had proved to be a very bumpy adoption journey. I had made this call before, without much to show for it, but I knew I needed to try again. Sometime after we had started vocalizing our concerns about Peter, but while we were still in the stage where everyone kept advising us "to give it time," I sent an e-mail to Dr. Aronson asking for help. She suggested we visit a therapist in the city, so we made an appointment.

Despite hearing the problem was Peter, the therapist asked to meet us alone, as a couple. So we arranged aftercare one day at the kids' preschool and dutifully drove into New York for our childless appointment. The therapist was stylishly dressed, older, and I distinctly remember her asking whether we'd like some iced tea. I smiled because the offer was so Southern. After thirty minutes or so of extracting our personal histories, she announced that our problems with Peter, and mine in particular, were a direct result of my not having sufficiently grieved over my miscarriages and infertility, as well as the loss of Ben, the baby we turned down in Russia.

I recall scrambling for the elevator, speechless and in shock, as Pat stayed behind to scribble out a hefty personal check. We were both fairly quiet in the car for the first few minutes, but then Pat slammed his hands on the steering wheel. "That was complete bullshit!" he screamed. "My God, did it not even occur to her that we're doing fine with Sophie?" I began crying after that, not because his outburst upset me but because it gave me permission to release all the pent-up confusion and frustration I'd been holding inside since that woman with her pitcher of iced tea first spoke. Needless to say, we chose against scheduling a second appointment. Pat drove home with my head resting in his lap, where the tears subsided in favor of the calming warmth his presence most always offers.

Luckily for us, I decided to give Dr. Aronson's recommendations a second chance. Maybe she didn't know the therapist she referred us to would suggest I was the one interfering with Peter's attachment and generally causing all our family's problems. And besides, by that juncture, we'd spent enough time with Sue, a known and respected expert in the field of attachment, to know in our hearts, once and for all, that Peter's problems were bigger than us and that neither of us had caused them.

So the second time I called Dr. Aronson's office to get the name of someone to whom we might bring Peter, she didn't mince words. "It's time to see my friend Ron Federici. He's the best, Mary. It sounds like this is a serious problem. I'll call him first to see if he can get you in sooner than later. Give me a day or two. Then call yourself. In the meantime, look him up on the web."

True to her word, Dr. Aronson made her phone calls, and we were able to plan a trip to Virginia to see Dr. Federici within three weeks. As far as I can tell, her intervention saved us about four or five months of waiting for an available appointment, and therefore further decline.

Ronald Federici is a clinical neuropsychologist with a host of other impressive credentials too numerous to list. He's also the adoptive father of seven children, many of whom were rescued from Romanian orphanages in the 1980s and early '90s. International adoption, and more specifically, the developmental, behavioral, and emotional issues that plague orphanage children, which in turn wreak havoc on the grossly unprepared lives of their mostly well-intended parents, is both his business and passion. The prospect of meeting this man and having him examine our son felt both exciting and scary. After reviewing the materials on his website, and watching some of the video clips from various interviews and public appearances, it was clear this man knew his business. He also seemed tough, a real roll-up-the-sleeves kind of guy. Though I couldn't predict exactly what he would say when our visit was through, I knew it'd be substantial, as well as life-altering. In the private chambers of my heart, where my deepest fears are lodged, I'd always felt there was something wrong with Peter, something serious and not amenable to an easy fix.

The waiting period flew by because it's not easy to prepare for a trip to see Dr. Federici with only three weeks' notice. The amount of paperwork to be filled out rivaled what I imagined an IRS audit process entailed. But we did it. The extensive background questionnaire, the rating scales, the teacher forms, and copies of all past evaluations. The list goes on and on, but I understood then and still do why he insists on being able to study the child's entire "knowable" past from every possible angle. With kids from Russia, and I'm sure other countries as well, there is no prenatal or birth history, no family medical history, no history of any kind prior to adoption. Even vaccination records, which some orphanages provide, are suspect. That's why parents often are encouraged to revaccinate their children after they come to the United States.

But none of this bothered me. As I was when filling out the reams of pre-adoption paperwork, I was very motivated, almost as though I was jump-starting the engine that would lead us toward our son's restored health. The only real difficult part of Dr. Federici's pre-appointment requirements had to do with his position on medication. He feels that children should be evaluated, whenever possible, without benefit of behavioral medications in order to establish a baseline and to accurately identify any underlying organic or psychological conditions. Although we agreed to this prerequisite, tapering Peter off Risperdal was no romp in the park.

I think after a time, most parents with children on behavior medications often start questioning whether the meds are still working. I know I did. However, all any of us have to do to disabuse ourselves of this notion is to slowly and properly withdraw the medication(s) and observe what happens. It's not a pretty process, at least it wasn't with our son, and it was painful to watch him backtrack. Every day a few more of the unbearable behaviors returned, some of which we'd almost managed to forget: playing with poop, "da tee tee da da," and spinning like a top on amphetamines, just to name a few. By the time we were ready to leave for our five-day sojourn, Pat and I were pulling our hair out.

Even so, there was still something invigorating, even hopeful, about embarking on this mission to Virginia. I imagine it's a little like fearing you might have cancer but being afraid to visit the doctor. Denying reality has its drawbacks and almost always backfires. There can be great relief in finally confronting the truth and then formulating a plan to address it. I decided I would rather try to remedy Peter's problems and risk failure than continue to fool myself about the seriousness of his situation. Many cancers can be treated, even cured, with proper intervention. Despite real trepidation, I was hoping the same held true for our son.

And we wouldn't be traveling alone. By this time, we had convinced Pat's mother to move from West Palm Beach back to New York to be closer to family. We bought a little house for her about a mile from ours, and Pat used part of it as his office, which worked out perfectly. His mom had company, and Pat had a quiet place to work, away from the noise and commotion of our thunderous household.

Despite her age (eighty-one at the time), Pat's mom insisted on taking the six-hour trip with us to watch Sophie during the first day of neuro-psychological testing and participate with the rest of us in the subsequent two days of behavior intervention. Pat's mother has this amazing ability to keep the two of us sane, and perhaps because we try harder to achieve some balance toward the kids when she's with us, we always seem happier as a family. She's somehow able to deflate our ever-ballooning feelings of despair and exasperation with her wit, advice, and example. Though she loves our kids completely, she worries about their futures as much as we do, especially Peter's. But she also accepts their pasts as part of who they are and never seems to take their behaviors personally. If she were only fifty years younger, I believe she would be the ideal candidate for parenting alcohol-exposed, attachment-disordered children. As it is, she's a godsend in my life.

Uncle Mark, Marbletown, NY (October 2004)

When we left early the day before the evaluation, car packed, DVD player poised for *Finding Nemo*, and the cooler filled with snacks and drinks, it almost felt like we were leaving for vacation. Poor Grandma, who's tiny even by Sicilian standards, was sandwiched in the back between Sophie and

Peter, who were both still in car seats. It was a long trip, to be sure, but we arrived early enough to get situated in our rooms and settled. The hotel unapologetically flubbed our reservations and gave away the adjoining rooms we were promised. So Pat wound up sleeping with Peter in one room and I stayed with Sophie in the other. Grandma deserved her own.

Late that afternoon we walked around Fairfax, a beautiful, historic city dating back to the 1700s and within shouting distance of D.C. We chose what looked like a kid-friendly restaurant and enjoyed a decent, if not spectacular, seafood dinner. Peter made himself vomit at the table, but luckily not until we were nearly finished. Thinking he was sick, the waitress was sympathetic. As is usually the case with those who briefly peer into our lives, she undoubtedly failed to understand, much less appreciate, why we left in a disgusted, embarrassed rush.

After the dinner that was cut short, we walked until we found a big green space where the kids could run off some energy before going to bed. Because we wanted Peter well-rested for the next day, both kids were tucked in by 7:45. I read for a while, and then Pat and I e-mailed back and forth from our laptops, neither of us savvy enough to have figured out "live chat" or Facebook. In a way, it was a little romantic; we'd never been separated in a hotel hallway before, and each time I clicked the send button, I'd wait anxiously for his cute, sometimes flirty replies.

Meeting Dr. Federici the next morning was an unforgettable experience. His office was nondescript, very low-key, the way I think all offices of this type should be, but as soon as he walked in, the waiting area sizzled with energy. Tall and a little lanky, he possesses this booming, fast-clipped voice that leaves no doubt about who's in charge. He spent forty-five minutes or so with Pat and me before he took Peter for testing. He wanted to hear our story, our adoption history, including the foul-up with the baby we called Ben and our decision not to move forward with that adoption.

While we were in Russia, the orphanage director told us that Peter's teenage mother came to visit him three or four times and brought an apple, but then stopped visiting. When we got to that part of our story, Dr. Federici interrupted and said, "I know—the mother brought him an apple." Pat and I just looked at each other. Despair and astonishment swirled inside our foolish brains with sickening synchronicity. How could we have been so naive as to accept as truth this pitiful, rote attempt on the part of the

Russians to prove a bond, a connection, to offer a hint of reassuring hope that someone nurtured and loved our child as an infant? They must think Americans terribly stupid, and, at that moment, I wasn't in a position to dispel any myths.

When we finished unraveling our tale, Dr. Federici paused for a minute, leaned toward us and said in a softer, more solemn voice. "Let's get this mess figured out." Standing up, he shook our hands, exchanged Italian niceties with Pat's mother, and then handed us a stack of additional forms and questionnaires to fill out while we waited. We were to take Peter with us at lunchtime and return him for more testing in the afternoon. Busy banging something on the floor, Peter failed to answer the first time Dr. Federici called his name, which I found surprising because I nearly sprang to attention at the sound of his commanding tone, and so did Grandma and Sophie. He didn't bother asking a second time. Instead, he leaned over, took Peter by both hands, and without a hint of roughness pulled him firmly to his feet. "It's time to come with me now, Peter," he said. I bit my lip as I watched them turn the corner. Our son never even looked back.

Although I had a sense of what lay ahead, at least partially, the diagnoses we were on the brink of receiving were terrifying to contemplate. Autism was already a key suspect because of the previous questionnaires we had answered. I had been asking "experts" for two years why Peter flapped his hands, walked on his toes, repeated his name, pulled his toys apart, was often unresponsive, threw tantrums excessively, and spun in circles. I still don't understand why, up until then, the various professionals in our lives couldn't see the obvious, because every single one of Peter's puzzling behaviors, which he exhibited routinely, was on the parent autism questionnaire. It was abundantly clear to me by the time we reached Dr. Federici's office that our Russian-born son was somewhere on the spectrum, so I was prepared for that. I was also prepared for a diagnosis of alcohol exposure, if not full-blown FAS. Jane Aronson had primed us for that culprit within ten days of our bringing Peter and Sophie home.

When the testing was over, Peter emerged bouncing and toe walking, with an odd little smirk on his face. We had brought plenty of toys and books to occupy Sophie during the long day, but Peter simply walked over to the stack of adult magazines and started robotically turning the pages of

Newsweek. Dr. Federici motioned us into a conference room, a tiny bit exasperated, maybe a little amused, and definitely shaking his head.

"The little bugger snuck one over on me," he said with a hint of disbelief. "You've got a sneaky one. When we were taking a break, and I saw he was doing a puzzle, I took the chance to use the bathroom. I was gone thirty seconds, no more. I swear." By this point I was fairly nervous. Looking over, I saw Pat squirming in his seat. Whatever happened was not good. "Somehow he managed to destroy my office!"

I remember thinking the damage must be substantial for the unshakeable Dr. Federici to sound so astonished. "In less than a minute, he took my letter opener and slashed my leather desk chair, he pulled every single plug out of the socket, swept my desk clear, he did something to my . . ." and then his voice trailed off. I didn't know what to say. Neither did Pat. We had become mutes glued to our chairs. Horrified, I envisioned getting slapped, unceremoniously, with a damage bill for $10,000 and a concurrent invitation to never return.

"I gotta give it to him," he finally continued. Then he looked up, shook his head, and, though I can't be certain, I think he smiled. He must have read our thoughts. "It's okay, guys. My fault. I got fooled. By a four-year-old. Honestly, it's a good lesson. I didn't think it was possible anymore."

Although we were relieved we wouldn't be applying for another equity line of credit, it was unsettling to hear that of all the thousands of children he'd seen, ours was the one to pull a fast one on him. I felt like I needed to apologize, profusely, but as soon as I started sputtering, he waved me off. "Listen. That's over. Here's what matters: I know what to do. There's good news and there's bad news." He paused to make sure we were listening. Taking his cue, I did my best to erase the image of Peter slashing a leather chair, but it wasn't easy. "Okay. I'm gonna start with the bad."

So we listened and took notes. Peter was autistic. Although his behaviors fell squarely in the moderate range of the spectrum, Dr. Federici felt other factors, including his early institutionalization, were the prime culprits. He therefore believed the most appropriate diagnosis was "high-functioning autism" or PDD-NOS, which stands for Pervasive Developmental Disorder Not Otherwise Specified. Seems like a catch-all, and maybe it is, but what it really means is that the person isn't "classically autistic" but is too impaired, including intellectually, to meet the criteria for a diagnosis of Asperger's

Syndrome. On the spectrum, PDD-NOS falls more or less in the middle. This was not good news, of course, but Dr. Federici made it clear that autism was the least of our problems. This was not a comforting statement to hear right after being told that our child was autistic.

Peter also had full-blown Fetal Alcohol Syndrome, his symptoms and impairments falling within the moderately affected range (Dr. Federici would later change his diagnosis to the "severe" range of the spectrum). This news, though not surprising, was particularly difficult to hear. It was the one possibility that truly terrified Pat and me since the onset of our adoption journey. We tried so diligently to protect ourselves, as well as our future family, against this devastating condition, but now we knew our efforts had failed. "But it could be worse," Dr. Federici interjected as he watched our faces fall. "Most kids I see with FAS are retarded. Peter's not. His IQ is low, but in the low average range. And with the right help, I'm certain we can raise it. The autistic traits too—they'll improve. The autism is secondary, like a side effect, to both his early institutionalization and the FAS. The point is, he can learn. He can improve. Believe me, I often sit in this very seat and tell parents there's really very little to be done. It's devastating. But Peter can be helped."

I have this embarrassing problem, or maybe condition, I'm not sure, in which my face turns beet red whenever I drink (which anymore is seldom), or get angry, upset, embarrassed, or even slightly overheated, or when I feel a migraine coming. Since this covers a lot of territory, I often look as if I'm drunk, sunburned, or suffering a hot flash. My mother had the same problem, so maybe it's hereditary. I could feel the heat rising in my face as I took in the news, trying desperately to understand how an IQ of 80, autism, and FAS were not such bad things.

Next, he said we should have our son evaluated by a neurologist because he was concerned Peter was having seizures. "Why?" I asked, puzzled. No one had ever suggested this before. "Because of the staring spells—lots of them. Also because most of these kids I see, like Peter, have abnormal EEG [electroencephalogram] findings that need and respond to treatment. And treatment means improvement." Then he took a breath, exhaled, and said, "But here's what really concerns me."

As my flush spread to the point I could have fried eggs on my face, I looked over to see Pat so slumped in his chair that he looked like he could have faded right into the fabric. How could there possibly be anything worse that what we'd just been told?

"What really concerns me," Dr. Federici continued, "are his dysregulated thought patterns—Peter shows little to no grasp of reality. He doesn't seem to know what's real and what isn't. And he's almost five. He should know, at least somewhat." Then he gave a few specific examples. "When I asked him to tell me the color of the horse in the picture, he said the sky had yellow acorns." One phrase from the written report that followed remains seared into my memory: that Peter displays "pseudo-psychotic logic patterns." Holy mackerel.

"But couldn't that just be a developmental thing?" Pat pleaded. After all, Dr. Federici had told us only a few minutes earlier that despite our son's low average IQ, he was functioning significantly below his potential. His adaptive IQ, meaning how he was using his intelligence to interact and problem-solve in the real world environment, was in the high 50s, which put him squarely in the retarded range.

"No. Significant difference between straight IQ and adaptive IQ always indicates brain damage, which is what we're dealing with here. Peter has FAS, maybe heavy metal exposure too. You're right in that he's functioning like a much younger child, but my concern about his thought patterns, well, that's a whole different thing. You're going to need to keep an eye on that. Keep a journal." And then he gave us a list of behaviors to watch out for and record.

Four or five months after our visit to Virginia, I almost hit a deer on the way home one day, with both kids in the car. A little shaken, I pulled over to settle my nerves. "Peter say go button," he offered. "Make car zoom on air. Flap flap." He was referring to something recently we'd watched on *Lilo & Stitch*, a kid's cartoon. He thought I could press a button and make the car hop and fly right over the deer, literally. When I tried explaining, for the zillionth time, how cartoons aren't real, that lots of things happen in them that can't happen in real life, he began to throw a tantrum. "Peter fly car. Peter fly car. Mama don't know. Peter fly car!" So into the journal it went.

By the time we were through with our post-evaluation debriefing, Pat and I were wobbly and on the verge of hallucinating ourselves. In addition to learning our son was autistic, and had FAS, possible seizures, and psychotic tendencies, we also learned that he suffered from ADHD, a mood disorder (probably bipolar-type), severe Post-Traumatic Stress Disorder (PTSD), sensory integration dysfunction, severe problems with attachment, and a host of learning disabilities across all domains.

When Pat and I lay in our separate hotel rooms that night, thinking our separate thoughts but occasionally e-mailing each other, we realized our reaction to the day was basically the same and went something like this: Oh my God! Now what do we do? Are our lives over? Should we dump the kids with family members and disappear into the Alaskan wilderness? But as our panic waxed and waned, we tried to remind each other that Dr. Federici had a plan that he promised would help our son and return some semblance of functionality to our home.

The next day, we arose and met downstairs for breakfast. Sophie was in a foul mood over the thought of spending another day in Dr. Federici's waiting room, and Peter was on the loose, medication restarted but still incredibly jumpy. I had wanted to switch rooms with Pat so that he didn't bear the brunt of spending every night with Peter, but he characteristically declined the offer. He looked so tired that morning, the kind of fatigue that derives from worry more than sleep deprivation, and I fought back a rush of emotions as I watched my deflated husband shuffle toward our table. I realized right then how angry I was, at Peter, at our situation, at the fact we were spending four days with a neuropsychologist when we should have been enjoying D.C.'s glorious cherry blossoms. I was angry at the world, at God, for what felt like perpetual punishment, and all because we wanted a family. Because I wanted a family.

Pat's mom sensed the change, the gravity, and as usual intervened. She suggested we finish breakfast quickly and enjoy the morning sun for a few minutes before we left for our appointment, which was Day One of Behavior Intervention. At this suggestion, Peter began his ceremonial purging at the table, but we caught it in time. In no uncertain terms Pat made it clear that he would be a very unhappy boy if he pursued this particular line of sabotage. Something in Pat's eerie tone convinced Peter to stop.

Despite the early hour, the day was already hot and hazy, as D.C. can be even in early May. We strolled slowly around a few neatly trimmed blocks. The characteristic brick buildings, with their blooming window boxes and glossy black doors, reminded me how much I enjoy Washington and Northern Virginia. Our leisurely pace stood in contrast against the hurried gait of business people rushing to catch their trains. I'm sure most, if they even paused to notice, thought us tourists. If only we had been.

I had the same feeling the morning my father died, as I waited in the airport to fly home, watching the throngs of people passing. No one knew or cared that my world had come to a crashing halt. The news received only the day before in Dr. Federici's office also had turned my world upside down, completely, and was just as difficult to process. This day for us would be frozen in time, forever. Our son was damaged, seriously and permanently. There was no turning back the clock of our lives. We'd have to find a way to move forward. I hoped Dr. Federici was right when he said he could show us the path.

❧

MAY 21, 2010. *Peter ambled toward the car after school yesterday, shoulders drooped and head hung low. He looked as pitiful as our little dog, Pippin, who has fallen into a deep depression over the recent installation of an Invisible Fence. On the way home, with Sophie and her friend Alexis chatting happily, I looked in the rearview mirror and asked what's wrong. To make a long story short, Peter's in love, big time, with the prettiest girl in class and maybe in the whole school, except, of course, our Sophie. But now his best friend is jealous. I couldn't get the particulars, but what matters is that Peter thought he'd lost his best buddy and the girl who's stolen his eight-year-old heart. I assured him these kinds of problems tend to work themselves out, but when we got home he asked if he could call "his girlfriend."*

So we looked in the school directory, but he didn't know her last name even though they've spent the school year together in the same class. We nonetheless settled on a probable identification, and I dialed the number. Bingo! He was standing next to me and I swore I could see his little heart pounding. He didn't know what to say, so I coached him along, in the faintest whisper, Cyrano de Bergerac style. The girl, whose voice I heard because Peter was so close, is obviously a winner, as beautiful on the inside as she is to the visible world. When my poor son's nerves couldn't take another second, he yelled into the phone, "I like you!" and nearly threw it at me as he retreated across the room. I quickly hit the disconnect button and rushed to make sure Peter had not, in fact, fainted. His color returning, his eyes lit with amazement, I found him all smiles. "She's not mad, Mommy!" With any luck, he'll patch things over with his friend today.

Those few moments with my son yesterday, alone in the kitchen, makes all the horror of the last few months more than worth the toll.

I realize I may not feel that way tomorrow, much less next year, but for now I'm content. My beautiful boy is love struck! There's nothing more normal, more typical, or more precious than that. Not even the certified letter that arrived earlier in the day could trump this good feeling, though it took work to resist the urge. From CPS, the letter informs us (me) of the time, date, and the exact allegations made by my mystery (hardly!) school accuser. This information had the potential of seriously upsetting me, except for the fact that my son's in love, and I knew the case had been closed and the file expunged, as there was not a shred of evidence.

But this letter contains a good deal of unsettling information nonetheless. First, the complaint wasn't filed against Pat and me, only me. Second, it says nothing about making Peter do chores when he wets, which is what the investigator told us was the basis for the complaint. I can only surmise that when he interviewed my vituperative nemesis and actually asked what evidence she had to support her allegations, the chores business was all she could think to say that didn't constitute a complete fabrication. I'm also concluding that the investigator, who indeed seems to be the kind of man we as parents and taxpayers actually want in this kind of position, didn't wish to upset me at the time any more than necessary. And maybe he was right. The actual wording used, obviously uttered with great disdain and little restraint, truly does indicate an unbalanced mind and a diseased heart, a woman intent on poisoning. Here's the narrative of the call: "The mother is excessive in her corporal punishment of Peter (8). Peter has medical issues which cause him to be incontinent. When Peter experiences incontinence the mother has beaten him up, including striking him in the head with excessive force. The mother has also thrown objects, including a book bag, at Peter. It is unknown if Peter has sustained marks or other injuries. Peter is frightened of the mother. The roles of the other individuals listed in this report are unknown."

And there's more. In terms of safety factors, she further alleges: "Caretaker [that's me—I guess my self-appointed archenemy doesn't consider me Peter's "real" mother] is violent and appears out of control. Child is afraid of or extremely uncomfortable around people living in or frequenting the home." The other people who live in or frequent our home are Pat, Sophie, Grandma, and Lindy. Now we know this woman always has had it out for Lindy, and I can see how she would view Pat as being malignant since he's married to me, but Sophie? As a seven-year-old second grader, surely she deserves immunity. Plus, she's really cute. And what about poor Grandma? Although at eighty-five she can run through an amazing litany of naughty Sicilian hand gestures if we beg her and she's feeling particularly puckish, I doubt the spectacle ever has traumatized Peter. Seriously, I just have to laugh. I have to find humor in my life so that I can continue to bear these petty assaults that nonetheless have real potential to devastate. Next month we go to hearing over the school district's refusal to place Peter in an appropriate school program. We're claiming, in part, that the school has become a hostile environment. If this nonsense over the last few months doesn't end the debate, then I may as well hang up my hat, both as lawyer and mom. But that's a month away. Right now, this mom-slash-caretaker is reveling in her son's love-induced misery. It seems love still blooms at times, even in hostile environments.

Chapter 23

Welcome to Boot Camp

When I reflect on this period of my life, two competing thoughts emerge like thunder on a sunny day. What Dr. Federici was asking of us was impossible. On the other hand, it just might work. The many hours in his office following the evaluation are fuzzy now, but the take-home message was clear: we had the power to break into Peter's mind and tear down walls formed from a noxious brew of terror and neurological insult. We headed home after two days of behavioral intervention armed with the tools and knowledge necessary to begin what Dr. Federici describes as thirty days of boot camp. The weeks that followed were simultaneously impossible to endure and transcendent in their unfolding. In all respects except the literal, it was the season I gave birth to our son.

I was still teaching at Bard College, and my semester wasn't over until the end of May. For this reason, the start of LoBrutto Boot Camp had to be postponed for a few weeks, so life in our home resumed, seemingly unfettered by the news and knowledge that Pat and I now carried. As soon as the semester was over, however, we withdrew Peter from preschool and jumped headfirst into the program we believed would heal our son.

Looking back, I must have experienced some quasi-religious measure of "faith" in Dr. Federici's methods to even contemplate doing what I did. On the other hand, sheer desperation may have driven me to try any approach that had any basis at all in logic and science. Whichever the case, we began what would become a profoundly moving and transformative journey at the start of Memorial Day weekend, 2006. The rules were few and easy to remember. Peter was to stay within six feet of one of us at all times, his days and evenings were scheduled in fifteen-minute increments, and all choice and free time were eliminated.

Boot Camp (Summer 2006)

Although Pat helped when he could, Peter and I were destined to walk this path by ourselves, side by side. We were confined to our property, and no one was allowed to visit. Radio, television, and video games were strictly prohibited. We also were encouraged to take Sophie to live with relatives for those four weeks and urged to allow Peter to sleep in our bed. I can understand why Dr. Federici wanted us to focus 100 percent on Peter, but removing our almost four-year-old daughter, who struggled with her own adjustment issues, was out of the question. So was the issue of co-sleeping. Peter thrashes throughout the night, waking every morning in a tangle of twisted bedcovers suggestive of a great, primal struggle. There was no way I would survive the month if I didn't at least have some time to recompose myself at night.

My mind slams shut, like a steel trap, whenever I try to recall what those first two weeks were like, because they were tough, really tough. I think I cried more during the overnight hours and stolen moments in the bathroom—with Peter kicking and banging violently against the other side of the door, than I ever have in my life. He spit, bit, screamed, vomited, and scratched at me to gain some distance and freedom, but I refused to allow him to scurry away like a trapped, feral animal. Intent on staying the course, I sometimes was forced to implement the holds that Dr. Federici taught Pat and me in his office.

These holds were intended to maintain safety when the intimate pressure of Boot Camp became more than Peter's rebellious nervous system could handle. Meant eventually to soothe and nurture and not to punish, Dr. Federici taught me to sit on the floor, legs spread wide, with Peter placed in front with his back against my chest and belly. I then would wrap my arms around him in a kind of forced snuggle. Once his mouth and body were quiet for three straight minutes, I could let go, turn him around, and offer what was hopefully a comforting, healing, face-to-face embrace.

The first time I implemented a hold, it took over an hour for Peter to reach the three-minute mark. I emerged from this experience bruised, dazed, exhausted, stiff, and barely able to summon the energy to resume our dizzying fifteen-minute time slots of puzzles, crayons, swings, books, floor time, and then meal preparation. My tiny son's vehement reaction to these holds left me feeling like I had been thrust into the middle of a stormy exorcism. I questioned, critically, Dr. Federici's method and second-guessed our decision to undertake such an arduous process that was exhausting and terrifying for both parent and child. More than once, Pat found me sobbing, tears streaming down my face in waves of silent agony, in the middle of one of these episodes. He would take over, literally, and I would dash from the chaotic scene, grateful to be free of the bonds of forced intimacy. Over the weekends, Pat almost always did the holds, demanding that I let him absorb at least some of the pain we were working so hard to expel.

And really, that's what we were doing. We were taking away Peter's pain. Forcing him to exorcise the rage, confusion, and distrust in a manner that looked violent but wasn't. I consoled myself by comparing this process to watching a child get his stomach pumped in the emergency room. It's unpleasant, and no parent enjoys watching her child suffer, but it's also unequivocally necessary. Although my mind concurred, my heart was reluctant, and harder to convince. On more than one occasion, I confessed to Pat that I felt like we were breaking a horse.

When we weren't immersed in an activity or embroiled in a tempestuous hold, Peter slowly learned to shadow my every move. At first, I had to physically pull him along by the hand, lunging for him whenever he tried to dart away. I began imagining that we were linked together by leg irons, like prisoners in an old chain gang movie. Peter did whatever I was doing and ate and drank whatever I ate and drank. If I was doing laundry, Peter was right there with me, sorting socks preschool style or tossing over baskets of clothes I had just folded. I ate nothing but kid food—peanut butter and jelly, cereal, or microwavable soups—because I couldn't safely use the stove or oven with Peter hovering so close by. Our son was as unpredictable as a newly launched pinball, and the requirement that he help me prepare meals was among the most formidable.

One of the worst aspects of this endeavor was making Sophie play second fiddle for an extended period of time. After all, her more ordinary, but no less important needs had been dwarfed since day one by Peter's five-alarm presence. But during Boot Camp, we purposely devised ways to keep her away from home as long as possible. We arranged for her to stay at her preschool's aftercare program, and Pat picked her up at 5:30 on his way home from work. We hated doing this, but we had little choice. Pat had to work and neither of us thought it was particularly healthy for Sophie to witness Peter's complete and utter collapse. The logistics of keeping Peter within arm's length, while managing to watch and keep his busy sister safe, were daunting. At the same time, exiling her to a relative's house for four weeks seemed potentially even more damaging, even assuming we could have arranged it. So we did the best we could. When Pat and Sophie came home at night, he took over Peter's program until dinner to give Sophie and I some time alone. He also did all the shopping and anything else that couldn't be accomplished from home.

I remember resenting Peter tremendously during the first half of this program. I was a prisoner in my own home, a captive of my own desire to parent, but instead of wearing an ankle bracelet, I dragged an unattached, angry, brain-damaged, and possibly psychotic four-year-old everywhere I went. Showering, using the bathroom, and dressing became challenges that

I had to plan well in advance and almost always when Pat was home. After a while, I couldn't remember why I was even doing this anymore. Peter was an alien to me, a whirling dervish of disability that I had neither created nor desired. What I wanted was a family, not a booby-trapped marathon that lacked a finish line. Pat's demeanor during this time was as puzzling as mine was distasteful. He clearly was trying to shore me up and offer the most support he could. But he also was eerily distant and aloof, as though he sensed that the forced intertwining of Peter and me was a journey he endorsed but could not himself take.

When my mother died in May 2001, Pat rubbed my back as he quietly recited a quote by William Makepeace Thackeray that I'll never forget: "Mother is the name for God in the lips and hearts of little children." I spoke those lines at my mother's funeral, for I knew in my heart they were true, and they came back to me in those first weeks of Boot Camp. To Peter, I was the antithesis of God, mother, parent, or caregiver. I was the devil. I represented everything he feared, everything that ever hurt him, and any and everything that ever could. Pat was right to take the back seat for this agonizing but cathartic journey. What had been hazily evident the day we first met in Birobidzhan was now abundantly clear: Peter didn't know or understand what a mother was, and it was my job to disabuse him of the notion that I was like every other woman who had entered his short life. To Peter, I was the one who neglected and abused him, drank prenatally, ignored his cries, opted not to change his dirty diapers, withheld nourishing food, and failed to rock him when he couldn't sleep.

Acknowledging this reality allowed me to keep most of my resentment in check and helped propel me through the Boot Camp process. Then, miraculously, the storm began to dissipate. Sometime around the start of week three, and in the midst of monotony born of cycling through the same sets of puzzles, chores, games, and outside activities, something barely perceptible happened. Peter began looking into my eyes, not straight on but with a definite sideways glance. Before then, he had only looked at me when he wanted to shock, like when he smeared feces all over himself or the bed. There were other signals too. He stopped darting away when I let go of his hand. Before long, both the frequency and duration of holds lessened, and, amazingly, when they did occur, he was noticeably less stiff when I turned him around afterward to hug.

We were making progress. If I was sitting on the couch, and I asked Peter to get a book, he'd pop up, grab one from the coffee table and plop back down, right next to me. He began clapping like an eighteen-month-old when I praised him for putting his shoes on correctly or using the toilet like a big boy. Though I scarcely realized it, tears of joy and relief slowly replaced those born of frustration, fear, and anger. It was working! Peter was awakening, slowly sloughing off the armor that had imprisoned his heart and mind since early infancy. After living a year and a half with a boy whose entire repertoire of behaviors was designed to inoculate himself against the dangers of love and intimacy, I knew enough to appreciate the significance of our accomplishments.

If the first two weeks of Boot Camp seemed endless, the last two flew by with unexpected alacrity. Feelings of fear and dread no longer dominated as Peter and I walked hand in hand toward the patch of land where our hammock hung lazily between ancient maples. Although he always enjoyed the hammock, any attempt to swing with him in the past had been greeted with kicks and flails forceful enough to leave ugly marks on my arms and legs. "Hammock, Mama, hammock. Peter wants. Please!" he implored, an easy smile spreading across his face as his eyes flirted briefly with mine. I couldn't say no, so I smiled back and nodded in agreement, careful not to show too much enthusiasm. His ability to process and regulate emotion was more delicate than a newly hatched chick. By then, I knew not to squeeze too hard or often. But as with so many other experiences in our deliberately cocooned world, things were indeed changing. And not just on his part. A few times a week I threw on an old bathing suit I kept stuffed under the sink and slipped into our oversized tub with Peter, hoping that his love of water and bubbles would mask, at least temporarily, his fear of intimacy. For me, the feel of his soapy skin against my own, luxurious moments snatched between playing endless rounds of nose-diving rubber dinosaurs, was heavenly. After a year and a half, I was no longer treated like the bedtime monster hiding in the closet.

Drinking in the features of his beautiful face and perfect form, there were moments when I caught myself looking at Peter, waves of emotion rippling through me. I began relaxing around our son, this boy who had seemed like an alien living among us for so long. Without fully realizing it, the torture of Boot Camp slowly blossomed into something truly beautiful.

My desire to reach Peter reemerged from the depths of impossible demands and instructions too great to fulfill. There was no room for doubt. Boot Camp was forcing the intimacy that both of us craved and needed. I wasn't breaking a horse. I was nurturing a helpless foal.

I often tell people that Boot Camp was the month I fell in love with my son, and it's absolutely true. Nothing about Dr. Federici's elixir was easy to swallow, nor was it a magic bullet. Peter continued to throw tantrums, though not as often, and his behavior was still erratic and unpredictable, as it remains today. What slowly disappeared from the tapestry of his psyche was the rigid isolation and terror. No longer did he need to rely solely on his own misguided impulses. The rigors of Boot Camp helped his body, mind, and heart understand that he was safe now, that he was worthy of love, and, maybe most of all, that a mother's love is meant to nurture and heal, not destroy or threaten.

As our month of romance came to a close, the children and I stayed busy putting the finishing touches on a scrapbook we made and called *The Fabulous Story of Peter and Sophie LoBrutto*. With the school year ending one week prior to the end of Boot Camp, Pat and I decided that Peter was doing well enough to allow Sophie to remain at home. Feeling like we had semi-banished one child for the benefit of another, I was relieved to have her back, all day long, where she belonged.

It was a magical time for me, and one I remember with great fondness and satisfaction. Both kids dove enthusiastically into the scrapbook project, something I hadn't anticipated. We cut out and glued down pictures of extended family members, as well as photos from Russia, family vacations, and favorite activities and outings. I wrote silly dialogue that made the children howl with laughter, and Sophie pasted the pages onto construction paper as fast as they flew from the printer. Then both of them would color around the borders and litter the pages with stickers. When our project was complete, I laminated the whole thing and bound the pages together to create a handmade narrative of how four strangers, from Florida, Brooklyn, and Birobidzhan, came together as a family in New York's Mid-Hudson Valley.

As it turns out, the completion of the scrapbook also closed the chapter on the most difficult and cherished month of my life, the month I fell hopelessly and forever in love with our son. Peter was damaged, yes, but those weeks, arduous, exhausting, and rewarding, taught me something far more valuable than any neuropsychological report could ever reveal. Our son was meant to be a beautiful, sensitive, loving, and caring person. Boot Camp helped me see that, and, moving forward, I realized it was my job, my obligation as chief protector of his spirit and heart, to make sure he and I never again lose hold of that truth. It's a promise I made to us both, and some days it's easier to remember than others, but it's one I'll never forget.

❦

JUNE 7, 2010. *Pat and I let the children sleep late because we didn't get home from our neuropsychological testing weekend until 10:30 last night. Bad weather and beach traffic conspired to rob us of a swift return. We hiccupped along the highway in stops and starts, the windshield wipers frenzied with effort, as the kids watched movies on the portable DVD player. Lindy made the trip with us. The inevitable lulls in conversation left more than enough time for Pat and me to immerse ourselves in silent hysteria. Two years and one month ago, Peter's IQ was in the low average range. After a long day of testing, Dr. Federici informed us our son has lost significant cognitive ground since he saw him last in 2008. About ten points in fact. His IQ is now considered borderline, he is experiencing visual and auditory delusions/hallucinations, which we unfortunately suspected, and he has made no academic gains whatsoever in two years. Our boy, to use Dr. Federici's words, is stagnating academically and deteriorating neurologically. His brain is not being exercised and it's dying, slowly but surely. That is the bad news, and it's devastating and hard to hear. But with the help of Lithium and our imperfect but devoted efforts at home, Dr. Federici also saw, for the first time, the sweet, loving, and compassionate child I'm honored to call my son. That in itself is a major miracle, and one I mustn't overlook in the midst of our grave worries. Peter was nothing short of feral, a regular jungle boy in madras shorts and fisherman sandals, when we first drove out of sheer desperation the six hours to see Dr. Federici in May 2006. But now this expert believes we're nearing the finish line in terms of solid and secure attachment.*

Given the extent of Peter's deficits, and all we've suffered and endured, my eyes filled with tears to hear this glorious pronouncement, even in the midst of Dr. Federici's accounting of our son's cognitive decay. Our due process hearing against the school district starts Wednesday. I don't hold out much hope the school will suddenly see the light and acknowledge that it can't meet our son's needs and that having him sit through the day and do as he's told, without an ounce of understanding about what he's doing or why, is literally causing his brain to melt. But strange as it sounds, I think I'm reaching some kind of peace about our situation. Peter will not be going back to that school. He can't afford to lose any more IQ points and we can't afford to have CPS come knocking every time we get in their faces about the inadequacies and misplaced emphasis of their efforts. Dr. Federici says the crime in all of this is that our son is educable, that he can learn, and that he can make progress. But the few hours a week Lindy works with Peter, one on one, using verbal behavior and other neurocognitive rehabilitation techniques, isn't nearly enough to maintain his functional skills. He needs Lindy-like interventions around the clock, all day long, but there's no way we can meet those needs privately. Lindy is too busy, she teaches severely autistic children all day long, and we are plumb out of funds. But we'll have to find a way. We'll either prevail at the hearing, or I'll do it myself. If we can take a feral child and transform him into the sweet, loving person he is today, especially when someone is with him, one on one, to help modulate his mood and impulses, we can improve his brain function.

None of this is rocket science. Peter is brain-damaged. He's operating academically and socially approximately three years behind his peers. So that's where we start. We find out what in fact he does know, what he's able to generalize across different settings and without being prompted, and we build from there. And when it gets too tough, when I think I can't do it anymore, I have to remind myself how far we've come. I'll remember back to Saturday night, when we sat in The Tombs, eating dinner with my nephew Jay, who is now a rising senior at Georgetown. A young man whose brilliance of mind and heart is incontrovertible, he was sandwiched between Peter and Sophie, happily indulging his little cousins as they clamored for every ounce of his attention. Peter now belongs, and he knows it. We've given him that. He has a family who loves him, a family hearty and jovial enough to try and laugh when he exasperates them. He's no longer alone, that tiny boy in Russia fighting for his own survival. He's part of us, and he'll never have to fight to survive again. It's our job now, and though it's the toughest work I've ever done, I'll never abandon him.

Chapter 24

When Rain Hurts

When our month of isolation ended, I thought very carefully about when and how to reintroduce Peter to the outside world. There's no doubt he began slowly to awaken as he emerged from the safety and rigor of Boot Camp, but he was fragile, like a newborn, and Pat and I treated him accordingly. Pat rearranged his schedule when he could so I could shop and run other errands without Peter in tow. Grocery stores, though not particularly loud, are crowded places where shoppers mill under the glare of harsh, fluorescent lighting. Peter is and always has been a wreck in those kinds of places and I think the intensely bright lights are a chief culprit.

The expiration of our voluntary confinement also meant dealing with a flurry of overdue doctor's appointments and evaluations. Dr. Federici encouraged us to have Peter evaluated by a pediatric neurologist, an ophthalmologist, a cardiologist, and others. He also recommended at least twenty hours per week of intensive verbal behavior therapy, which is a kind of applied behavior analysis used mostly with children on the autism spectrum. I managed to persuade the county, which oversees preschool special education services, to provide an hour a day of Applied Behavior Analysis/Verbal Behavior in our home, five days a week. ABA/VB is a method of teaching children with autism and is premised upon the theory that appropriate behavior, academics, and life skills can be taught using scientific principles with measurable outcomes. Given the expense involved, Pat and I considered ourselves lucky. The county was also providing in-home occupational, physical, and speech/language therapy. We would do our best to provide the other fifteen hours of intervention by teaching ourselves the pertinent strategies or if necessary, privately paying for additional services.

I remained very hopeful during this transitional period. I thought of Peter like a tiny hummingbird, beautiful and full of energy but delicate and jittery. It was my job to protect him, to provide the sustenance and stimulation he needed to flourish and grow but within the boundaries of what his frazzled nervous system could handle. Dr. Federici thought that with intensive neurobehavioral rehabilitation, Peter could significantly improve, both in terms of intellectual capacity and functional behavior. The stakes were high but presumably within reach.

Committing to this goal meant substantially changing the tenor of our lives, and it wasn't always easy. At the completion of our first post-Boot Camp dinner, for instance, Pat's eyes danced with mischief, catching my attention. I knew exactly what he had in mind. He wanted to resume our after-dinner chant, "Abu De Abu Da." I loved the way the children would howl and scream as they banged their tiny palms against our farm table, Pat's furrowed brow relaxing whenever he joined the cacophony. But our home was a different place now, so I shook my head in disagreement. Peter didn't like loud noise. In fact, he could barely tolerate it. We simply hadn't known before—I thought Peter was howling and screaming because he enjoyed the cacophony, but I was wrong. It was just one of the many lessons that Boot Camp taught us.

Another lesson with which I struggled was the need to continue what I call "distance parenting." My natural parenting style centers on activities such as snuggling beneath a cozy blanket while watching a movie and making decorations during the holidays. I crave intimacy and love to the same extent and for the same reasons that Peter craves predictability and sameness: to make my world feel safe, beautiful, and secure. But Sunday morning snuggle sessions in front of the fireplace were not what Peter needed, at least not then. He needed me to be firm, patient, unyieldingly consistent, and unfettered at all times by his behaviors. It was a tall order for a mush like me, a woman who, embarrassingly enough, can be brought to tears by listening to *Annie's Song* while running errands in the car. It's also something with which I continue to struggle. The behaviors of both of our children at times seem purposely hurtful, leaving Pat to coax me out of my melancholy by reminding me that their actions aren't caused by callousness so much as impulsiveness and dysregulation.

When Peter and I began venturing beyond the confines of our eight-acre property, I at first limited our excursions to Peter's doctor appointments, which thankfully went without a hitch. His heart was fine, but the doctor put him on a yearly monitoring schedule because children with FAS have on average a 40 percent chance of having or developing cardiac issues. The ophthalmologist concluded that Peter's vision was normal but that his eye muscles were weak. It was something to watch and address if time and maturation didn't resolve the problem on its own. The only hiccup in the physician lineup occurred at the neurologist's office, where the doctor, who would become chief champion of Peter's health, reviewed Dr. Federici's report and conducted a thorough exam. A youngish man with a great smile and an unabashed love of children, he agreed with Dr. Federici's recommendation and ordered a twenty-four-hour ambulatory EEG to rule out any seizure activity. The process involved gluing a few dozen wires to Peter's scalp, attaching them to a recording device, and then lugging the contraption around for an entire day and night in a nylon backpack.

The entire ordeal sounded implausible to me. I had a hard time imagining how Peter or the rest of the family would cope with this. My initial reaction was "I can't do this," but I reminded myself that Dr. Federici was the one person who was capable of unraveling the mystery of our son, and he felt the procedure was necessary. Pat and I would have to find a way to help Peter endure yet another shock to his continuously overloaded sensory system.

The wires were scheduled to go on the following week. At the time, I didn't know that epilepsy could be present in the absence of obvious convulsions. Dr. Federici, and now Peter's new neurologist, were concerned that he was experiencing absence seizures, little spurts of unresponsiveness that can be mistaken, especially in children, for simple inattention or daydreaming. Depending on the frequency, children with this kind of disorder blank out for a few seconds without realizing it, missing vital words, gestures, and other information necessary to make sense of and interact normally with their world.

I mulled over this information in my head, again and again, as we left the neurologist's office. I didn't know whether I wanted Peter's upcoming test to reveal that he was seizure-free or seizure-impaired. It sounds horrible, but absence seizures are treatable, and both Dr. Federici and the neurologist explained that significant cognitive improvements are often seen once this kind of disorder is diagnosed and properly controlled with medication. Peter was already taking medication to control his behavior; the notion that his fuzzy thinking and lack of memory might improve with the addition of an antiepileptic held a certain undeniable appeal.

Peter was in a particularly good mood as we marched across the vast expanse of the medical center parking lot. It was breezy and surprisingly cool for early July, and I remember the luxurious feel of his little hand in mine, how he exerted just the right amount of pressure and refrained from squeezing too hard. Focusing entirely on the treat he knew would follow, he showed no interest in knowing why he was being hauled from doctor to doctor. Sometimes the treat was a lollipop or a coloring book, but that day I wondered whether he could handle going out for lunch. Other than the medical appointments, he and I still hadn't ventured out much. The gains made during Boot Camp had brought hope, real hope, to our family, and I was reluctant to risk losing even a smidgen of improvement. On the other hand, I yearned for human interaction and rationalized that our self-imposed solitude eventually would be breached anyway.

Heading home, we passed a sandwich, soup, and salad spot I had always wanted to try and so I turned the car around and told Peter we were stopping for lunch. The restaurant was filled with the working busy, and I had to negotiate our way through crowds of people in suits to find a table. I thought about leaving but didn't. Something about the mass of people was exhilarating, and I craved the sight of other adults. Once seated, I did my best to relax us both by engaging Peter in a thumb war, a game he usually enjoyed despite the physical contact required. "I win," he yelled, rocketing to his feet. I smiled in agreement and tried to get him to play again, but the commotion surrounding us was too much of a distraction. When he began the dreaded "da tee tee da da" refrain, fingers dancing in his face, I knew what was in store. This time I truly was about to leave, but then our waiter approached, a college-age kid with a goofy smile. He saw the panic rising in my face and assured me that nobody would notice a rowdy little boy during Friday lunch hour. "Relax," he said. "What'll you have?"

Realizing I had been holding my breath, my bangs fluttered as I exhaled and slumped against my seat. I ordered soup and a half sandwich for myself and peanut butter and jelly with apple juice for Peter. While we waited, I sang little songs to calm him. "One little, two little, three little Peters . . . four little . . ." Though far from normal, his eye contact was improving, and I beamed knowing that he was able to look at me, however briefly, while I sang. His ability to allow me to help calm him in a busy restaurant was further proof that Boot Camp had worked.

But right after the waiter brought our food, Peter began destroying his sandwich because the bread was too thick and generally just different from the kind I buy at the grocery store. I was about to stop the carnage when he stopped, looked up, and asked me a question. To my knowledge, Peter had never asked a question before. I put my spoon down, cleared my throat, and did my best not to act surprised. This was a major milestone. "Why Mama that man talk to Peter?" he asked. On the cusp of entering kindergarten, his words still were garbled and unclear, and he rarely used verbs or pronouns. I wasn't sure if I heard him correctly, so I listened intently as he continued. "Man is talking of me," he nodded anxiously. "Lady talk Peter. The whole place talks Peter."

It took me a while to make sense of what he was saying. I looked around and took in the dozens of conversations that were swirling around us. I hadn't noticed before. Like most people, I had tuned them out. But not Peter. He was communicating something important, a fact that made perfect sense and yet never occurred to me: my almost five-year-old son couldn't filter noise. We had been a family for nearly two years, but I only learned, that day, that Peter *hears* everything whether he wants to or not. It was a horrifying realization, a eureka moment in the middle of a popular restaurant. I stared transfixed at my son's face. For the first time since our relationship began, he possessed both the trust and tools necessary to confide in me, to let me know he needed help. Pulling some cash out of my wallet to throw on the table as I hopped from my seat, I slung him into my arms, his body stiff and resistant, and headed toward the exit.

I'm sure I looked like a madwoman darting from the restaurant, but I knew Peter needed help. He wanted me, *me*, to stop the pain and discomfort, the assault to his auditory processing system, and I would not let him down.

The first of many twenty-four hour ambulatory EEGs (Summer 2006)

Two days after the EEG, I received a call from the neurologist's office telling me that I needed to pack a few things and get Peter immediately to the hospital. As calmly as possible, the neurologist told me that Peter's EEG results indicated that he had experienced more than a hundred seizures while awake and even more when he was asleep. Vassar Brothers Hospital in Poughkeepsie has a pediatric video EEG ward that allows doctors to correlate EEG findings with changes in demeanor, movement, behavior, and responsiveness. They wanted Peter admitted immediately because of both the frequency and pattern of his seizures. Seizures that occur more frequently at night and are accompanied by developmental delays or regression can indicate an intractable and devastating type of epilepsy called Lennox-Gastaut syndrome. It was imperative that a diagnosis be made as soon as possible because every day lost to untreated Lennox-Gastaut equates to another day of brain insult that cannot be undone.

Terrified, I called Pat at his office and waited for him to arrive home. Peter's neurologist said that he would need an MRI before getting hooked up to the monitoring equipment and that he would remain hospitalized until a definitive diagnosis could be made, probably five to seven nights. The rooms all had DVD players and video games and controllers, and we were encouraged to pack favorite books, movies, toys, and puzzles. Thanks to the compassionate design of the ward, I would be allowed to stay with Peter around the clock.

A lump the size of an orange clogged my throat as I whirled around the house, preparing for this unexpected sojourn. Though I had been braced for the diagnosis of a seizure disorder, the possibility of a type of epilepsy that carried a devastating prognosis had not been considered. An hour or two later, as Pat drove the four of us to the hospital, thoughts raced through my mind. Would Peter be okay? Were seizures to blame for his bizarre and erratic behaviors? Would he continue to deteriorate until he became a mere shell of his potential, the promise of a fulfilling life forever and elusively beyond his grasp? My eyes filled with tears as Pat reached over and took my hand. I knew this would open the floodgates further, though, and I didn't want to completely fall apart in front of the children. So I calmly freed my hand. "I can't," I apologized. As always, he knew just what I meant, patting my hand as he wrestled to contain his own worries and emotions.

Our time at Vassar Brothers is mostly a blur, but bits and pieces, like stubborn sprigs breaking through a barren terrain, remain rooted in my mind. To begin with, the people who were in charge of Peter's MRI were not helpful. All agreed that Peter would need anesthesia, yet Pat and I could not convince the nurses handling our son to sedate him *before* they tried inserting an IV. Peter couldn't even tolerate tooth brushing, which we explained, but they were cocky enough to ignore us. Of course, they were wrong. Peter bit, flung, spit, kicked, and almost injured himself to avoid the IV needle. I was howling, Pat was livid, and our wild-eyed son was banging his head against the metal rails of a hospital crib. Finally, a nurse with some sense intervened and suggested that Pat take him into the MRI, where they would sedate him with a mask over his face and then deal with the IV. Isn't that what we requested in the first place?

The only positive part of that awful experience was the fact that the MRI showed no structural abnormalities. If the MRI was a sprint, the rest of the week was a marathon. Peter barely had survived the ambulatory EEG a few days earlier, and he responded to being hooked up again by acting like a cornered animal. He clawed and cried in protest. Thankfully, the woman who hooked him up was phenomenally skilled and kind. By the time the forty-minute procedure was over, she had him laughing. From then on, I did my best to put aside my considerable worry and focus on keeping Peter entertained and comfortable. Pat brought Sophie and Grandma at night, along with a little surprise or a couple of pints of ice cream. Somehow we made it through five long nights, the first couple of which were spent listening to the torturous screams of the poor child next door. Peter became so agitated and overwhelmed by the screaming that he waffled between rounds of banging tantrums and downright catatonia.

On the sixth morning, Peter's neurologist walked into the room and gave us the news we had been waiting for: he did not have Lennox-Gestaut syndrome. Peter suffered from common absence seizures, and, though they were occurring with astounding frequency, they were certain to abate with proper medication. Two hours later, Peter's wires were unhooked and we were on our way home.

Considering I slept about six hours over the course of the entire hospital ordeal, I reenergized quickly. To control the seizures, Peter began Lamictal, with the dose ratcheted up in small increments over time. The neurologist said we might see some behavioral improvements because the drug is also used as a mood stabilizer. That was good news too. For several weeks I carefully checked Peter's body for signs of rash, a harbinger of a potentially dangerous Lamictal-related allergy, but, other than that, our lives resumed and the rest of the summer unfolded more or less according to plan.

The revolving door of therapists required a large white calendar board to prevent me from double scheduling or, more likely, running an errand only to find a therapist waiting in our driveway because I had forgotten an appointment. Though we mainly stuck close to home, the world came marching to our son in the form of various professionals carrying plastic bins filled with the tools of their trades. I did my best to give Sophie the attention she needed while also trying to learn different techniques from watching Peter's therapists that I could implement myself. Sometimes a therapist invited Sophie to join in, which was a great relief because then my parenting attention felt less divided.

That summer I learned joint compression—how to sandwich Peter between couch cushions as if he were the hamburger and the cushions were the bun—as well as techniques to teach him to play. I also learned how to make a sensory box from uncooked beans and rice, littering them with coins, plastic dinosaurs, and other small treasures, and how to design obstacle courses that would promote motor planning and strengthen weak muscles.

Peter's ABA/VB therapist would become a friend and source of much needed support and advice. An older woman with a college-age daughter and a great sense of humor, she at first doubted the extent of Peter's problems, but nonetheless dove into her task with steadfast professionalism. She began by laying out a mat with a city design and placing rubber cars, buildings, trees, people, and houses in a pile. Then she asked Peter questions like "Where should the fire station go?" When he stared blankly at the mat or put the station in the middle of the town pool, she first made sure she had eye contact and then corrected, "The fire station goes here." Then she physically laid her hand on top of his and together they placed the station in the appropriate spot. This is called hand-over-hand assistance. "Now where does the station go?" she repeated. If he was able to point to the correct spot, or better yet, indicate with language, he received a reward: a preferred toy to play with or a token. At least from a mother's perspective, this is what constitutes verbal behavior: the asking and repetition of questions that require a child to process and sequence information until the task is mastered. To this day, I still interact this way with my son. "Peter," I say. "Please put your clothes in the drawer." And then, as he turns, I repeat, "Where do the clothes go?" With any luck, he'll answer, "In the drawer."

At other times she would have me hold one end of a blanket while she held the other, and we would swing Peter back and forth and side to side. One direction calmed him down, we soon discovered, but the other revved him up. She constantly interwove physical activities and more sedate ones, like using photos of different people to help Peter recognize emotions. "Which boy is sad?" she asked, holding up two pictures, one of a boy about to cry and the other of a child sitting happily in the grass. "The sad boy is frowning," she prompted, exaggerating her own facial expression. "Now which one is frowning?" And so it went.

Although Peter's needs were being met that summer, perhaps for the first time, truly, in his life, I worried whether Sophie was getting the attention and support she needed. Pat and I had devoted much of the last year, and at least the last six months, trying to figure out the peculiar cadence of our son's mind and actions. Most days, I fell into bed soon after telling the children good night. Keeping Sophie safe from Peter, and Peter safe from himself, was exhausting, unrewarding work. There was little time for more ordinary experiences that Sophie both craved and deserved. Like it or not, she was forced to conform to the same rigid schedule we maintained for Peter. Though we discussed it at great length, Pat and I could never come up with a plan that offered the flexibility to parent Sophie one way and Peter another. They were just too close in age, background, and proximity.

We tried to compensate for the inequities inherent in parenting a special needs child by having frequent outings to the local swimming pool, playground, and hiking trails, places we knew that Peter could navigate and that would provide Sophie with the physical outlet and freedom she needed. It wasn't enough—she needed so much more— but it was all we could afford. When one child is acutely ill or injured, the child with the sniffles must by necessity fall to the back of the line. She was too young for day camps, and I couldn't bear the thought of putting her in a summer day-care program. I wanted her home with us no matter how imperfect the environment or circumstances. I tried to find baby sitters and mother's helpers, but it was a futile task as one after another quit on us.

Another way I tried to engage both kids while always keeping an eye on therapeutic benefit for Peter was to invent crazy sensory opportunities. Peter was and still is a sensory avoider, meaning he's hypersensitive to physical touch. Sophie, on the other hand, was and still is a sensory seeker, meaning she craves input from physical sensations. Where I got this idea I'll never be sure, but one day I put the kids in their bathing suits and goggles, took them outside, and gave each of them a can of whipped cream and a bag of cheese doodles. I encouraged them to spray me as well as each other, and then we took turns flinging cheese doodles at one another in an attempt to get them to stick onto our bodies. Given the expression on Pat's face as he watched the spectacle from the back step, we must have looked possessed. Sophie laughed with unabashed glee, and Peter did his best to avoid the sticky, gooey mess, but, in the end, we all had fun.

Despite the hardships of that summer, the heartbreaking news from Dr. Federici, the seizure scare, and the almost constant presence of therapists, it was one of the happiest seasons of my life as Sophie and Peter's mother. For the first time in eighteen months, we were no longer alone. We had real help, real experts, making a difference in the life of our child and thus in our lives too. We said goodbye to the summer therapists, listening knowingly as they confessed that despite first appearances, Peter was one of the most complicated kids with whom they'd ever worked. Although kindergarten was around the bend and new challenges and obstacles awaited, I felt more confident than ever.

One day in early September, the kids and I were walking to the car when a soft rain caught us by surprise. Sophie laughed with delight, tilting her head toward the sky to catch any droplets, but Peter screamed. Pulling his hand away from mine, he was gone before I knew it. Though parked in a big, but mostly empty lot, I was scared because he was acting so erratically and had no innate regard for danger. Lifting Sophie quickly into the car, I ran after him. Bug-eyed and shaking, I one-armed him around the waist and hauled him back to the car, kicking and screaming. Getting him strapped into his car seat with all limbs flailing was a challenge, but I was becoming an expert at corralling unhinged preschoolers. After a minute or two, he calmed down and started rocking. Reaching his gaze through the medium of the rearview mirror, I apologized for acting roughly but explained that his bolting was not acceptable and had frightened me. When I asked what made him so scared, he looked at me puzzled, as though he couldn't imagine that I didn't already know. "Mama," he whispered, "the rain hurts Peter."

❧

SEPTEMBER 13, 2010. *These last few nights have been wide-open-window nights, a sure sign that autumn lurks around the corner. I lay awake, unable to sleep, my thoughts racing in seeming synchronicity with the breeze that tickles my hair as it gently spirals through the room, an uninvited but welcome companion. Rest eludes me, this time, because the head of special education is saber rattling, and not in a subtle way. Because we don't expect a ruling on our due process hearing before September 30th, our son's psychiatrist, who is well known and respected in the community, wrote a letter to the district requesting homebound services until the hearing process is resolved. She agreed to this course of action, in part, based upon Dr. Federici's recommendation. Under New York education law, the district is required to provide such services upon written request of a child's physician. But the head of special education is balking, trying to scare us with poorly disguised threats and vague, sinister language that conjures up images of truant officers and the reappearance of CPS. He's gone so far as to say that the fact that we are in the D.C. area today and tomorrow does not constitute "legal excuse for [our] children's absence." The fact that he's targeted both kids with this pronouncement, and not just Peter, isn't lost upon us.*

Our son has recovered substantially from the disaster of last year, physically, emotionally, and psychologically, and we have no intention of compromising his health and welfare by putting him in harm's way again. The double whammy of psychological abuse delivered at the hands of "educators" intent on turning him against us, coupled with the emotional damage and physical stress of having to sit through day after day of a curriculum that for Peter might as well have been delivered in Swahili, turned his brain to mush. Now that we know what really occurred last year, it's no wonder he came home raging every day and began suffering from visual and auditory hallucinations. Peter's mind is fragile, yet, as these past few months have proven, it's also incredibly resilient. Our son is healing, he's coming back to us, and, until this sordid affair is settled, home is not only where the heart is, it's where safety resides as well. So if the school thinks a nastygram or two can scare us into submission, they're sorely mistaken. Our child's life is at stake. Safeguarding who Peter's able to become—his soul, his happiness, his very potential—is our sacred obligation. It's an obligation from which we will not run and for which intimidation tactics are destined to fail.

I take a phone call during a break today from a new friend who lives in Minnesota. She too is an adoptive mother of Russian-born children and knows a thing or two about loss, love, and primal struggle. We have so much in common, it seems, but mostly we share an eerily similar tale of family dynamics. We're able to speak for twenty minutes about a number of issues, and the very sound of her voice releases some of my festering tension. We talk about how the Peters of the world, and their parents, have no organized voice, certainly no lobby power, and therefore little means to convince the decision-makers in their children's lives—be they social workers, educators, physicians, mental health providers, or clergy—of the extent of impairment. Because there are no established or widely accepted treatment protocols for post-institutionalized, alcohol-exposed children, those in a position to render decisions affecting our children's future tend to take one of three courses: (1) they treat our kids like throwaways—the most catastrophic approach; (2) they apply a one-size-fits-all mentality, which is dangerously simplistic; or (3) they borrow from other models, such as those developed for Down's Syndrome. Using Down's protocols to treat our kids, especially those with normal or above-average IQs, makes about as much sense as forcing a husky child into slim-fit jeans. Such a decision only makes sense in the absence of other options.

As my friend and I hastily say our goodbyes, I hang up the phone thinking about this predicament, how our lack of voice as a community and our society's lukewarm interest in our children's welfare are largely responsible for the grief and trouble our families have endured.

I want to break this cycle of tragedy, suspicion, and misunderstanding, in ways large and small. I want to help find a way to form a voice, a united voice, that advocates not only for our children, but for parents scattered across the country, well-meaning people who either suffer in silence or bear the unmistakable brand of righteous battles fought and lost. There's something terribly wrong when it's not safe for a nine-year-old boy to attend school, when lines in the sand are drawn not only from ignorance and indifference, but because there's no clear solution—no path toward recovery, that ordinary, everyday people can follow.

I know a little about how those "refrigerator mothers" of the 1950s and '60s must have felt as they tried to raise their autistic children in the midst of constant misunderstanding, accusation, and lack of science. Fifty years later, I'm still outraged on their behalf. They were unwilling pioneers (and victims) in a field not yet born. I wonder whether fifty years from now the science of raising FASD children will have made similar advances. Better yet, maybe we modern "refrigerator parents" can band together with courage and unity of purpose to eradicate the problem, along with the accompanying stigma, once and for all in our lifetimes. Now wouldn't that be something?

CHAPTER 25

MITOCHONDRIAL WHAT?

IN THE LONELY hours before dawn, I occasionally hear Jane Aronson's throaty, commanding voice echo through my soul. "You can heal the body, but not the brain." This statement constitutes a precautionary slogan that I now know should run like a ticker tape across adoption websites worldwide. She delivered this unwelcome but much needed wisdom in late August 2004, over long-distance lines between our hotel room in St. Petersburg, Russia, and her home in Maplewood, New Jersey. We wouldn't meet Peter for two more months yet, Pat and I still in the throes of trying to understand what was wrong with the baby we called Ben.

A few years ago I learned that another American family adopted "Ben" shortly after we turned him down and set about the cruel task of erasing all evidence of the intersection of our lives. I've heard through the grapevine that he's as impaired as Dr. Aronson predicted, but I take solace in knowing he's receiving better care and more love than a Russian orphanage ever could have provided.

Like so many other things in life, including our encounter with Ben, we soon realized that taking Peter to Dr. Federici was not the end of our problems, but rather a new beginning for our family. Peter's neuropsychological report, thirty pages thick without attachments, became dogeared, underlined, scribbled on, covered in stains, and creased from constant use and reference.

Boot Camp saved our family, there is no doubt, and we owe an enormous debt to Dr. Federici for his expertise, compassion, and continued commitment to improving our son's prognosis and our family's future. But it wasn't and never will be a magic bullet. The weeks that turned into months and then into seasons were riddled with many of the same challenges that we grappled with before and that we will most likely struggle to understand and cope with for the rest of our lives. FAS is permanent brain damage, an unscalable wall of misfiring neurons and erratically wired impulses that imprisons its victims in a perpetual state of disability.

I never appreciated what living with an FAS child meant until we brought Peter into our home and lives. On the one hand, Dr. Federici helped us discover that our son possesses a truly beautiful heart. When we were alone together for an entire day not too long ago, I asked what he thought we should do. I was thinking along the lines of going for a walk or riding bikes. "Whatever you want, Mom," he replied. "You like the antique places, maybe we could do that," he said with a smile. "I just want to be with you." Oh, how my heart soared, as it always does in these transcendent moments, the impossible difficulties slipping away in favor of these delicious, joyful moments. Never in my life could I have envisioned reaching the point where Peter might suggest antiquing as a pleasant way to spend an afternoon. Our triumphs are enormous, we have earned them together, and they deserve celebration.

But then inevitably, the reality of coping with his many disabilities returns, often with bruising, unforgiving intrusion. For instance, ten minutes after Peter made his endearing suggestion, I asked him to use the bathroom, a request that can be greeted with grumbling or even outright hostility. When I realized he'd been closeted in the bathroom off the kitchen much longer than necessary, I knew to check. What I found was a sink filled with chunks of splintered bar soap floating atop a sopping wet hand towel. I don't know what he intended exactly, but urinating in the toilet wasn't topping the list. My catching him in the act set off a chain reaction of explosive temper that culminated in his violently shaking the glass shower door, throwing his eyeglasses against the wall, and spending time in his room. Once there, he continued the rampage by banging the walls, stomping the floor so violently that the house rattled, and then lifting and dropping the top end of his metal-framed bed until he physically was spent.

Mystic, CT (Spring 2008)

I've more or less learned to accommodate these wild swings of mood and action and so has Pat, though to a somewhat lesser degree. The intensive therapy made available to us the summer before Peter started kindergarten ended abruptly when he became school age in September. In New York, the county transfers special education responsibilities to the local school district once a child enters kindergarten.

For the next five years, Pat and I would battle principals, special education chairpersons, teachers, school psychologists, school nurses, and various other service providers, such as occupational and speech therapists, to obtain the kind of intervention that Peter needed to improve his brain function. We did this at enormous cost to our health, finances, careers, reputations, and sanity. To this day, I believe the infrastructure of Peter's mind might function more smoothly if he had continued to receive the level of services provided by the county. At barely five years old, Peter's brain was still highly elastic, meaning that damaged parts were capable of self-repair if properly stimulated, and that healthy, intact parts also could have been trained to take over and compensate.

This kind of neurological rewiring, however, does not come free of charge. Applied Behavior Analysis/Verbal Behavior (ABA/VB) is one way to coax the brain into reorganizing itself, but there are other methodologies that can be equally effective, depending on the child. Neuro-cognitive rehabilitation is expensive, time-consuming, and requires a great deal of professional training to implement correctly. Although it would take years, literally, for us to regain from our school district the level of services we lost that summer, we did have one ace in the hole. Her name is Lindy, and at the time she was in her twenties working to earn her master's in special education with an emphasis in ABA/VB. Today, she is dually certified as a special education teacher and a behavioral analyst, and she is an integral, much-loved part of our family.

Sometime between Dr. Federici's visit and the start of the school year, I began searching for someone to work with Peter on a private-pay basis. My efforts eventually paid off when I received a call from the chairperson of the College of Education at SUNY New Paltz. She told me there was one student she thought might fit the bill, but she had no idea what she was doing or whether she was available. With a little effort, I tracked Lindy down, and, fortunately for us, she was looking for a new family to help because the child she had been working with for years had just been placed in a residential autism school. In many ways, it was kismet.

Although Dr. Federici gave us invaluable information and a blueprint for action, Lindy gave us direction, hope, expertise, and an occasional respite. She began working with Peter toward the end of the summer, as many as four afternoons a week. Like everyone else, she at first underestimated the extent of his problems. She confessed this to me a few years ago after we had just weathered a particularly difficult meltdown that involved end tables flying across the room. Within six months of joining Team Peter, she realized that not only was her newest challenge significantly impaired, but that it was nearly impossible to identify patterns and triggers in his behavior and responses because he was so different day to day, hour to hour, and sometimes even minute to minute.

Tall and slender, Lindy keeps her curly brown hair pulled tight in a ponytail or bun and mainly dresses in close-fitting athletic outfits. After we knew each other a while, she explained that the autistic preschoolers she worked with during the school day had a penchant for pulling hair and ripping clothes. She had learned to take precautions. Having grown up under bumpy circumstances, she also keeps her heart closely guarded. Wary of adults both young and old, she pours her considerable energy and intellect into the autistic children, to whom she is fiercely devoted. Lindy understands the autistic brain better than anyone I've ever encountered. Temple Grandin, the well-known autistic writer, professor, and animal behavior specialist, once approached Lindy at a conference, singling her out in a crowded room like a hawk circling its prey. It seems Dr. Grandin instantly recognized Lindy's innate ability to understand what autism feels like and therefore was eager to speak with her.

We joke about it now, but the first few months with Lindy were all business all the time. When we began asking her to stay for the occasional dinner, she often said she couldn't, but sometimes she would falter and mumble, "If you want me to stay, well, I guess I could." Though we took her ambivalent answers to mean yes, we also knew she needed to be added to the list of people under our roof in need of help with trust and attachment. Today, more than five years from the summer we first met, we still encourage Lindy to move in the direction of openness. Given that she now calls us Mama and Papa, I think the effort has brought rewards.

Lindy organizes Peter's mind in a way that Pat and I never have been able to master. Their classroom is the basement playroom and our expansive, rural backyard. Pat and I designed a room just for Lindy, in fact, when we decided to finish the basement in our current house. It's a simple room with soft lighting and neutral walls, and it's sparsely furnished with a table and chairs, a futon, and a single bookshelf. She uses the room for table work, listening to books and songs on CD, and for playing educational games. Among her bag of tricks is a token board, a timer, a box of art supplies, a weighted vest, and a whiteboard nailed to the wall. In between sedentary activities, they use the playroom to create obstacle courses, practice walking on stilts, jump in the inflatable bounce house, swing on the indoor swing, or do various exercises with a therapy ball. When the weather's nice, most of the physical activity gets taken outside.

As with virtually all strangers and acquaintances, Peter tried to jump into Lindy's arms whenever he saw her. Though she found it difficult to accept, she was understanding and respectful when I explained that Dr. Federici cautioned us strictly to limit hugs and kisses to immediate family members. In those first weeks of kindergarten, she and I would wait for him together in our driveway, waving as the minivan that transported Peter to and from school came into view. Sophie usually would still be upstairs, taking her nap. We often found him comatose across one of the benches, the demands of the day more than his fragile mind and body could absorb. I would rouse him as I chatted with the elderly bus driver, urging him off the bus as if he were a stowaway drunk, while Lindy continued waving her big, exaggerated wave, intent on getting Peter to notice her and reciprocate. Even now, at age ten, he still greets nearly everyone with the "Lindy wave," an endearing, humorous gesture teetering somewhere between a parade float wave and a distress signal.

One Sunday afternoon, when we were in a Sports Authority buying sneakers for the kids, Peter stopped dead in his tracks and screamed. Pat was milling around the store absent-mindedly but sprang into action at the first shriek, reaching our panicked son before I did, and I was only a few yards away. Whisking him up without first investigating, Pat ran straight for the sliding glass doors. By the time Sophie and I caught up, Peter was beginning to come out of his trance-like state and had begun crying. "Peter no see, Papa," he wailed. "All the things went away. Peter no see." Pat and I stared at each other dumbfounded. Peter is difficult to question, even today, because he often can't articulate his thoughts, but after numerous attempts, Pat and I concluded that he had suffered some kind of temporary vision loss.

We were terrified, of course. The next day I made an appointment with a pediatric ophthalmologist in Albany. I told Lindy about the strange incident that afternoon and asked whether she ever had observed anything remotely similar. Her answer surprised me. Although she hadn't noticed any visual disturbances, she had been noticing some shakiness and weakness in his legs. After some discussion, we agreed that Peter didn't look quite right—he had dark, purple circles under his eyes, his hair seemed thinner, and he was tiring too easily for a child his age.

I think I was so focused on treating Peter's cognitive and behavioral problems that I overlooked some obvious physical symptoms. When we first brought the children home, improving their physical health was our only objective. Treating them for latent TB infection, giardia, rickets, and severe malnutrition topped the list of priorities. Despite Peter's stagnant growth those first six months home, he thereafter grew nearly a foot and gained over twenty pounds. Sophie's physical transformation was nearly as impressive. New clothes and shoes were worn for weeks or even just days at a time instead of months, and I celebrated each next size up as the victory that it was. But late that summer in 2006, just as autumn was inching toward the Hudson Valley, green leaves beginning to crisp at the edges as overnight temperatures dropped, I was forced to acknowledge that Peter was transforming too. A slow but undeniable wilt.

Though this would not always be the case, the pediatric ophthalmologist at the time found nothing abnormal about Peter's vision. Still, he listened closely as Pat explained our concerns. Although I normally took the kids to their appointments, Pat gave me a break on this one. Putting dilation drops in Peter's eyes was not going to be a picnic, and, as we feared, he had to be held down. When the two of them returned home, Pat explained that the ophthalmologist suggested we take Peter to a specialist in Albany who might be able to help. The eye doctor was as concerned as we were that something wasn't right.

I delayed making the appointment for a few weeks, however. I'd had enough of hospitals, labs, and doctor's offices, and I knew my son felt the same way. Barely five years old, Peter had been poked and prodded more times that summer than I had in my entire life. Pat and I hated the idea of putting him through more, so we decided to push bedtime up and make sure he was eating enough. Boot Camp may have cured Peter's habit of vomiting during meals, but he was still a fussy, often petulant dinner guest, one of those kids who simply doesn't enjoy eating.

But then the breathing thing happened. Checking on the kids before I went to bed, I tiptoed into Peter's room and stopped dead in my tracks. He was sound asleep, cocooned as usual under his blanket and quilt, but breathing rapidly, very rapidly. After pulling Pat up the stairs to have a listen, I fumbled for my watch to measure his respiration rate. Not trusting my calculations, I tried counting again and then asked Pat to do the same. Our results more or less matched. Peter was taking approximately sixty breaths per minute, highly abnormal according to my quick Internet search. A day or two later, the nurse from Peter's school called to say that he again was experiencing bouts of rapid breathing and a higher than normal pulse rate.

I made the appointment with Elaine Schulte, the pediatric specialist in Albany, that afternoon. I was happily surprised that she could see Peter sooner rather than later. By the time the appointment arrived, Peter was also experiencing bouts of unexplained sweating and night sweats severe enough to drench his bedding and pajamas. On certain days, and without discernible pattern, he would be too exhausted to run and play in the yard. Even on cool days, there were times when even the slightest physical exertion resulted in his being covered in sweat. When I asked him what was wrong, he almost always replied that his legs felt wobbly and his head hurt. I'm not sure whether these symptoms were unfolding one after another before our eyes or whether they had been there, in lesser form, all along. I do know that the storm in Peter's head had calmed significantly, allowing us to see through to other problems a little more easily and without constantly dodging flying objects.

Explaining my concerns to Dr. Schulte was a bit daunting because his symptoms were all over the board and intermittent, and I couldn't say for certain how long they had been present. It didn't help that Pat and I had no idea what conditions or diseases might be lurking in his genetic makeup. I drew lines across entire pages of the pre-appointment paperwork, scribbling "n/a, adopted." Luckily, Dr. Schulte is an adoptive mother herself. She understands all too well the added worry that results from not knowing your child's medical or birth family history. Also, like Jane Aronson, she has a keen eye for detail and a reputation for unraveling complex medical problems. She is so adept at what she does, in fact, that several years ago the prestigious Cleveland Clinic recruited her to become the director of its international adoption program.

Having already guessed (correctly) that Peter had autism and FAS, I thought myself quasi-qualified to guess the nature of these bizarre medical ailments. I shared with Dr. Schulte, only somewhat sheepishly, that I was concerned Peter might be anemic and/or suffering from diabetes. Of course,

I was making a fool of myself. To this day, I appreciate her tactful response, suggesting that we run some blood and urine tests and take care not to jump to any conclusions. Talking in soothing tones as she examined him head to toe, she noted, as others had, that he was tactilely defensive and particularly unwilling to undergo a genital exam.

"Any confirmation of sexual or physical abuse?" she asked as Peter writhed in protest on the examining table. "We're not sure," I began. I did my best to explain what Dr. Federici had explained to us—namely, that we'll never know the answer to those questions because the brain "files" extreme neglect and deprivation the same way it registers or "remembers" sexual or physical abuse. In other words, regardless of the cause, Peter responds like an abused child. Nodding her head knowingly as she worked to calm my frightened, uncomfortable son, I felt more confident that bringing him to yet another specialist was the right choice after all. One thing I've learned from our journey with Peter is that many pediatric physicians, no matter how well-trained or well-intended, just don't get post-institutionalized children. Add FAS to the mix and they might as well throw their hands in the air and retreat. It can be a very frustrating experience, to say the least. That's why the Jane Aronsons and Elaine Schultes of the world are so vital to and appreciated by adoptive parents.

We left Dr. Schulte's office that afternoon with the name of a pediatric geneticist, Darius Adams, who also practiced at Albany Medical Center, and her promise to be in touch as soon as the lab results came back. She wasn't able to offer an explanation yet regarding Peter's symptoms, but she clearly had a hunch. Though worried, I felt we were in competent hands. "We go to Donald's now?" Peter asked, bouncing his way down the catwalk toward the parking garage. Sometime around the TB scare, I began taking Peter to McDonald's as a reward for tolerating doctor appointments and blood draws. I honestly had no idea back then that we'd become such frequent visitors of medical establishments. "Sure," I agreed, quickening my step to keep pace. The mom who rather naively vowed to spare her kids the dangers of fast food was becoming an ardent believer in the palliative effects of a Happy Meal.

Dr. Schulte called a few weeks later to give us the results of the lab work and to encourage us to go ahead and make the appointment with the geneticist. Peter's blood and urine contained numerous abnormalities that indicated potential problems across multiple organ systems. She went on to explain that she was concerned about a possible genetic problem involving his mitochondrial DNA.

I listened dumbfounded while she rattled off phrases like pyruvate-lactate ratio and carnitine deficiency. "Mito what?" I finally hiccupped, not grasping the news. I vaguely recalled that mitochondrial DNA was passed from mother to child because I once watched a program about hemophilia and the Romanov royal family where this type of genetic testing was used to identify successive carriers in the bloodline. The rest of what she said went in one ear and out the other. Although I had never heard of mitochondrial disease, the clip in her voice told me that I would soon need to become a lay expert on the subject.

She was kind enough to speak with me again the next day, patiently recounting what I was too shocked to process the first time. According to Dr. Schulte, Peter's labs were suggestive of a mitochondrial disease, which in simple terms is a disorder of energy production. She wasn't in a position to name which of the nearly three-hundred different types of dysfunction he had. Nonetheless, she felt strongly that his strange constellation of symptoms—seizures, muscle weakness, gross motor problems, ptosis (droopy eyelids), vision disturbances, developmental delays, headaches, and bouts of rapid breathing and heart rate—in all likelihood were part of the same disease process. As I would later learn, mitochondrial cells are responsible for converting food into energy to power our various organ systems, including the heart and brain. The range of possibilities discussed on the Internet was too vast to grasp, but an hour of Googling told me that Peter's lab results were no small concern. Many mitochondrial diseases are fatal and many others are degenerative, drastically reducing both life span and quality of life. In addition, the field of mitochondrial medicine is still brand spanking new; it didn't exist thirty years ago, so diagnostic and treatment protocols are still in their infancy.

In less time than the seasons take to change, Pat and I would learn that our perplexing but plucky son suffered from FAS, autism, a mood disorder, epilepsy, PTSD, various learning disabilities, and now, perhaps most damningly, a potentially life-threatening genetic disorder. Making the situation even more confusing was the fact that many of Peter's "mitochondrial" symptoms could be explained by some combination of his other already-diagnosed conditions. Finding out that we would have to wait four months to see the geneticist was almost more than we could stand.

❧

October 6, 2010. *Two days ago I received an e-mail from the school district's attorney, with a copy of the hearing officer's decision attached. We won. Across the board, on all counts, and on all points. Even though we shouldn't need the outside verification, it's rather satisfying to read that a neutral third party doesn't think we're nuts, or crazed parents, or unrealistically looking to our public school to provide Peter with a designer, top-of-the-line, private-school-caliber program. We were looking for the district to adhere to the require-ments of state and federal law, and to respect our rights under the same, as parents. I can't say the last three years of sparring with the school have been worth it—the manufactured abuse charges, the lies and coverups, the damage to our son's fragile mind and bewildered heart, as well as the substantial collateral damage to our daughter, which we're only now fully beginning to appreciate. But winning cer-tainly helps.*

Regardless of whether the school district appeals, for us, it's over. The day after tomorrow, Peter will start his new school, a program that will provide him one-on-one learning and life skills training within an intensive, neurocognitive rehabilitative framework. It's a day that's long overdue, but hopefully not too late. Lindy asked him yesterday whether he was excited about starting the new school. "I don't want to go," he replied. The next part is what made my heart skip and my eyes well. When she asked why not, his response was simple and matter-of-fact. "Cuz I want to stay home with Mommy." Wow! How very far we've come, the two of us. Last night I looked back through my journal and reread some of the entries I wrote just a little over two years ago. Though I haven't forgotten the all-encompassing sense of hopelessness, rage, and absolute chaos that daily life with Peter entailed, those worries no longer hold me captive. Never could I have imagined then that our son could ever feel, much less absorb, the love for him that I've fought so hard to first find and then instill. My words feel awkward today, I know, but I think it's because my heart's so full. Peter's courage, his vivacity and plucky determination, have touched so many lives, and, of course, transformed my own.

Yesterday I received a call from a woman who lives about an hour south of us. She raises golden retrievers, has an autistic child, and has been following our story. Her dogs, which sell for about $1,200 apiece, are bred specifically with mellow temperament and family companionship in mind. This complete stranger wants to give Peter one of her female pups. To top it off, the call came on the same day that I spoke to our vet about whether the time has come to say goodbye to our crotchety but cherished Jack Russell terrier, Scout. At fifteen and a half, she's deaf, incontinent, uncomfortable, and very disoriented. Her quality of life is diminishing quickly, and I worry that we may be keeping her alive for selfish reasons. I don't know when her time will be up, though it's likely to be soon, and it's something Pat and I dread. I also don't know whether we'll be able to bring the new pup into our home, despite how eerily fated and connected this chain of events feels. For me, the love and companionship that our pets provide outweigh, several times over, the undeniable labor involved. I'm a true animal lover, and, though it may sound silly or perhaps even juvenile, the very presence of our pets shores me up, helps me feel less homesick when those moments come, less alone, more needed, and yes, more unconditionally loved. But I don't think Pat feels the same, and I can't much fault him. We have so much on our plates, and for him a puppy means work (which it is), added stress, and everything else that goes with the territory.

But still, even if we end up declining this incredibly generous, almost fortuitous offer, I'm grateful beyond description. The fact that Peter, and his story, has touched so many lives gives me hope, real hope, that we'll be able to heal the hurt that's been hidden so deep inside Sophie, a hurt that's only now beginning to surface, and one we only barely understand. Our cherished little girl has the tenacity, stubbornness, and the agile mind of a Jack Russell terrier. In fact, Pat and I often joke that she and Scout must be biologically related. She has all the right stuff, so I have to believe in my heart that she can overcome these troubles. As I quietly relish our victory over the school, all the while preparing for Scout's farewell, Peter's new school experience, and Sophie's worrisome struggles, I reflect on how far we've come, as individuals and as a family. I hope love continues to blossom in our home, despite setbacks and emerging issues, or the inevitable loss, now and then, of one of our much-loved furry friends.

CHAPTER 26

OVER THE RIVER AND THROUGH THE WOODS

TIME SLOWS TO a crawl when waiting to learn whether your child has a serious illness. My imagination drifted unyieldingly toward horrible possibilities and a growing sense of dread throughout the wait. Although Peter's appointment with the cardiologist went well and no abnormalities were found, the visit did not quell my growing anxiety, because the doctor told me he was glad to have a baseline on our son should his cardiac status change in the future. They were ominous words impossible to ignore. Explaining that children with FASDs are at much higher risk of developing heart-related health problems, he added almost apologetically that the possible addition to the mix of a mitochondrial disease increased the risks many times over. What I wanted the cardiologist to say was that Peter's heart was in ship shape and that there was no reason for us to return to his office. Instead, he put Peter on a six-month follow-up cycle that would need to be adhered to until he was at least eighteen.

Having no choice but to keep an ever-vigilant eye on his health, Pat and I put Peter on the small van to kindergarten every day. Though grateful to have the break from his behaviors and demands, I worried he lacked the stamina and skills to handle the pressures of a busy, noisy classroom. Almost daily, Peter confirmed my worst fears, barreling from the van into our home like a wild bull. Eyes bulging, he'd catapult himself about, nonsense words bellowing through the halls as he alternated between laughing hysterically and screaming as if he'd just seen a ghost. On the days Lindy was there, she'd whisk him into the sunroom to calm him with joint compressions or other sensory-calming tricks. Sometimes it worked, sometimes it didn't. There were days when he stuffed the toilets with garbage and scratched our leather furniture with his nails, as though he were inoculating his fragile mind and sharpening his talons for the next day's battle.

During this time period we constantly battled Peter's behaviors, histrionics we felt were a direct consequence of his overstimulating school environment. Although we had no problem getting him classified as a student with a disability, and thus eligible for special education services, we were at odds with the school district from day one regarding placement. Insisting that he was a good fit for an integrated classroom, they placed him against our wishes in a combined kindergarten/first grade with a single teacher and one aide. The teacher was dually certified in both special and regular elementary education, a neat little fact that allowed the district to justify having only one teacher in an integrated classroom when New York law requires two.

The result was a combined class with more than twenty-four special education and mainstream kids, including a blind child, a Down's child, four children on the autism spectrum, two or three with other disabilities, and Peter. The classroom itself was adorned from floor to ceiling with colorful, twirling mobiles, reflective posters and other pinups, and various artwork and photographs. The space was so visually overwhelming that it reminded me of the "It's A Small World" ride at Disney World. Because it was both a mixed grade and integrated special education classroom, the children worked in groups, more or less at their own pace, moving from station to station throughout the day for their various lessons. In addition to the visual overload, the schedule was orchestrated like a spirited game of musical chairs. While one group of children worked on reading, another might be doing a craft or shouting out the names of coins. ("Nickel!" "No, it's a penny!") The district might as well have stuck our son in the middle of a tornado.

There was no ABA, no special programming for any of his disabilities, no anything. The accepted educational protocol for children with FASD recommends that classrooms be modified so that they're plain and uncluttered, sparingly adorned, with neutral colors and soft lighting, and, above all else, quiet and orderly. I don't know whether parents of the mainstream children felt the magic, but all we experienced was the inevitable aftermath of Peter spending six hours a day in a taxpayer-funded amusement park.

Summer 2008

That fall was the beginning of what would become a years-long struggle to find a school or program that even arguably could meet Peter's needs. His IQ and range of abilities and disabilities, not to mention his psychiatric issues, render him unique in the educational world. He doesn't fit nicely into any category and never will. He is too high-functioning for the kinds of programs designed for the mentally retarded. But by the same token, he lacks the memory capacity, the processing ability, and the language and life skills necessary to navigate a classroom filled with kids coping with mild to moderate learning disabilities, such as dyslexia or even Asperger's. He's the square peg forever being pushed with stubborn resolve into a hopelessly round hole.

The federal law that protects children like Peter, the law that protects each learning disabled child's right to receive a free and appropriate public education designed individually to meet his or her unique needs, is a land-mark piece of legislation. Called the Individuals with Disabilities Education Act, or IDEA, it requires schools to modify the curriculum and the class-room to meet an eligible child's individualized educational and psychosocial goals. What it doesn't do—and I can appreciate why—is grant disabled chil-dren the right to gold-standard programming. Instead, schools need only show that their programs are "appropriate," that they offer a "continuum of services," and that their classified students are making "reasonable progress" toward their individual goals.

During the entire first semester of Peter's public school education, Pat and I repeatedly were told that the district was only required to provide the educational equivalent of a Ford, not a Cadillac. The district's team of educators and administrators remained unswayed by our assertions that Peter was deteriorating before our eyes, losing a little more of the gains made over the summer as each overtaxing school day passed. They blamed his after school behaviors on poor parenting and insisted that Peter was making significant progress in the classroom. We butted heads so many times that we eventually hired an educational attorney to represent us. Dr. Federici had made clear that there was a window of opportunity in which to make significant rehabilitative brain improvement, and we knew that Peter's window was closing fast. The elastic ability of the brain to heal itself, to forge new pathways of functionality, begins to close around ages seven or eight and becomes nearly closed around ages twelve or thirteen. In all respects, we felt the oppressive weight of time. Peter was already five and a half. Although we had secured through the county a summer of ABA/VB services, and were providing what we could afford through Lindy in the afternoons, the school was sabotaging our efforts.

About the time Peter's genetics appointment arrived, Pat and I made a life-altering decision. Charging us over $10,000 to attend a few meetings, write a few letters, and eventually throw up her hands, our lawyer gave up. She angrily proclaimed that never in twenty-five years of practice had she dealt with a more ignorant, obstinate, unreasonable, and unprofessional group of people. She suggested we move to another school district if we re-mained committed to improving our son's cognitive potential. Although we had the option to file for hearing, which essentially entails suing the school district, she pointed out to us that such a path would cost at least $40,000.

The icing on the cake, she said, was that given the current budget climate, there was no real likelihood of prevailing.

Keeping in mind that Sophie would start kindergarten the following fall, we took our attorney's expensive advice, cut our losses, and put our 1733 Dutch Colonial "forever home" on the market. We began looking at houses and property in Red Hook, a quaint village across the Hudson River from where we lived. I knew from my years teaching at Bard College that the school district there was among the better ones in New York state and certainly the best in our region.

We met Dr. Adams, the geneticist, in early spring. By then, Peter's physical symptoms, for the most part, were holding steady. Because his seizure medication was still being adjusted, it often was difficult to tell whether changes in his stamina or level of alertness were a medication side effect or something more. Not wanting to stress the children, Pat and I limited our house-hunting excursions to school hours. The morning of the genetics appointment, we must have looked at three or four houses before picking Peter up for the hour drive to Albany Medical Center.

I was so shocked by what we heard in Dr. Adams' office that afternoon that I never have been able to recall what houses we saw earlier that day. First, he confirmed Dr. Federici's FAS diagnosis, which was no surprise. But after examining Peter's lab reports and giving him an exam that included his walking up and down the hall and performing a number of other easy physical tests, Dr. Adams sat us down and gave us a crash course on mitochondrial disease. Essentially, he advised us to seek a diagnosis because our son showed all the classic symptoms of a mitochondrial problem. He explained that families sometimes wait several years to get a definitive answer, and many never get an answer at all, because the available diagnostic tools are new and relatively crude in their ability to pinpoint a single disorder among so many hundreds of possibilities.

The best chance of securing an accurate and relatively quick diagnosis, we were told, was to obtain a muscle biopsy from Peter's thigh. We could travel to one of two clinics in the country that processed fresh muscle biopsies, which have the highest rate of diagnostic success, or we could have the procedure done locally and have the frozen sample shipped to one of them. Regardless, the procedure would not be easy on Peter as it involved taking a square inch of muscle from one of his thighs. Further, there were no guarantees that a muscle biopsy, whether fresh or frozen, would give us any answers.

Flying to another state to put Peter under general anesthesia for the purpose of wresting a chunk of muscle from his unblemished thigh, with no guarantee it would yield any answers, held little appeal. In addition, Dr. Adams explained that there really was no treatment for these diseases, only management of symptoms and secondary complications, such as cardiac involvement, should they develop. Finally, in terms of prognosis, he told us that Peter could slowly get worse over time, he could improve, or he could suffer a "catastrophic" event. I admire and respect Dr. Adams, but how are parents expected to live with that kind of prognostication? Why would anyone tell distraught parents that their child could suddenly drop dead, especially when that child only has symptoms and some funky lab results, not a definitive diagnosis?

Pat and I left the appointment stunned. Gripping a script for additional blood and urine tests, we trudged back to the parking lot with Peter in tow. February in upstate New York can be bitterly cold. Peter yelped as the elevator doors opened onto the parking deck, the wind stinging his defenseless face. On the drive home, Pat and I mulled over the fact that Dr. Adams strongly felt that a diagnosis would benefit Peter because new drug and treatment trials were popping up all over the country. With a diagnosis, we stood a strong chance of getting our son enrolled in one.

In the end, we agreed to the procedure but only because he already was scheduled for surgery to remove his tonsils and adenoids. One hospital stay, one general anesthesia, two different surgeons. Coordinating their schedules, convincing the ENT and the general surgeon that one surgery was more humane than two, no matter how personally inconvenient, was a monumental task that took considerable time and coaxing. The biopsy would have to be analyzed frozen, not fresh, but the psychological and physical trauma to Peter would be minimized. By the time the surgery day arrived, we had moved across the river to Red Hook in hope of a better special education experience. The decision would prove financially disastrous—the real estate market collapsed a few months later—but we thought it was a necessary step on our path toward some semblance of educational salvation.

So on September 5, 2007, Sophie started kindergarten and Peter was placed in a first-grade inclusion class with a one-to-one aide. His first-grade special education teacher had experience with FAS kids and knew firsthand the kinds of struggles we dealt with on a constant basis. That fall and winter, Peter experienced three episodes of what Dr. Adams described as "metabolic strokes" while at school. His teacher told us that he would become unresponsive for a few minutes, drooling and listing to one side, and then he'd slowly return to a more wakeful, though disoriented state. He seemed to spike a fever during these interludes and remained lethargic, weak, and confused the rest of the day. There were days his legs were so weak that he couldn't walk. He pulled himself along the floor like a drunken snake, and Pat and I would carry him up and down the stairs and help him to a chair or the couch.

When I flew to Atlanta that spring with the kids to attend our niece's high school graduation, Peter had another episode. By this time he was gaunt and often listless, and Pat and I were terrified that our son was deteriorating slowly before our eyes and we were powerless to stop it. A frantic call to Dr. Adams staved off our whisking him to the ER, because he said there was little doctors could do other than make him comfortable and keep him hydrated. Dr. Adams suggested I feed him milkshakes with protein powder, to give his slumping metabolism a boost, and keep a close watch on his respiration and heart rate. I don't know whether the milkshakes helped, but at least I felt like we were doing something.

We returned to New York with Peter in a wheelchair, but within two days he was stronger and able to walk again. Why these episodes happened, and how his body was able to overcome them, remains a mystery. A few months later, when the muscle biopsy results began trickling in, we learned that the entire effort largely had been futile, leaving Peter with a traumatic memory and a two-inch scar for no good reason. The sample had gone to two or three different labs across the country because different pathology methods were used to test for different groups of mitochondrial disorders. Half of Peter's biopsy went to a lab that, as it turns out, used a contaminated medium, rendering his sample, and thousands of others across the country, useless. It was a devastating blow because Peter's symptoms and blood work suggested that the kind of disorder he suffered from fell into that lab's purview.

The other test results were ambiguous. One indicated nothing out of the ordinary, and the other "pointed to" the possibility that Peter had a disease called Mitochondrial Depletion Syndrome, which means his mitochondrial cells functioned normally but they reproduced and replenished abnormally. In other words, old cells were dying at a faster rate than new cells were being produced. After a while, this has a snowball effect. The body simply cannot produce the energy necessary to keep the organs running because the total quantity of mitochondrial cells continuously declines. Literature indicates that children diagnosed with this condition do not survive beyond age seventeen.

With the sound of my heart pounding in my ears, I strained to listen to what Dr. Adams was saying on the phone. The diagnosis wasn't definitive. We could get a new, fresh muscle biopsy to shed more light on the situation. Geneticists really don't know how many people are living with a mild form of this condition, so try not to panic about the grim statistics. Though there is no treatment, exercise increases mitochondrial cell production, so make sure he receives physical therapy and stays as active as possible. Keep him on a high-fat diet and pump as many calories into him as he'll tolerate. Enzyme supplementation and vitamin therapy benefit some kids. New tests and treatments are being developed every day. Hang in there.

The only good news that came from this conversation was the realization that Peter was actually improving by the time Dr. Adams' grim forecast reached us. His neurologist had put him on a new drug, Periactin, to control his headaches, which he felt were migraines, and to increase his appetite. Always eager to look at the whole picture, he knew Peter had some sort of metabolic issue, whether mitochondrial or otherwise, and he also understood that kids with FAS in general have a hard time maintaining weight. He felt that stimulating Peter's appetite would help his functionality no matter what the cause. As it turns out, he was absolutely right. Risperdal, Abilify, and Lithium, drugs notorious for their weight-gain side effects, never had any impact on Peter's appetite or weight. But taking Periactin twice a day not only curbed his debilitating headaches, it precipitated his using a phrase we had never previously heard: "I'm hungry."

As the weeks went by, I learned to accommodate Peter's suspected disease and accept the fact that we might never know for sure what was plaguing our son's physical health. Pat and I spoke at great length about the utility of taking Peter to Cleveland or Atlanta for a second, fresh muscle biopsy, and in the end we decided against it. If Peter had this disease, there was nothing to be done anyway. Even his doctors grudgingly began to appreciate the fact that we were being asked to continually subject our son to a needle-in-the-haystack investigation that might benefit medical science but would bring little, if any, relief for our child or us.

For this reason, we never have been able to pin down the exact cause of Peter's mitochondrial and/or metabolic issues. After living in a state of near panic for several months, wondering how long Peter might be with us, or whether a period of cognitive regression was a normal part of his highs and lows or a more sinister signal, we received another phone call from Dr. Adams. Baylor University had come up with a blood test to quantify the amount of mitochondrial deletion in kids like Peter. It was an important breakthrough in the burgeoning field of mitochondrial disorders. This test would tell us whether Peter was destined to decline rapidly or whether his body could hold its own for the foreseeable future. More importantly, it didn't require scalpels, anesthesia, or travel. The test cost over $2,000 to perform, and it certainly wasn't covered by our insurance, but Dr. Adams assured us that Albany Medical would foot the bill.

When the results of the blood test came back, after endless weeks of waiting, I didn't know whether to laugh or cry. The part of the muscle biopsy that wasn't ruined by contaminated chemicals indicated there was a genetic abnormality that affected the way in which Peter's mitochondrial cells replicated. But according to this brand-new, breakthrough, $2,000 genetic blood test, Peter's mitochondrial cells were replicating normally. So what did that mean? Did Peter have Mitochondrial Depletion Syndrome? Did he have a different mitochondrial and/or metabolic disease? Or did he not have a mitochondrial problem at all? Dr. Adams couldn't tell us. He just didn't know. This was a new test, and the consensus was that it was a definitive test, but the muscle biopsy results could not be ignored and neither could Peter's symptoms and other blood work. In other words, after almost two years, we were back to square one.

Today we watch Peter for signs that he's not getting enough calories, try to make sure he takes in plenty of fats and gets adequate rest, and resist letting our imaginations wander into dangerous territory over whether and when our son might rapidly deteriorate again. The fact is he's generally healthy, at least for now. He doesn't have the stamina that other kids his age have, his muscles twitch and he can sometimes become shaky and exhausted with even modest exertion, but he's holding the course. Periactin and a high-fat diet are key to maintaining his health, and we hope and pray these tools continue to give Peter what he needs to grow and move forward in life. Other children and their families struggling with mitochondrial disease have not fared as well. We should, and do, consider ourselves lucky.

ᘍ

OCTOBER 25, 2010. *Happy Adoption Day to us! Six years ago today, we vowed in a Russian court of law to love and cherish two orphans now and forever known as Sophia Katherine and Peter Thomas. I think we've done a pretty good job honoring that pledge, if I do say so myself. I've read so much about adopted kids' struggles with identity, grief, and loss, how they so often wind up thinking they weren't wanted by their birth parents and were merely a consolation prize, of sorts, for their adoptive parents, couples who, like us, may have dealt with infertility. How my heart aches for these children, and how I hope ours are able to work through those doubts and realize just how much they are prized. Sophie and Peter are my heart and soul, the reason I fight battles with impassioned zeal, when necessary, and celebrate our triumphs, big and small, with fervent enthusiasm. They are why I constantly practice becoming the mother and role model they so deserve, and why I crash, sometimes hard, from the exhaustion the effort so often produces. But despite the hardships that litter the course, theirs are the only faces I see whenever in a quiet moment I escape into the private recesses of my own thoughts and envision a more traditional means of forming a family. If they had been ours from conception, I like to believe life would be easier for them, and also for Pat and me, but then maybe that's nothing more than lousy fiction and fanciful thinking. Our children are who they are because of the myriad influences in their lives, both pre- and postnatal. Their pasts are as fixed and unalterable as the color of their eyes, and yet still we fight to help them shed the heavy cloak of their early experiences. And that's okay, I suppose, and certainly our obligation.*

But today we celebrate not who our children were but who they are and might become, who we are together as a family, and how fortunate we are that technology, an increasingly global community, and timeless desire have brought the four of us together in a wonderfully unconventional union that sustains itself through hope, determination, humor, and humility. No one is perfect in our family, least of all me, but we are improving, individually and as a unit. One of the great gifts that the kids, especially Peter, have given Pat and me is the desire to stretch the limits of our patience, to deepen our capacity for kindness, and to strengthen our collective will to succeed, allowing us to overcome obstacles that once seemed too formidable realistically to even broach.

Six years ago, Peter constantly screamed at me whenever I came near or even risked establishing eye contact; otherwise, he occupied himself by repeating the same bit of gibberish over and over, like a scratched vinyl record. This time four years ago, Peter was spitting on me, stealing my most cherished possessions, vomiting purposely at the dinner table, and injuring himself and Sophie, sometimes without any provocation. He had no inkling of how to approach or interact with other children. Two years ago, he still didn't trust us, his speech was still nearly indecipherable, his muscles ached so badly there were days he couldn't walk, and he was more or less kicked out of Irish step dance, karate, tennis, and swim lessons due to behavioral concerns and intolerant instructors. Now, at age nine, Peter is a polite and happy child, and he looks to us, especially me, for support and guidance. He's mostly healthy, and he's finally in an appropriate school setting. He has an amazing best friend, and he plays soccer on the weekends. On our Adoption Day six years ago in Birobidzhan, I dreamed so many dreams for Peter, but then, as reality set in over the weeks and months that followed, I watched these dreams fade into the obscure darkness of terrifying diagnoses and my own wild imagination. How remarkable, then, to see them resurrected, not perfectly envisioned the way only dreams can be, but played out on the real stage of our lives, accomplishments fought for and won, affections systematically sought and acquired, skills always, always, a work in progress but now with a more predictable, reassuring, forward momentum.

    Don't get me wrong. There's nothing perfect or even "normal" about our household, not even close. Peter's needs are enormous and require constant supervision, intervention and vigilance. Even our Happy Adoption Days are difficult, especially for Sophie, a fact I used to discount as mere coincidence. Thanks again to Dr. Federici, I now more clearly understand that she struggles deeply with profound issues of preverbal trauma and that she misbehaves, actually sabotages this particular family celebration, not so much out of spite or ugliness, but out of fear, confusion, and insecurity. Today's intended celebration is no exception, but given how far we've come with Peter, I know we can help her too. In fact, Peter intervened directly today to ease my growing discontent over Sophie's reaction to this milestone. As she was fussing over this and that and everything in between, Peter took the time to write me a note. It read: "Sary mommy I hope y fele beter." Then he drew a heart with a smiley face below the writing. He may not know it, but my precious little boy gave me the best Happy Adoption Day gift I could ever hope to receive.

CHAPTER 27

DUE PROCESS

I ACTIVELY RESIST the temptation to view our journey with Peter as a series of epic challenges, one after the next. But the effort to identify the cause
of and put a name to his medical concerns seemed to fly on the wings of our
earlier effort to obtain a better educational placement. There are days where
I wonder when Pat and I will be allowed to stop riding the roller coaster
of crises and settle into a more predictable existence. On the other hand,
there are days when I realize that our lives are richer, more deliberately led,
because of the obstacles we've overcome. My son had no future before 2004,
and today he's getting the help, love, and support he needs and deserves.
We simply can't afford to take a break from our quest to give him the tools
needed to grow into the loving, kind, better-connected person we know
he's becoming.

Our last major battle came not in the form of hospitals or moving vans,
but draped in the fundamental principles of fairness, justice, and integrity.
Perhaps it's fitting that as a lawyer, I eventually would be called upon to defend our family and advocate for Peter before a hearing officer in what's called
a due process hearing. As I've mentioned, The Individuals with Disabilities
Education Act (IDEA) is a federal law that guarantees the right of disabled
children to receive a free, appropriate, and public education. In this context,
"appropriate" means an individualized program tailored to address a dis-

abled child's unique educational, physical, social, and emotional needs and created hand in hand through a partnership with the child's parents.

This is a wonderfully forward-looking law that has many of the ingredients necessary to revolutionize special education in American public schools. Passed in 1997 in large measure as a result of parental outcry over having their disabled children sequestered from the general student population, its power is invoked today as both weapon and shield. Because the IDEA was enacted to liberate disabled children from self-contained schools and classrooms, the law requires school districts to meet these educational mandates within what's called the "least restrictive environment." This means that mainstreaming educationally disabled children is presumptively the best placement option. And for most, I believe this is the right course. I appreciate how mainstreaming children with disabilities is preferable where there are adequate supports and accommodations in place to help special education students succeed in that environment.

But the reality is that the Peters of the world do not and cannot succeed in a "modified" regular education classroom. Instead, they fall through the cracks, landing all too often in an educational abyss where they're propelled through the public school system not by improvement or achievement, but by carefully orchestrated scripts and paper trails designed to create a record of legal compliance. Pat and I endured four long years of watching Peter stagnate, and often regress, under the guise of integrated special education services.

Every marking period we were told how much progress Peter was making. By the end of third grade, his teachers even suggested that he understood what an obtuse angle was and could explain the basic principles of electricity. When asked at home about an obtuse angle, he told us confidently that it was the name of one of the characters in *The Lion King*. He referred to Abraham Lincoln as Hamburger Lincoln Log and said that President Obama was a slave that died in a grocery store but now lived with George Washington. Concepts, principles, and facts whirled randomly about his overloaded brain until they came rushing out in contorted spurts of meaningless rant. No one at school, other than his first-grade teacher, had done anything to help our son sort through the mass of information fed to him, conveyor-belt style, on a daily basis.

After four torturous, overstimulating years of "inclusion" education, our son could barely count on his fingers and was reading on a beginning kindergarten level, which meant he really wasn't reading at all. It was a crime. Peter learns differently, certainly, but he can learn. Watching him struggle to write simple words on a piece of paper was torture, for both parents and child. Homework assignments inevitably ended in tantrums, with pieces of broken pencil flying like shrapnel across the kitchen.

The experience finally became unbearable when Pat and I found out his third-grade teacher was taking his soiled clothes home at lunch to wash so we wouldn't find out that Peter was wetting at school. According to the school, Peter couldn't be mainstreamed if he was incontinent, and because the school refused to send him to a more appropriate program, despite our numerous pleas, they made sure that the appearance of continence was maintained. Of course, to carry this off, they had to wager that Peter would be unable to rat on them. The same group of people who sat across from us stone-faced, meeting after meeting, asserting that our son's language skills were close to normal were nonetheless counting on his profound language impairment to help them maintain the coverup.

The question of Peter's deteriorating behavior and growing psychiatric instability was another major concern. With no behavioral management plan in place, not to mention appropriate programming, the school's solution to the problem was to physically remove him when he became too disruptive or overcome with anxiety and let him babble or run in circles around the school grounds with an aide. Coming back every afternoon to our highly structured home, with rules and expectations in place to help him self-regulate, was akin to having a household of kids return from an overstimulating day at Disney World and then expecting them to get down to business, immediately, with homework and chores. It was a setup for full-blown revolt.

Luckily, there is a provision in the IDEA law that affords parents a right to have concerns about their child's special education heard before a neutral third party, called an independent hearing officer. Although not as formal as a trial, both parents and the school can call and examine witnesses, submit supporting documentation, such as academic and neuropsychological assessments, and testify directly. This quasi-trial is called a due process hearing; it's intended to interject principles of fairness and justice into a bureaucratic system steeply stacked in favor of school districts.

Our due process hearing began in the middle of June 2010 and concluded nine long weeks later. The decision was issued by the hearing officer in early October. Though we did solicit the help of a nonprofit education attorney, I conducted the majority of the hearing and did the vast amount of legwork that went into it. Pat transformed into the paralegal and document assistant I desperately required to keep up with the mounds of exhibits being proffered on both sides, and, by some grace of God, we fumbled our way through the murky, often funky waters of special education law that fateful summer. It wasn't pretty, and I made mistake after mistake, sometimes with humiliating consequences that the hearing officer frequently highlighted, but we made it through.

Lindy with the kids

Armed with three separate neuropsychological assessments by Dr. Federici spanning a period of six years, as well as solid documentation and testimony by Lindy, Peter's home teacher, regarding what our son actually could or could not handle academically and socially/emotionally, we chipped away at the district's well-greased and smug defense.

Lindy kept meticulous notes regarding Peter's abilities, including periodic assessments of whether he could reproduce at home any of the work the school sent home or otherwise claimed he had mastered, and I laid them out for all to see. Dr. Federici's reports and direct testimony further cemented the fact that Peter was not learning and could not learn in his current placement, and, perhaps even more damning, that the district actively was causing him harm, academically, emotionally, and psychiatrically.

In short, we did our best to illustrate that Peter wasn't accessing any of the curricula, that he was actually regressing as a result of the inclusion setting, and that the district systematically took extraordinary, collusive, and at times immoral steps to suggest otherwise in an effort to protect their own self-interests. Peter's school had put all of us through hell, and Pat and I long ago had reached the tipping point in terms of our desire to play nice.

The straw that broke the camel's back had occurred two months earlier, when the school psychologist, we believe, reported us to CPS after learning that our request to have this person removed from Peter's team, due to various incidents of what we viewed as serious misconduct, had been granted. The CPS investigator would later tell us that he had never seen such a clear case of school retaliation in his thirty-year career, and when asked whether a particular school psychologist had filed the report, he simply responded, "How did you know?" It was a horrible time for Pat and me, and one we appreciate could have had a disastrous outcome had a less-seasoned investigator been in charge. The district wasn't fighting fairly, that much was evident, and it was time to take off the boxing gloves and come at them with a few punches of our own.

On more than one occasion, the attorney for the district cried openly in response to my hammering of her clients during the proceedings, leading the hearing officer to order adjournment so the opposing counsel could pull herself back together. During one of these breaks, the hearing officer drove to the neighboring town of Rhinebeck and used his cell phone to snap a picture of former President Clinton, in town for the wedding of his daughter, Chelsea. It's no wonder that this process, dripping with vehemence on both sides, consumed the entire summer.

Legally challenging the wisdom of your local school district in a town the size of Red Hook is an unpopular move. Red Hook residents (sometimes called "Red Hookers") are proud of their school and of the education their children receive. In fact, if Sophie were our only child, we might well be waving the same flag of solidarity and good fortune. There's little argument that Red Hook knows how to provide quality education to children who are developing normally. It's quite possible that it even knows how to adequately educate special needs children whose disabilities are addressable and fit squarely within the parameters of an inclusion setting. But Red Hook didn't and doesn't know squat about helping our son. However, bringing this undeniable fact to the district's attention, as well as that of the larger community, is a socially isolating decision and one with which we still grapple.

Despite numerous pleas, only three socially minded friends, including my old director and dear friend at Bard, showed up at any one of the numerous hearing days to support our efforts. No doubt that's why their show of allegiance and their straight-backed, eyes probing, in-search-of-the-truth body language still resonates in my memory.

As the proceedings finally concluded in late August, it became clear that the hearing officer would not render his decision prior to the start of school. It also was clear that the district intended to force our hand and send Peter to the fourth-grade inclusion class pending the outcome. Having promised Peter (and ourselves) that he would never set foot in that school again, we hunkered down for yet another skirmish. Ominous letters were sent from the district threatening legal action if we continued to keep our son from school. In response, I scrambled desperately to obtain the paperwork to illustrate, if necessary, our intent to provide home schooling. If the police showed up at our door, I needed to be ready.

Otherwise, Peter and I spent the four weeks it would take the hearing officer to render his decision reading books from the library, working on life skills, and just enjoying each other's company. In the afternoons we picked up Sophie from school, often among a sea of stares, some judgmental and others sympathetic. Despite the obvious hardships, this time of turmoil and uncertainty also turned out to be a window of opportunity for deeper bonding between mother and son. By age nine, Peter finally was beginning to grasp, and believe, that Pat and I were his protectors and that our chief mission in life was to keep Sophie and him safe. Despite our efforts to shield both kids from the particulars of the hearing, they knew there was a fight and Peter knew he was the focus of it. But he also knew, perhaps for the first time in our lives together, that we were firmly and resolutely in his camp.

We weren't optimistic about the hearing's outcome, as we were well aware that parents rarely prevail, especially in the midst of today's very real budget issues and other political realities. The IDEA law provides due process for parents, but the threshold necessary for schools to show that they're meeting a particular child's needs is so low that most districts' actions, no matter how deficient, survive legal challenge. Furthermore, hearing officers are compensated, and sometimes chosen, by the school districts themselves. The system can work fairly, and sometimes does, but there are certainly no guarantees.

As it turns out, though, our case was one of the exceptions. For the first time in the district's history, the parents prevailed. The hearing officer concluded that Red Hook had failed to provide Peter any meaningful education for the entire three years that he had been enrolled there. It was a victory for our son, our family, and the larger community of children and families living with the effects of FASD and post-institutionalization. After the decision was published, phone calls and e-mails came flooding in from lawyers and advocates across the country, congratulating us on accomplishing something that had remained elusive for so many: namely, successful advocacy for the unique educational rights of those with FASD, as well as for children whose minds and hearts have been crippled by orphanage care. To quote the decision of the hearing officer:

> I find that the parents are entitled to compensatory services based on the denial of FAPE [free and appropriate public education] for the 2008–2009, 2009–2010, and 2010–2011 school years. As indicated above, despite the overwhelming evidence that P.L. is a very complex child, with significant educational needs, the District failed to offer P.L. an appropriate program for three consecutive school years. For all the reasons set forth above, I find the District's inclusion class is not the appropriate educational setting for P.L. *Red Hook Decision*, p. 31 (October 4, 2010).

The hearing officer ordered the district to send Peter without delay to a nearby autism program that emphasized data-gathering and taught academic subjects and life skills on an individual basis. For the first time in his life, our son was afforded the opportunity to walk into a classroom—composed of five other boys, a teacher, and two aides—where he didn't have to struggle to fit in or even just survive the day. This classroom, finally, would be built to fit Peter.

∾

DECEMBER 3, 2010. *I've not written in my journal lately because I don't know how or whether to put into words the events of the last few weeks. The good news is that our lives are back to normal again, at least relatively. The bad news is that Pat and I, and perhaps even the kids, glimpsed a reality regarding Peter's future that we had never allowed ourselves to consider before. To put it bluntly, Peter fell off the sanity wagon for a few days, without precursor or other obvious explanation. It was the scariest experience of my life, and it's left me a little shell-shocked. I don't want to rehash the details, the particulars of those few days that are now branded into the consciousness of our lives, and so I won't. But I will describe some of how the incident has left me feeling.*

Suffice it to say there was a break, a sudden, catapulting crack in the fragile chemical balance that is our son's brain, his personality, his heart, his very identity. Fortunately, it lasted only a few days, because with the help of some pharmaceutical intervention, bam! He was back. A little dazed, a little more confused, but he was with us. All of this happened the week before Thanksgiving, a time when I'm usually preparing for our annual twelve-hour road trip to Blowing Rock, North Carolina, where my family gathers for the holiday. We weren't sure we'd be able to go, because stabilizing Peter, and keeping him stable, was our main priority, but his recovery was faster than his descent, which is remarkable. We aren't quite clear about what happened, and we're still waiting on some test results, but his psychiatrist thinks he experienced a manic episode.

I know my siblings were worried about our coming for Thanksgiving, for Peter, and for themselves. The news that his psychiatrist cleared him for the trip—she actually thought it would be restorative for us to proceed as originally planned—was received ambivalently. It seems that no one, not even my family, wants to insert himself or herself into the maelstrom of a mental health crisis. Peter's problems, and Sophie's too, have a way of pulling Pat and me slowly but inevitably away from the comfort and easy companionship of friends and family. Our daily lives, aside from attempts to stay solvent, are filled with doctor's appointments, therapists, psychologists, special education, strict routine, and therapeutic parenting.

    While in North Carolina, I caught up on all the comings and goings of my many nieces and nephews, all of whom I cherish. One is heading to Australia for a college semester abroad, another just got her driver's license, and a third is a foot taller since I saw him last March. Their lives, and the lives of the others, are proceeding more or less according to plan and with great expectations for their very bright futures. My children's lives are proceeding too, with accomplishments that dwarf by comparison those of even their most accomplished cousins, but their achievements aren't as obvious, and Pat and I have had to move mountains, always, to further even the smallest progression. And it's taken a toll, a fact never as obvious as when I'm with my siblings, who are immersed in the important and blissfully ordinary business of making sure their kids get into a good college, have nice friends, are well-traveled, and learn to navigate different kinds of social and professional circles. Theirs is the world in which I grew up, but it's not the world our children will occupy, nor is it a life to which I'll ever return, and therein lies the rub.

    I don't know what our children's futures hold—I don't allow myself to envision an outcome beyond self-sufficiency, intact self-esteem, and hopefully the capacity to give and accept love. Sophie is an amazing child whose talents could take her to heights she's never imagined but whose skeletons rattle her confidence and cloud her way. Peter has a beautiful heart but a damaged brain, and he's more vulnerable, I realize, than I ever allowed myself to believe. I hope and pray he never loses his capacity for love; beyond that, his future is uncertain. Maybe the uncertainty is what drives my present melancholy, that and the growing feeling of loneliness that continues to gnaw at me. I miss my family so much, and yet I worry that there may be more than just geographical distance coming between my siblings and me. Our lives have become so different that I wonder whether we are losing the glue that is our commonality. Pat knows I'm struggling with this, the unacknowledged gulf that's growing like a lazy tumor due to our difficult circumstances and the isolation that it breeds, and night after night he holds me tight to let me know that he's there, and that he always will be. He is single-handedly nurturing my sanity these days and I cherish him for it. He appreciates as well as I that my siblings can no more understand, for instance, the extent of the trauma we've endured with the school district, or why we lack the money to pay our income taxes, than I can presently fathom the freedom that their lifestyles afford.

On the heels of Peter's breakdown, I craved more than ever the companionship of my siblings. I was homesick in a way I haven't felt in years. But in North Carolina this past week, in the summer home of my childhood, where I always felt safe and supported, I was genuinely lonely. It's not their fault; my family's done nothing wrong. In truth, and maybe in part because I'm the youngest, I worship, adore, and admire each of them more than they will ever fully appreciate. I'm just seeing reality a little more clearly these days.

As we prepared to head back home, I had the strange sensation of looking into the window of normal life, my siblings' lives, and catching only a flickering glimpse of memories formed long ago, back when I naively believed a true heart and conscientious mind were the only ingredients necessary for building a fulfilling life. Though the camaraderie of shared experiences and common interests, as well as the comfort it offers, permeated the air around me, what I so yearned to grab hold of this Thanksgiving seemed impossibly past my reach, and eons beyond my current circumstances. Our son's challenges are fixtures in my life with which I clearly still need to come to terms. I've made a lot of progress, but there's more to go. My post-Peter life will never resemble my former life, but it's rich in love and purpose all the same. I have to remember that and work on new ways of embracing what we have rather than dwell on what we've lost, or what will never be.

CHAPTER 28

GREEN CHIMNEYS: A CHANGING VIEW

DESPITE WHAT SOME have called a historic victory against our school district, it wasn't easy for me, and especially Pat, to let down our guard and relax. This was true even though Peter began his new school without incident. For a few months, our home and lives, along with the easier, more predictable routines we settled into, seemed to magically normalize. Sophie was less anxious and more relaxed. Peter was proud of the work he was doing, of his small but noticeable strides toward continence, and he enjoyed his new friends, who were much like him. His need for constant supervision, for one of us to act as his external brain around the clock, never lessened, but at least he didn't embark on a rampage every time he returned from school. That alone was a blessing worth counting.

The holidays came and passed and I accepted a part-time teaching position at Marist College in nearby Poughkeepsie. I was beyond ready to pour some of my nervous energy into endeavors other than parent advocacy, to close the book on the roller coaster nature of our past and commit to a gentler, more predictable future. As I would soon learn, however, there were still plenty of obstacles ahead, formidable hurdles fully capable of thwarting any and all efforts at starting this new chapter in our lives.

In short, Peter lost his tenuous grip on reality sometime in early 2011. Like a gentle swell that stealthily transforms into a crashing wave, our son began showing increasing signs of a very fragmented, fractured mind. His ability to distinguish fiction from fantasy had always been fragile, but that January, a near total decompensation took hold. The phone calls, e-mails, and notes from school illustrated, with increasing intensity, his teacher's concerns over Peter's erratic behavior and her ability to keep him safe. He was bolting from the classroom without obvious cause, and it sometimes took a flock of adults to find him hiding in places like a janitor's closet or under the desk of the school principal. He was hearing voices and seeing things, such as the Grinch and a group of men he said were "robbers," and this caused him to grow increasingly terrified of being alone. His teacher also reported that he would scream in class without provocation, as though utterly terrified, and would often verbally, and sometimes physically, incite the other boys.

The same kinds of behaviors were happening at home. One day in the parking lot of Target, he began screaming. Wrestling free of my hand, he threw himself so forcibly into the side of the car that he bounced off like a rag doll into an agonizing heap of hurt on the pavement. His only explanation was that he was being chased. Another day I found him swinging a baseball bat at our cars, all the while screaming that he would not let "them" win. No matter how many calls and emergency visits we made to his psychiatrist, there was nothing we could do to relieve his tormented condition.

Eventually, he was admitted to Four Winds Hospital, a psychiatric facility about an hour south of our home. It was both the hardest decision of my life and one that brought unexpected, perhaps even unwanted, relief. Peter spent the majority of the intake interview babbling incomprehensibly while alternating between attempts to climb the walls and slithering about the floor like an epileptic snake. He was nervous, I realize, but he was also experiencing psychosis. There just was no way around this conclusion. Afterward, while we waited, Pat feeding Peter one snack after the other to keep him calm, I called my brothers and sister and took some comfort in hearing their voices, one by one, as I sobbed uncontrollably into the phone.

The afternoon we took him to Four Winds marked the beginning of an undeniable change in my view of Peter and our role in his life. The atmosphere of our home transformed instantly the minute Peter was absent. When we got home that night, exhausted, cried dry, and worried not only about Peter but also Sophie, whose apprehension over learning of her brother's hospitalization was palpable, we knew the house felt different. Definitely lighter, as though the accumulated stress of our lives had flown from the windows in synchronized measure to the rushing swoosh of the car as we sped down the Taconic State Parkway toward the hospital.

That night I began to truly accept, for the first time ever, that maybe Pat and I weren't capable of providing Peter's needs 100 percent on our own. It was the start of a horrifying but necessary revelation. We had been hearing this litany for some time, from Peter's mental health care providers as well as from Sophie's therapist, who was unshakeable in his assertion that our daughter would never resolve her past trauma in the midst of the chaos Peter's constant presence brought. But now we were beginning to share their viewpoints.

Early Fall 2010

Three months and two lengthy hospitalizations later, Pat and I began to integrate the idea into our everyday working lives. I had spent the last seven years working to find a solution to Peter's problems but was now faced with the realization that in many ways they couldn't be fixed. The staff at

Four Winds told us that our nine-year-old son was the most complex child they had ever treated, acknowledging further that he was only slightly more stable both times they discharged him. A week or two after Peter's last discharge, when he tried to jump from his second-story bedroom window (Sophie heard the noise and alerted Pat), the hospital declined to take him back, claiming they lacked the staffing to ensure his safety or that of the other patients.

We were clearly at a crossroads. We had fought the school district and won, but the victory now seemed hollow. Perhaps we should have brought our legal challenge earlier, when Peter's brain was more pliable and capable of healing. Maybe by the time he enrolled in the autism program the damage was too great to be reversed or substantially altered. I don't know. What I do know is that his psychiatric issues were snowballing in both momentum and weight, leaving us powerless to reverse the course and with few viable options.

All the professionals who had been involved in Peter's life over the years agreed that it was time for us to face the need for residential treatment. The young boy we liberated from an orphanage in Russia, a child whose love and trust took years to cultivate and nourish, was being discussed as an attractive candidate for reinstitutionalization in the State of New York. It was a hard pill to swallow. Although we had batted the idea around in our heads over the years, especially during heightened times of stress and frustration, we had never seriously considered the possibility.

And yet there it was, a list of residential schools we were expected to consider, laid out for us on the table to mull over like items on a Chinese dinner menu. Sophie's therapist went so far as to gain our reluctant permission to allow crisis intervention services into our home. Customarily, these services are utilized in a community for the express purpose of keeping a troubled family together. In our case, however, crisis intervention was sought so that a social worker could come into our home, observe our routines and methods used to corral Peter and keep both kids safe, and disabuse us of the notion that we could stay our present course. I remember the social worker asking Peter, upon meeting him, that if he could make one wish come true, what would it be. She posed this question after enduring my twenty-minute monologue about our son's virtues and our various parenting accomplishments. After considering the question for several seconds, Peter looked straight into her eyes and replied flatly, "To not have parents."

To this day, Pat and I refer to those gut-wrenching weeks of uncertainty and looming decision as our "reverse intervention." In the end we relented, or, perhaps more accurately, surrendered, to the unpalatable conclusion that keeping Peter at home was not in the best interest of the family nor was it helping to move him forward. We had brought him as far as we could on our own. The time had come for us to broaden our support system and allow others, even strangers, into the interior fabric of our lives.

Peter later apologized for the comment, which I knew had sprung from his feeling like a cornered animal. He knew that he wasn't doing well and that lots of frenetic activity was occurring because of it; he felt threatened. His apology tore at my heart even more than the insult because, despite how lost he was in his own psychiatric storm, he cared enough about our relationship to mend what he knew was an unkind remark. A few short years ago, I wouldn't have dreamed such a moment possible—the bites, scratches, kicks, and insults abating only through the inevitable process of his body and mind succumbing to exhaustion, and never with so much as an inkling of purposeful reflection or regret. I was terrified that this fragile but growing connection between mother and son would fray as a result of enrolling him in residential care.

Once we had made the decision, however, I forced myself to stay the course. Pat and I had spent countless years second-guessing our parenting abilities, the nature of our love for Peter, and our commitment to family. We had been through hell and back any number of times and were still nursing battle wounds, despite our ultimate victories from the CPS investigation and the due process hearing. Sending Peter to a residential school on the heels of lengthy, torturous hospitalizations would require more fortitude than all our past challenges combined.

In the end we chose a residential treatment facility and school called Green Chimneys in Brewster, New York, which is about an hour's drive from our home. After we knocked the breath out of our school district in the hearing, the anticipated battle with the district over placement and payment never occurred. Peter would enroll as a residential student in June 2011.

Green Chimneys has a sprawling campus that has evolved over the years to meet growing demand. Originally begun in 1947 by Dr. Bernard Ross as a small private school intent on having typically developing children interact with farm animals, it grew over time into an oasis for kids requiring more specialized care. Today the campus is recognized worldwide as a model for reaching children with behavioral, emotional, and developmental delays through therapeutic animal-assisted therapy. The nonprofit organization's stated mission is to "develop a harmonious relationship between people, animals, plants, nature and the environment through an array of educational, recreational, vocational and mental health services."

More importantly for us, the population of the school has evolved over the years to include not only troubled kids considered "at risk," but a growing percentage of children on the autism spectrum and at least a dozen or so kids adopted from Russia. As we spoke with staff, it quickly became apparent that they understood how to embrace the Peters of the world, as well as the challenges, heartaches, and triumphs faced by parents desperate to reach them. In addition, we felt Green Chimneys was attractive because it had a Health Center staffed with registered nurses, pediatricians, psychiatrists, a dentist, and other health care providers. Given Peter's health issues, the availability of full medical services was a comforting and necessary attribute.

It's impossible to walk around the two-hundred-acre campus and not run into something furry or feathered. The campus is brimming with farm animals and wildlife, and the children who attend the school—one hundred residential students and more than eighty day students—interact with them constantly. There is an indoor pool as well as a sizable lake suitable for swimming, fishing, canoeing, and kayaking. The kids grow their own fruit and vegetables in the campus garden and operate a country store in the summer, offering their harvest for sale as well as various knickknacks they create in art and woodworking class.

Through these activities and more, the children learn respect and self-reliance, improve self-regulation, and develop crucial daily living and interpersonal skills necessary to transition back to the home and eventually into adult life. They are paid for the work they do on the farm and in the garden, and their "salaries" are put into a college savings account, with a little reserved for personal spending. Children with continence issues like Peter are put on strict, around-the-clock toileting schedules. Other daily living skills, such as showering and dressing, are practiced with the same level of commitment and repetition.

The folks at Green Chimneys also appreciate the fact that idle time is the worst enemy for children who struggle to self-regulate and modulate their own behavior and emotions. For this reason, kids at Green Chimneys are kept physically active and mentally occupied from the moment they wake up until they make their drowsy bedtime calls to parents. A busy, active campus, it pulsates day and night to the pervasive rhythms of positive reinforcement, growth, and healing.

The day we brought Peter to Green Chimneys, knowing he would be living in a dormitory with seven other boys with various special needs, ranks among one of the most difficult of my life. Pat's mother came with us for moral support, and we brought Sophie too because we felt that showing her the school and Peter's newly decorated private bedroom within the dorm, along with the rest of the state-of-the-art facilities, would help allay her substantial anxiety.

We entered the Health Center on Peter's first day hauling three bulging bags filled with clothes, shoes, stuffed animals, photos, books, and toys, all carefully marked "PL" for identification and safekeeping. Peter looked like a lost lamb when we said our goodbyes. There were no tears or clinging hugs, but I knew to search beyond the façade of our son's stoicism and see into his heart, where so many of his feelings stay hidden. He was scared and nervous, and I did my best to let him know that his worries were normal and would lessen with time. He would not be allowed home the first month, as per Green Chimneys' transition policy, but we were permitted to visit and speak on the phone as often as desired.

It would take me some time to overcome the enormous fear that on some fundamental level I had failed our son. Three rocky months of psychiatric hospitalization culminating with placement in a residential treatment facility is not the storybook ending I once envisioned for our family. I tormented myself for months trying to figure out where I went wrong, what I could have done differently to produce a result other than that of a fractured family. The fact that Pat expressed more relief than mourning or regret made my own guilt more pronounced, even pernicious. He was at peace with the decision, as evident in the measurable improvement in his outlook, mood, and energy level. In fact, he was as calm and centered as I remember him being prior to the adoptions.

In some ways I resented Pat's apparent willingness to shed the burden of day-to-day responsibility for Peter, but I also realized that my husband, at sixty-two, had reached the zenith of his capacities. It was unrealistic and unfair, I realized, to examine my own feelings and needs apart from his, or those of our children. Our family was in trouble, there's no doubt. It wasn't Peter's fault, but his disabilities were overtaking our lives to an increasingly destructive, unhealthy, and unsustainable degree. And so with this in mind, and using Pat as an example, I began to pick myself up.

The fact that Peter soon thrived in this new environment helped. He's been assigned a one-to-one aide in school and is supervised heavily at all other times. There is little or no opportunity for him to fail and every incentive to become more independent and succeed. In addition, he met other kids with challenges very similar to his own. Instead of feeling like the only boy on the planet who couldn't stay dry, control his emotions, or understand social cues, he's now surrounded by children with whom he has more commonalities than differences. After years of struggling to make Peter fit into our world, I began to appreciate that my focus was misplaced. Peter will never fit fully into our world, but there are plenty of opportunities and incentives for us to fit more neatly into his.

I'm not sure I would ever have reached this epiphany without the respite and example provided by Green Chimneys. When Peter comes home on the weekends and holidays now, I've learned to enjoy him without expectations or the unyielding need to improve his circumstances or functionality. Emotionally, we are closer than we've ever been, in large part because I no longer have to do the work on a 24/7 basis that Green Chimneys accomplishes through a large, rotating staff of trained individuals. But even amid children with significant developmental and emotional issues, Peter's needs continue to stand out. His issues with impulse control, attention span, mood swings, and memory require the highest level of redirection and supervision. At the same time, though, he also is heralded as a role model in terms of his capacity for kindness, love, and forgiveness. When the occasional wave of guilt sweeps over the terrain of my heart like a passing dark cloud, I do my best to remember this. I'm very proud of the fact that Peter has blossomed into the caring, loving person that he always was intended to be.

In the end, the real triumph of this story is that I reached Peter's heart. There are Russian-adopted children at Green Chimneys who can't accept or give love, who want little or nothing to do with their parents, and whom I fear are destined to lead lonely, troubled, and unsatisfying lives. My heart aches for those children, as well as their parents. The plight of these families helps me appreciate how lucky we truly are. Peter knows that he is loved, that Pat and I are the chief protectors of his heart, and that we will always stand beside him.

In September 2002, on the first anniversary of 9/11, when the streets and theaters of Broadway were still largely empty, Pat and I had dinner at one of our favorite restaurants and then headed to the theater to see *Hairspray*, starring, among others, Harvey Fierstein. Closer to the tragic events of that day than I care to remember, Pat wanted us to spend the evening doing what typical New Yorkers love to do, and apparently we weren't alone. The performance that night was sold out, and the crowd consisted almost entirely of locals. The growing symbiosis between the audience and the cast as the musical unfolded was impossible to ignore. Each time the audience roared its approval, the performers bumped up their energy level and enthusiasm in equal measure. It was as though this small enclave of New Yorkers, nestled for an evening within the larger environs of the city, would not be deterred from celebrating our way of life, our freedom, and the unassailable ability to make meaningful choices in our lives as Americans. When the performance ended and after bows were taken, Harvey Fierstein came back on stage, and with an emotionally charged voice, delivered a speech about the resilience of Americans and New Yorkers in particular. He then burst into a raspy rendition of "God Bless America" as he swatted away the tears streaming down his face. One by one the rest of the cast and crew joined him on stage. In no time, the entire audience was on its feet, singing, holding hands, and shedding healing tears of remembrance and hope.

It was one of the most beautiful, transcendent moments I've ever experienced, not entirely unlike our journey with Peter. In the midst of horrible tragedy and its aftermath, resiliency of spirit can and does prevail. Just as New Yorkers at *Hairspray* were struggling to come to terms with the horror that assaulted the city and nation only a year earlier, I continue to struggle with Peter's disabilities and the uncertainty that his future holds.

But I've come a long way. No longer do I consider ours a fractured family, but rather one that is proceeding on a course designed to fit our unique needs. Peter has taught me that love and commitment have many layers of depth and that the journey undertaken to discover them is far more rewarding and meaningful than one premised on achievement of concrete, measurable outcomes. For this I am truly thankful.

Mudge Pond, Sharon, CT (Late Summer 2011)

Afterword

I CHOSE TO END this book at the point at which Pat and I widened our circle of support so that Peter could continue to grow and heal. Obviously, this isn't the end of our story. The journal entries are meant to be snapshots in time compared with the narrative of the story, which the chapters provide. They are a "where we are now" juxtaposed with the backdrop of how we arrived. But as I reread the manuscript in preparation for publication, I realized that a lot of what I wrote in the chapters, starting in late 2006, was also a reflection of the moment.

For instance, friends we believed would remain constant in our lives regrettably, and often without explanation, have drifted away. At the same time, people we thought would never comprehend the rocky terrain of our family have lifted us up and provided immeasurable support with more than a dollop of humor and compassion. Our son's physical health has become less problematic over the years than any of his doctors predicted. Remarkably, Peter is making more and greater strides, at the conclusion of this writing, than he's ever made before. Sending him to Green Chimneys turned out to be a providential decision.

And then there's Sophie. She did not emerge as unscathed from her pre-adoption experiences as I once allowed myself to believe. Pat and I were overwhelmed with our son's needs and could not or would not see the extent of her trauma. I needed to believe in the fantasy of her wholeness. What she needed was a therapeutic, healing home; instead, in many ways, she escaped from one war zone only to emerge into another. But she is resilient, plucky, bright, and determined. She is still every bit the child I met and fell irrevocably in love with almost eight years ago on a hazy August day in Russia. I have no doubt that she can and will reconcile her past, moving with grace toward a future rich with possibility. Every day she invites me to stand with her arm in arm as she finds her way. It's a great privilege and testament to her courage and capacity for love.

But this book was never meant to focus on Sophie. Though Pat and I decided to make much of my journey with Peter public, we also made a conscious decision, for the most part, to shield our daughter. Peter's wounds have found purchase mostly in his brain; Sophie's are lodged deep within her heart. By necessity, they require different treatment and sensibility. Although I allude to her struggles—they are typical post-institutional effects too often brushed under the rug by pre-adoption professionals—the particulars have been left out. However, the fact that Sophie appears less frequently in the book, and is rarely the center of focus, doesn't mean that she's been relegated to a supporting role in our family. I like to tell her when we kiss goodnight that I love her more than the sun, the moon, and all the stars in the sky. Remarkably, joyfully, she knows it's true.

I have spoken to both children about the book, about the difficult things said and the reasons I wrote them. I've read parts of it to them, even painful parts. I believe Sophie and Peter understand when I tell them that I wrote this book so that we can help improve the lives of orphaned boys and girls around the world and prevent pregnant women from consuming alcohol. Sophie is ten now and suddenly worried over what her friends might say. It's a legitimate concern and one I can't ignore. My hope is that eventually any of her friends or schoolmates who someday choose to read this book will realize that the blonde beauty they sat next to, that they played, laughed, even quarreled with, is even more remarkable and deserving of admiration than they remembered. And if someday Peter is able to read *When Rain Hurts*, I hope with all my heart that he will feel my love for him rising like mist from the pages.

Because our story continues to unfold, I've added as many recent journal entries as I could before Red Hen Press necessarily wrested the manuscript from my hands. It was hard to write that first year Peter was in Green Chimneys, but I managed a few. Writing these entries over the years has proved both cathartic and restorative, allowing me to reexamine motives and decisions previously made as well as chart a more deliberate path toward the countless tomorrows that await. Thank you for traveling this road with my family and me.

Spring 2011

❦

JUNE 30, 2011. *"Don't forget to bring my Pokemon cards," Peter repeats as I tell him Lindy and I plan to visit today. "I need ALL my stuff, Mom." Hearing his voice, so upbeat and focused on the here and now, his mind incapable of worrying over the future or dwelling on the past, offers both comfort and distress. Ten days ago, Pat, Sophie, Grandma, and I took Peter to Green Chimneys School, a nearby residential treatment facility, to live, grow, and hopefully heal. It turns out that I've been living a lie these last few years, telling myself I could handle Peter's escalating needs, his unpredictable thoughts and warp-speed impulses. No one wants to admit her child is more than she can handle, especially an adoptive mother, and especially someone like me, who takes pride—or at least solace—in a certain stubborn resolve to march through adversity. But his attempt a few weeks back to catapult himself from a second story window in the middle of a tantrum, disabused me of that notion once and for all. No psychiatric hospital would take him after the window incident; we were told his management needs exceeded their current staffing capabilities. So we held our breath, crossed our fingers and said a little prayer until his admission day at Green Chimneys arrived. We also bolted his bedroom windows shut, put an alarm on his door, and kept him downstairs all day every day until bedtime. He's been at his new school for ten days now; after his one-month acclimation period, we'll bring him home every other weekend and for holidays and school vacations.*

My hope, laced with regret but steady with resolve, is that this experience can soothe his tortured soul in a way our home, our love, our daily family life could not. A child like Peter has a way of consuming one's thoughts, and it's no different—at least not yet—now that he's at Green Chimneys. The unfulfilled farmer in me drinks in the many sights of the lush, well-tended fields, barns, and pens that adorn this renowned school. Peacocks roam the grounds freely, as do guinea hens and other birds. The year's lambs, kid goats, and calves are still small and cuddly enough to elicit involuntary sighs of joy, and there are miniature horses, ponies, and standard horses at almost every turn. Some children are riding horseback while others help train a group of four-month-old golden retriever puppies slated to become therapy dogs. I immediately wish I could work here, both to be closer to Peter, whom I ache for despite the obvious peace and calm his absence has brought, and to be a part of this healing community of people, live-stock, and pets. Right now Peter is uninterested in the animals—the flies, the odors, and the work involved are more than his sensory sys-tem can navigate. But with time, and tremendous support, he may come to understand that there is a path, a way to live in and view the world that makes sense, where effort produces results and where good choices lead to positive outcomes.

Maybe these animals will help lead the way. Right now his mind, his world, his every waking minute is filled with fiery chaos, and, for any number of reasons, Pat and I aren't the ones who are going to be able to douse the flames. It's a difficult thing to admit, but I know it's true. We have brought him so far, but we reached a wall we simply could not scale. He needs more. Does he mourn the tear in our family's fabric? Is he wondering why he's sleeping away from home, or consider when he'll be returning? For Peter's sake, I hope not. It's our job to shoulder those burdens, to decide what's best for him in the context of what's necessary for the rest of us. So right now I assure him that I'll do my best to locate his beloved Pokémon cards, and I look forward to taking him in my arms so I can feel his silky skin and hopefully con-vey—on a cellular if not conscious level—that he is cherished. I need him to know that he is and always will be my special boy, a child who held my heart hostage for years but who with bravery and brawn has transformed us both into persons with unexpected capacity for resil-ience, compassion, and love.

ɬ

AUGUST 29, 2011. *I've been a halfhearted insomniac most of my life, teetering on the edge of clinical significance, as seems the case with so many other challenges in my life. As I lay awake at 2 a.m. watching* Mystery Diagnosis *in the bonus room—a show Pat claims is at least partially responsible for my insomnolence—I can't help but giggle to myself. Our dog, Pippin, loyally snug in the crook of my arm, looks up at me, sleepy but enthused. It seems we share synchronicity of mood, a divine pleasure I think any dog lover understands and cherishes. I was joking with Pat the other day in the car, accusing him, at age sixty-three, of vacillating between adolescent rage and geriatric forgetfulness. He was a little erratic behind the wheel, and I honestly couldn't tell whether he was experiencing road rage, absent-mindedness, or some combination of the two. He thought my description funny, and the memory of that drive had me laughing in the middle of the night despite the weight of worries that kept me awake.*

But all kidding aside, I think he and I are suffering from the same symptoms, they're just manifesting themselves differently. It's been nearly ten weeks since Peter entered Green Chimneys as a residential student, but we've yet to reach a new equilibrium. I've read The Out-of-Sync Child *cover to cover, maybe more than once. If only it provided guidance for the out-of-sync parent, which is surely what Pat and I have become. Before Green Chimneys, we were on a tumultuous ride with our now ten-year-old son, and one that didn't always produce desired results. But it was a ride we nonetheless came to understand. Now things have changed for Sophie, Peter, Pat, and I. It's like we've been flung into the realm of some metamorphic process, and we're waiting with bated breath to see how we'll emerge. Will we all become butterflies, or will some of us become newts?*

Peter left Green Chimneys for his first lengthy break on Friday afternoon. He doesn't have to go back until Labor Day. He has lost a little weight, seems more wistful than I remember, and is acting more than a little shy. Despite the awkward mood, we picked up his meds at the Health Center, said our goodbyes to staff, and headed straight to the county fair, which was a good thing because we later learned it was closing at midnight in anticipation of Hurricane Irene. Our kids look forward to the fair almost as much as Christmas or Halloween, and I would have hated them to miss it. When we finally got home, exhausted, grimy, and smelling of corn dogs and fried dough, I watched as Peter brushed his fingers lightly along the kitchen island and then the kitchen table. The excitement of the fair had pushed the melancholy aside, but now it was back. When I asked what he was doing, he whispered, "It feels like a new home, Mom." A punch to the gut, surely, but uttered without intention to harm. I knew exactly what he meant. Despite the fuzziness that coats so many of his thoughts, in that moment he experienced complete clarity of mind. I almost broke down in front of him, but I fought back my emotions, bit my quivering lip, and gave him the biggest hug he could handle. "Your home will always be where I am," I managed.

We have changed, our little family of four. But instead of slumbering peacefully until the final transformation is complete, I remain alert and restless, pensive but also steadfast in my conviction to stay the course. I must have faith in myself, my husband, of our decision to place Peter in a residential school, and in the strength and resilience of our two remarkable though disproportionately wounded children. Our metamorphosis, it seems, has only just begun. But I believe we have the stuff from which butterflies are made.

November 11, 2011. *Peter comes home for the weekend this afternoon and I can't wait to see him. When he was with us for Halloween, he admitted that Green Chimneys was helping his brain. "I know it's good for me, Mom," he says, smiling shyly. When he's with us, he doesn't want to do much. I watch as he drinks in the familiar surroundings, the scents and sights of home that he surely loves but can't always handle. He's content to play with his toys or snuggle with me in front of the television with a blazing fire to keep us company. Sophie senses that Peter and I are very close and at peace in these moments, and there's no denying that this fact unsettles her. She's*

not used to Peter and I sharing that kind of intimacy, and she feels threatened. I understand, of course. Our youngest has been terrified that Pat and I are going to send her away too. I try reassuring her by explaining that Peter has a problem in his brain that requires 24/7 support and that Green Chimneys can help him in a way that we just can't. It's a hard pill to swallow. Parents are supposed to be able to fix all their children's problems. Sophie deserves to be able to believe this, especially given her own traumatic past, but I've been put in the unenviable position of dissuading her from such notions, at least of late. However, the child who constantly stated she hated her brother now waits impatiently by the window for his arrival on an every other weekend basis. At least Green Chimneys has taught Sophie that she does indeed love Peter, an unintended consequence for which I'm grateful. Sophie knows we'll have a quiet weekend because we're beginning to understand that Peter just can't handle the noisily thronged outside world, preferring instead the newfound quiet of home. Everybody, including educators, therapists, counselors, and us, has finally stopped trying to force, coax, and cajole Peter into living a neuro-typical life despite his very obvious neuro-differences.

At night, after the children are asleep, the phone rings. It's Peter's psychiatrist from Green Chimneys. She wants to discuss Peter's hallucinations, specifically the Grinch that he sees, hears, and feels on an eerily regular basis. I'm a little annoyed at first; it's Friday night after all, and I was just settling into the luxurious feel of knowing that everyone I love is safe and sound and under one roof. But she's a busy woman, I realize that, and so I shake off the intrusive vibe and listen closely to what she says. She's been talking with Peter lately, as well as his teachers, aide, and dorm staff, and she's come to the conclusion that our son is suffering from separation anxiety. She thinks the Grinch materializes, more often than not, when he's not in my presence. Yes, mine! I can hardly believe my ears. The psychiatrist explains, "He says 'Mommy makes him go away.'" Dumbfounded, I make her repeat her theory, as well as any supportive evidence. Could it possibly be that the boy who spit and hissed at me for our first years together is now counting on me to keep his demons at bay? Could it be that I have actually become the person in the world he *most trusts to keep him safe? My heart beats so loudly I can barely hear her speaking.*

I do my best to convey maternal concern, but I can't shake free of the sensation that I've just won the lottery. I'm sorry that Peter struggles with these experiences, I know they scare him witless, but this worrisome news cloaks a brilliant nugget of gold. After we hang up, the salty taste of my own tears takes me by surprise as I pad down the hall to kiss Sophie and then Peter one more time. I realize with bittersweet surrender that we have reached the end of our journey to create a mother-son bond. My quest to make Peter understand that he is loved, unconditionally and forever, has been a success. I hate that he's feeling, hearing, and seeing things. but my heart nearly cartwheels knowing that he believes I can stop the Grinch dead in his tracks. The rub, of course, and the reason for the tears, comes in appreciating that this moment may have remained elusive had Peter not gone into a residential school. The dogged diligence required to keep him and the rest of us safe and at least somewhat functional was clouding the path. It seems that in our case distance between mother and child has actually bridged, rather than widened, the gap between us, and perhaps I shouldn't be surprised, or even disappointed. FAS is a cunning disability, and early neglect, abuse, and deprivation only serve to exasperate an already faulty mindset.

But despite the irony, the aching sense of loss that hovers around the edges of even this most prized moment, I'm more optimistic than ever about my son's heart, and our futures together. Whether rain or Grinch, Peter has empowered me to shield him from the ravages of his past as well as the obstacles in his future. There's so much ahead, challenges I don't even want to fathom, but for now I'm content. I've given him my love, and in return, he's shown me his trust. I can fall asleep tonight feeling luminous and light. Having reached for the unreachable, I now know that reality created through effort and resolve, from a contour of love that never seemed possible, is eminently more satisfying than the unreliable, sometimes disappointing stuff from which dreams are made.

❧

MAY 1, 2012. *I struggle to keep my voice calm and cheerful as I listen to Peter on the phone, which has become our lifeline to each other as surely as it was when Pat and I were long-distance dating, NYC to Atlanta, fifteen years earlier. Dropping him off at Green Chimneys last night, we endured the now familiar ache derived from having a ten-year-old child separated, more days than not, from the rest of his family. "When I'm discharged, Mom," he asks plaintively, "can I join the Boy Scouts?" It's an unexpected question, Peter never having expressed any interest in Boy Scouts in the past. "I don't want to be bored when I go home," he explains. "I know I gotta stay busy." On occasion we carpool with another Red Hook family whose teenage daughter also attends Green Chimneys. When we arrived back at school Sunday night, the teenager announced that she was being discharged in August and will be attending a less restrictive special needs boarding school next fall. Peter didn't catch the part about her going to another "sleep away" school, only that she was being discharged from Green Chimneys, and I didn't have the heart to correct his thinking. I know Sunday's conversation is what sparked his sudden interest in discharge, which is of course the ultimate goal of all Green Chimneys residential students.*

Despite knowing that this has stirred up his homesickness, I'm struck by the fact that he has developed enough self-awareness to know that he needs constant structure, that free time is one of his mind's worst enemies. When I speak to him on the phone, listening to his doleful voice, I long to tell him that soon he'll be back with us on a permanent basis, that "sleep away" school one day will be a thing of the past, but I reply more carefully. The truth is I don't know when Peter will be coming home. He's making great progress in so many areas—social skills, continence, speech/language, and daily living— but at the same time he's demonstrating only modest gains in terms of his constant, chronic need for supervision and redirection. It's only been ten months, but the reality is that he may always need the 24/7 external brain that Green Chimneys provides.

I fully appreciate that his improved emotional and psychiatric sta-bility might quickly deteriorate if he were back home where the level of care that Green Chimneys supplies simply cannot be replicated. It's a harsh reality and one that I push from my mind with some frequency. I miss Peter terribly but console myself by recognizing that I might never have felt this way, that we never might have been capable of this closeness, had I not fought for and won his love and trust. When he's home now, whether for just a weekend or a longer break, I've learned to relax in his presence and enjoy our relationship without the constant burden of having to teach, reteach, redirect, or provide consequences. For the most part, I no longer have to teeter along the precipice of enjoying my role as mother and protector while constantly being aware that disaster and chaos could strike at any moment. But Peter doesn't understand this, he couldn't possibly, and frankly, I hope he never does. I don't want our son ever to think that he's a burden, that the effort needed to care for and protect him is more than we can handle on a constant basis.

And so as I speak to him on the phone, I distract him by reviewing when he'll be home next and what our plans are for the upcoming weeks. I acknowledge that he misses home and that I miss him too, but I do my best not to let his wistful voice rip away at the confidence I have in our decision to enroll him at Green Chimneys. In so many ways, the school is an oasis, both for students and parents. I have to remember that it's a place of growth, acceptance, and healing and that its existence is an extremely positive presence in our lives. But here's the thing: I also can't forget that positive change, at least in our case, is not without its toll. As we say goodnight, I propose that we meet on the moon in our dreams, a game Peter and I always have played and one that makes him truly smile. I tell him to look for a polka-dotted spaceship and he tells me that his will be blue with a big yellow star on the tip. We agree that I'll bring snacks and he'll bring a soccer ball. I tell him I love him and kiss the phone knowing that in our dreams, we are always together.

❧

JUNE 4, 2012. *It's been ten days since we saw Dr. Federici in northern Virginia for Peter's biannual neuropsychological assessment. Dr. Federici is a significant reason why we've made so much progress with our son, his evaluations providing a measuring stick for past efforts as well as an invaluable road map for the future. These visits are difficult for Peter, though. They demand his focus and attention in a way he's not quite equipped to handle, and the information gleaned from them hasn't always been easy for us to digest. Words and phrases like psychosis, autism, lifetime care, FAS, significant support, mood dysregulation, and cognitive deficiencies—they're enough to scare anyone. But those particular descriptors didn't loom so heavily this time. Something has changed—something really significant, and great.*

The very best part is that Pat and I knew it before Dr. Federici even told us. Peter is better. Not just a little bit better but about 40 percent better in every area of functioning (except academics, where there's been only modest gain). I've never seen Dr. Federici look so pleased. I couldn't decide whether he was beaming like a proud papa or looking more like a small child ready to burst with exciting news. Either way, we sat in his office after the testing, relaxed and full of banter, trading compliments and accolades like a small band of combatants who've just conquered a formidable enemy. After almost eight years of constant effort and struggle, we may have turned the corner with the boy I once described, quite accurately, as feral. Today Peter is happier, more centered, more trusting, showing better reasoning and problem-solving skills, demonstrating improved language skills, and exercising more independence and ability to adjust to changing circumstances.

Dr. Federici credits this positive leap to two things: the cumulative effect of our efforts and our success in finally getting him placed in an appropriate therapeutic environment. The only asterisk that looms over my otherwise warm and glowing feeling is the knowledge that Green Chimneys School is achieving what Pat and I could not. I realize that we've brought Peter a great distance, and in some ways I recognize that many others might have given up where we persevered, but I still ache with the wish that this last, most victorious push could have been achieved in the intimacy of our home. I'm thankful that Green Chimneys is achieving what we couldn't, but the truth is, I'm also a little resentful and jealous. Peter wants to be home, he clings to me during our visits and his eyes well up with tears on our drive back Sunday nights. It's hard to reconcile this Peter with the boy who used to smear feces on himself and spit on me, but I suppose knowledge of our troubled past only makes the hopefulness of the present that much more luscious and remarkable. The only problem is that I want to whisk my son away, back into my arms, to the love that's grown as steady and unstoppable as the rising sun, but I know I mustn't. Sometimes I feel like an estranged mother contemplating parental kidnapping.

There's a cost to progress, at least in our case, and it comes in the unwelcome form of mutual heartache and homesickness. Peter needs the 24/7 supervision, the one-to-one staff who help keep his impulses in check and his distractibility minimized, and who constantly talk him down from his various tirades and skewed perceptions. We can achieve this at home—I've become particularly adept at various strategies—but I can't sustain it indefinitely. I realize that it's only a matter of time—ten days, maybe two weeks—before Peter's challenges begin to outwit my stamina, patience, and commitment. I realize, with more than a little melancholy, that the reason he's 40 percent better is because Green Chimneys and its plethora of strong young men and women on eight-hour shifts don't give his mind or body an opportunity to unravel, at least not for very long. I should be grateful for this, and, in fact, I am. It just stings a little. A wise doctor told us almost two years ago that Peter needed a system of supports, a circle of providers that extended further and deeper than two parents could simulate or sustain. I need to realize and believe that Green Chimneys' victory is our victory too, that the endeavor is a collective one, and that it's not an either/or proposition. Although my mind knows this to be true, my heart requires a little more convincing.

After the testing, we drove to Ocean City, Maryland, for Memorial Day weekend and spent most of the time on Assateague

Island, enjoying the beach and the wild ponies. Watching Peter navigate the cold, crashing waves, the gritty sand, the always changing conditions of the shore, without his stiff and bracing posture, his usual guarded, super-sensitized body language, truly was exhilarating. For the first time ever, he wasn't the boy on the beach with obvious issues and challenges. He was just a boy on the beach, a wonderfully happy boy, who, alongside his sister, was filled with the ordinary joys that we as parents all hope color our children's memories. When we got home, and Peter was tucked into bed before going back to school the next morning, he hugged me fiercely and asked, "Did I have a good trip, Mommy?" Knowing he was asking about his behavior and not whether he had a good time, I smiled into his eyes, fighting back my tears. With as much composure as manageable, I assured him that he did. And it's true. Peter, our beautiful, enigmatic, and resilient son, had a wonderful trip indeed.

JUNE 9, 2012. *Peter's home this weekend and something curious has begun. It's happened a few times in the past month or two, but it's taken me a while to assimilate this new chapter in our relationship. A few weeks ago at dinner he reminisced, with more than a measure of self-deprecation, how he used to be such a bad eater, and misbehave so terribly at the table, that we sometimes resorted to having him eat separately in the dining room. "But then I just dropped it all on the floor for the dogs!" he said, laughing. "There was really nothing you could do." His grammar, word choice, and articulation are still works in progress, but this is essentially what transpired. And then a few days ago, along the same line, he comments, "Can you believe I used to stuff the toilets till they spilled everywhere? And then make my nose bleed all over me?" Yes, I can believe it. I survived those phases and, to date, all the others. The part I can't believe is that he remembers these destructive patterns and now can laugh about them. I had no idea he possessed that kind of self-awareness, either then or now.*

On days like this I can imagine our son when he's twenty-two or maybe twenty-five, a young man with a strong, chiseled body, darkly tanned in the summer, and a mischievous smile that draws women like flies to sugar. He is handsome, yes, but he is also kind. He'll struggle with memory, processing, money management, and, perhaps most worrisome, the ability to distinguish between those who wish him well and those with more predatory intentions. But I imagine him standing on his own. He'll have a job, hopefully in an area that interests him, like video games or landscaping, and with any luck, he'll be proud of his accomplishments. I hope he'll continue to look back on his journey with the same brand of humor he's demonstrating now, the good-natured ability to acknowledge his past in order to help propel him toward the future. Miraculously, he regularly proclaims that he intends always to live with his mom, or at least next door, a fact that both astonishes and comforts. It was an intense struggle to open my heart to this child—the boy who hurt himself as much as, or even more than, he hurt me—but now the door to my affections is wide open, and the view grows more spectacular. As long as I have a home, so do our children.

The four of us spend the rest of our day together lazily, with me doing my best to pry Peter and Sophie away from their cavernous playroom toward the beautiful day outside. When I finally succeed, I wonder whether my prediction that Peter might like landscaping is too ambitious. He loves to help outside in the fall and early spring, but I'm reminded now that summer is a different matter. The insects make him swat and spin and growl with consternation. He jumps on the trampoline and squeals, his body suddenly arching, whenever a gnat or fly swirls past. "I want to go inside!" he howls. And so I concede. The presence of insects remains a major sensory problem and creates in him marked overreactions. Maybe the bugs, or the absence of bugs, are the reason I spend so much effort getting us to water during the summer, either the town pool, our favorite lake, Mudge Pond, or the ocean. Water is a weapon against the creepy crawlies, at least the kind that dominate the skies. Plus, the kids and I are as drawn to water as beetles are to roses. Pat would rather spend the summer hiking in the mountains, but he's forever the good sport. Between

Peter's bug issues, my mangled ankle, and Sophie's inevitable cries of boredom and exhaustion (that ensue after only ten minutes on a trail), the opportunities for hiking are few and far between.

Like all parents, the two of us occasionally wonder when we'll get to resume, on our own or as a couple, some of the activities we enjoyed pre-children. Given the dynamics of our family, and our undeniably increasing ages, it seems possible that "our" time might never come, but that's okay. We're growing, we're stronger, and we're seeing progress where before we saw only disaster and hopelessness. The kind of mountain climbing we do these days is virtual, but there's no doubt we've scaled countless precipices to reach and help Peter, and there's bound to be more ahead. We try and will continue to do the same for Sophie, though her needs are subtler and in many ways trickier to traverse. But for now, with the bugs filling the airways and the sunny day to lure us along, I think I'll pack the beach bag, load up the kids, and head to the lake.

JULY 14, 2012. *The sun hot and lake levels low from lack of rain and blistering temperatures, we bring our own folding chairs and stake out a spot in the dusty shade. Sophie, Pat, and I have taken the one-hour trek to Green Chimneys, where the annual family picnic is being held at their nearby sister facility, Clearpool Educational Center. There is an inflatable obstacle course on the lake for the kids to climb and navigate, but the water is too low, so the kids, mostly boys, stare longingly, arms folded over bare chests, at the now unattainable goal. Pat and I play volleyball with Sophie and Peter, and before we know it, boys of various age and ability have joined us on either side of the net where an energetic game ensues. Sophie, no longer the epicenter of her parents' attention, feels put out and walks away. She doesn't handle our interest in other children, her brother included, as graciously as we'd like.*

Later, Pat and I enjoy a few minutes' chat with the founder of the school, Dr. Sam Ross, an octogenarian zealously devoted to his mission and the kids he serves. He is a beloved leader of young minds and hearts, and I watch as he surveys the picnic, the mass of healing children and parents, his eyes benevolent and proud without apology, a pride that derives from a lifetime of selfless work and accomplishment. Peter is glad to see us but a little grumpy from the heat and the realization that we are together for only a few hours. The separation between child and family is unnatural, intuitively wrong, and we all do our best, in our own ways, to ignore this fact so that the reality doesn't overwhelm and smother what is meant to be a happy day. I try to stay busy with both kids and spend a lot of time swimming with them in the lake. My family shouts playful jeers as I'm made to pass the deep-water swim test, just like the children. Peter and Sophie both clap as the lifeguard writes a fat "X" across my hand, memorializing my success. Pat watches from the dock with towels in hand. Sophie is fine as long as it's just Peter and me, but when I start talking to other kids or adults, she slinks off sulking, her face transformed into an angry caricature of herself. Sophie resents these outings and doesn't understand why the parenting we give Peter is sometimes less intense that the parenting she receives at home. She doesn't appreciate that our time with Peter is limited and that the nature of our relationship is different, at least temporarily, from our relationship with her. Though I try to reassure her, there is little I can do to alter this fact. She has us 24/7, for better or worse, and Peter does not.

After trying to eat a few rubbery burgers and downing several too-small plastic cups of cold water, we head over to another part of the grounds where a climbable water slide has been set up. One of the counselors sits atop the inflated climbing wall, ostensibly to maintain order and safety, but he's spraying the kids in line below with a water hose, which sets off rounds of gleeful screams. Pat and I, seeking yet another spot of shade, strike up a conversation with a couple who recently enrolled their six-year-old as a day student. It's not long before we're swapping war stories of contemptible treatment by our respective school districts. Forever amazed by the fact that although individual circumstances differ, the overall plot remains unchanged, I listen with amusement as the mother, an educator herself, shares with us that she shoots certain individuals in her district a not so discreet bird whenever their paths cross. So many Green Chimneys parents are combat veterans who've fought their districts tooth and nail to get the appropriate placement for their special needs children. I'm glad we've met a few more veterans today; shared experience breeds hope and comfort and reaffirmation that the prize was worth the fight.

Earlier, one of Peter's friends eagerly approached, wanting me to come meet his mother, whom he doesn't often see. He is a sweet but troubled boy with a difficult background, always happy to lap up the extra interest and attention I try to show him whenever possible. The mother matter-of-factly tells Pat and me that when she works through her own issues, she'll be able to bring her son home. The love in her eyes is apparent, but there's also a deep sadness and lack of confidence emanating from within. She is the other face of Green Chimneys, a mother fighting just as hard for her child but for very different reasons.

When the picnic winds down, we decide to take Peter for an early dinner and ice cream. We aren't quite ready to say goodbye and are grateful his social worker approves the impromptu off-grounds request. When we drop him back at school, later than we planned but earlier than I'd like, we remind him that he'll be home the following weekend and that it's only a few days away. We kiss goodbye and hug each other tightly. Then, as I plunk myself back into the car for the long, often silent ride home, I turn my attention as a mother back to Sophie, 100 percent. This unnatural shifting of familial rank and place throws her and the rest of us off. I've come to appreciate that this pendulum effect is just one of the many forms that payment for the price of progress takes.

August 18, 2012. *I think this will be the last journal entry I write before irrevocably handing the "final" manuscript over to Red Hen Press. It's so hard to know what to say, or where to find conclusion. Peter is at school and won't be home until Friday, though he'll be with*

us then until after Labor Day. Sophie is starting a new school, a small Catholic school across the river, and I know the anticipation of new kids and routines looms heavy. Pat and I thought seriously about re-joining the Catholic Church—after all, we're sending our daughter to Catholic school—but in the end we decided against it. Neither of us is ready for the suspension of certain convictions that such a move necessitates. We want our kids to have spirituality in their lives and the chance to have a meaningful relationship with God, but it won't be as Catholics, at least not for now.

Pat and I met with Peter's treatment team at Green Chimneys last week, and we're very pleased with his progress. "He's definitely a kid moving toward discharge," words from the attending psychiatrist that resound like song in my heart. The when and the where and the under what circumstances are yet to be determined; I continue to struggle but am working hard to resist the urge to plan for and accommodate the future beyond the next few weeks or months.

We stop by Peter's classroom before leaving to say hello and steal a hug. The room is naturally lit (no overhead lights), the handful of boys who occupy it quietly attending to their separate endeavors. It's the complete opposite of the raucous, crowded classrooms he was made to endure for so many years. Time to process is needed even when it comes to recognizing Mom and Dad's faces, and so we wait for him to as-similate our unexpected presence. When he does, when that light bulb finally flicks on, his pleasure overflows immediately, filling the room with contagious energy. He nearly bowls me over as he races to grab hold, jumping us both up and down while exclaiming, "Mommy! Mommy!" I never heard him call me this happily when he was three or four or five, but hearing it now, at eleven, is more than enough. Soon everyone is laughing and saying hello, the vibe celebratory, as when a holiday awaits. I've shed so many tears over the years that moments like these, unexpected moments that cause my eyes to water with joy rather than sorrow, can never go unmarked.

On the drive home, I carefully wrap the memory like a present. There is plenty for which to be grateful. As I lay awake last night, somewhere between worrying about special needs trusts and our out-standing tax bill, I thought of a Tim O'Brien story called The Things

They Carried that forever will stick in my mind. It chronicles how a soldier in the Vietnam War stripped away his memories, his hopes, his dreams, and the accompanying physical possessions he carried in his rucksack as reminders, little by little with each passing day, until he carried nothing. At first he clung to certain keepsakes but soon realized they added physical and emotional weight. In the end, the soldier is left with nothing but the raw instinct to continue living, to kill or be killed. His memories of being loved and of having loved are erased, forever, leaving the reader to ponder whether physical survival alone can ever really constitute living.

It's a haunting story and a cautionary tale. I'm keenly cognizant that I find myself in the opposite position these days. I don't want to take the analogy too far—after all, family struggle is a far cry from combat—but there was a time when I also actively engaged in the shedding of self in order to reemerge as something different, stronger, harder, more impenetrable. I thought I had to, but it was a mistake, and I'm finished with it. Parenting my son has made me stronger, yes, but if my heart hadn't been open, at least cracked a little, we never would have found each other. I never would have known that Peter's soul is lush and rich, the opposite of what I feared in those first unbearably difficult years. Sophie never would have had the benefit of seeing, firsthand, that even impossible obstacles are capable of being hurdled. And Pat and I, if we didn't know before, now appreciate that for us, The Things They Carried, that thing or memory that keeps all of us bound to a world beyond our own existence, is each other. Never in a million years could I have guessed that two Russian toddlers, both abandoned, neglected, and deprived, and one with significant brain injury, would ever teach me so much.

Biographical Note

Mary Evelyn Greene, an environmental attorney and college professor, adopted two children from Russia in 2004. Ever since, she has doggedly devoted herself to improving her alcohol-exposed son's condition, publishing articles in *Adoptive Families Magazine* and *Adoption Today* along the way. Dissatisfied with her son's educational progress, she gained local notoriety in 2010 when she took their local school district to court and won. She is a contributing author to *Easy to Love but Hard to Raise* (February 2012), a collection of stories written by and for parents of special needs kids. Born and raised in St. Petersburg, Florida, she remains an avid University of Florida football and basketball fan. She currently lives in Montgomery County, Maryland, with her husband, two children, and multiple furry friends, and is the Senior Managing Attorney for the Environmental Integrity Project. This is her first book.